I0878149

The Democratic Ethos

MOVEMENT RHETORIC/RHETORIC'S MOVEMENTS

Victoria J. Gallagher

THE DEMOCRATIC ETHOS

Authenticity and Instrumentalism in US Movement Rhetoric after Occupy

A. FREYA THIMSEN

THE UNIVERSITY OF
SOUTH CAROLINA PRESS

© 2022 University of South Carolina

Published by the University of South Carolina Press
Columbia, South Carolina 29208

www.uscpress.com

Manufactured in the United States of America

31 30 29 28 27 26 25 24 23 22
10 9 8 7 6 5 4 3 2 1

Library of Congress Cataloging-in-Publication Data
can be found at http://catalog.loc.gov/.

ISBN 978-1-64336-317-2 (hardcover
ISBN 978-1-64336-318-9 (paperback)
ISBN 978-1-64336-319-6 (ebook)

‘I can’t believe what you say,’ the song goes,
‘because I see what you do.’

JAMES BALDWIN

CONTENTS

SERIES EDITOR'S PREFACE

The University of South Carolina series "Movement Rhetoric/Rhetoric's Movements" builds on the Press's longstanding reputation in the field of rhetoric and communication and its cross-disciplinary commitment to studies of civil rights and civil justice. Books in the series address two central questions: In historical and contemporary eras characterized by political, social, and economic movements enacted through rhetorical means, how—and with what consequences—are individuals, collectives, and institutions changed and transformed? How and to what extent can analyses of rhetoric's movements in relation to circulation and uptake help point the way to a more equal and equitable world?

In her timely and engaging work, A. Freya Thimsen examines different conceptualizations of democracy in US political opposition to corporate rights since 2010, focusing particularly on the legacy of the Occupy Wall Street Movement. Thimsen advances the case that the *democratic ethos*, as consolidated and disseminated by the Occupy demonstrations, is a flexible set of rhetorical tactics by which collectives (organizations, campaigns, and other groups) go about presenting themselves as being "authentically" committed to democracy. The book's chapters illuminate the relationship between traditional and innovative rhetoric in contemporary politics and demonstrate that the *democratic ethos* is not a simple cultural ethic, attitude, or character trait but rather a flexible, repeatable set of tactics by which a collective discloses its own habits of self-composition as it simultaneously pursues persuasive goals.

ACKNOWLEDGMENTS

This book was conceived and pushed along during a time of political upheaval. The analysis has benefited from all kinds of conversations, some of which happened well before even a sentence of the book had been written. My memories of these conversations had slipped away until a conceptual soft spot or knotty problem demanded that I return to them.

My time at the University of Pittsburgh gave me an unexpected appreciation for the questions and problems of the rhetorical tradition. The education I received at Pitt has shaped my thinking so thoroughly that I have trouble seeing that influence clearly. This specific project began in earnest at the University of North Carolina at Chapel Hill. Larry Grossberg and Carole Blair, whose vastly different but complimentary approaches to reading, guiding, supporting, challenging, and criticizing were endlessly important to how I related what I wanted to say to how I wanted to say it. Della Pollock is quite simply an inspiration—to me as to so many others. I wish I could claim to have done justice to the richness of her sense of performance. Many others made my experience of UNC a compelling one. Their voices and ideas will camp out and echo in my mind for many years to come: Brenda Balletti, Bill Balthrop, Grant Bollmer, Lucy Burgchardt, Rich Cante, Andrew Davis, Sarah Dempsey, Murat Es, Natalie Fixmer-Oraiz, Maggie Franz, Kate Harris, Marjorie Hazeltine, Elizabeth Hennessy, Rolien Hoyng, J. Nikol Jackson-Beckham, Srinath Jayaram, Chris Lundberg, Robert MacDonald, John McGowan, Alex Mcvey, Liz Mason-Deese, Jennifer Mease, Dennis Mumby, Julia O'Grady, Mike Palm, Kashif Powell, Adam Rottinghaus, Allison Schlobohm, Sarah Sharma, Tim Stahl, David Supp-Montgomerie, Jenna Supp-Montgomerie, David Terry, Armond Towns, Stace Treat, Eric Watts, Alia Wegner, Grover Wehman-Brown, Jes Speed Wiley, Shannon Wong-Lerner, Heather Woods, and Sindhu Zagoren. During my time teaching at Northeastern University, I learned a lot from my students and colleagues in Boston, especially Dale Herbeck, Pamela Pietrucci, and Anjali Vats.

I have been grateful to work in a supportive, intellectually rich community at Indiana University while writing the bulk of this book. This community has been populated, defined, lead, and nurtured by my generous colleagues at IU, who have supported me in many different ways. I have relied on and learned from Robert Terrill's tremendous patience, John Arthos's ability to dwell in ideas, Scot Barnett's love of theory, Vivian Halloran's generosity, Purnima Bose's sharp insight and humor, Katie Silvester's sympathetic ear, Rebekah Sheldon's everything, Nikki Skillman's gracefulness, Dana Anderson's enthusiasm, and Patty Ingham's determination. I'm also grateful for Stephanie Li, who unlike so many others fearlessly and repeatedly asked the question: "How is the book going?" My large and diverse department at IU has been a joy to me, particularly Michael Adams, Chris Ferris, Rae Greiner, Justin Hodgson, Ivan Kreilkamp, Joan Linton, John Lucaites, Monique Morgan, Walton Muyumba, John Schilb, Ranu Samantrai, Brando Skyhorse, Cindy Smith, Alberto Varon, and Shane Vogel. Thanks for everything, including all the help I know you would give if I were better at accepting it. It has also been my privilege and delight to work through ideas related to this project with the talented students at IU, including Caddie Alford, Collin Bjork, Sage Boyd, Phil Choong, Joanna Chromik, Erika Coe, Eryn Johnson, and Ben Luczak.

In addition to Laura Plummer and all the participants in the Scholarly Writing Program at Indiana University, I am grateful for everyone who has written companionably by my side in coffee shops, libraries, classrooms, meeting rooms, dining halls, lounges, offices, and kitchens. When you were there, it was more fun *and* I got more done.

I learned a lot from colleagues in the Rhetoric Society of America Summer Institute workshop on democracy led by Pat Gehrke and Jeremy Engels as well as the workshop on ethos led by Pete Simonson and Carolyn Miller. Ira Allen and Zornitsa Keremidchieva have listened to me talk about the themes of this book on more conference panels than I care to admit. Z, your generosity and intellectual enthusiasm are infectious, and your creativity is boundless. Ira, you are right that liberalism is tired. Matt May gave me gentle, indefatigable counterpoints for many years. Megan Foley showed me what it means for intellectuals to follow their hearts. Ron Greene's cheerleading and thoughtful perspective has helped me see a home for this work. John Lucaites, Bob Hariman, Purnima Bose, and Dave Tell each exemplified a commitment to rigor that helped me focus and refine this project. Barbara Biesecker's commentary has proved both thought-provoking and delightfully honest. Ralph Cintron's sympathetic skepticism about democracy has been bracing and made me see how this project might spark things I can't yet see.

This project was supported by a fellowship from the American Association of University Women. Olivia Little and Bee Smale pitched in on hunting down some things for me. Laresa Lund's patience, diligence, and precision have made this manuscript far more presentable than I ever could have achieved on my own. Kurt Zemlicka's humor and support saw me through a decade's worth of work on this topic. The final push would not have been possible without the companionship, love, silliness, and kindness of Baxter and Amma. They made it possible for me to finish this book during the most intense phase of quarantine.

Introduction

Radical-left academics loved Occupy, even when they loved to hate it. There is a decent argument to be made that Occupy basically *was* the street performance of radical-academic leftism, notwithstanding the substantial divisions within that group. The outpouring of radical-left love for Occupy was in part the result of how leftism in the United States had not translated easily into popular politics during the past half century. Yet the 2011 Occupy demonstrations in the United States affirmed the capacity of radically antistatist academic leftism, deeply influenced by anarchism, autonomist Marxism, and Latin American practices of *horizontalidad* (or horizontalism), to take to the streets in the twenty-first century.

Some left-leaning progressive and liberal intellectuals, however, were unconvinced that Occupy actually demonstrated the political viability of radically antistatist leftism. This dissatisfaction was often framed as a reaction to Occupy's refusal to make specific, state-oriented demands.[1] Thomas Frank, for instance, wrote that Occupy was "uncritical groupthink," the "most over-described historical event of all time," and a failed effort that wasted its promise because it didn't seek concrete reforms.[2] Frank's critique encompassed the elitism of academic leftism, which (he argued) has ensured the increasing distance of academic leftism from what he imagines as "the common people" and their values and ways of thinking and speaking. Frank lamented, "For all its intellectual attainments, the Left keeps losing. It simply cannot make common cause with ordinary American people anymore."[3]

From the vantage point of a decade later, Frank's disappointment seems premature. Occupy continues to live on in the rhetorical forms that it consolidated and disseminated. As part of a larger, ongoing dynamic of innovation and ossification, Occupy has contributed a set of technologies, techniques, and epistemologies to the democratic repertoire of US politics. If Occupy is evaluated solely in terms of specific policy outcomes that happened in the year or two after the demonstrations, as Frank does, it cannot help but be found wanting. But the longer view now available suggests different questions about the lasting impact of the radicalism of the 2011 demonstrations.

This book argues that the performance of democratic values rooted in practices of left radicalism and horizontalism play an important role in the way that more mainstream contemporary US prodemocracy advocacy groups disclose their practices of self-organization to prove their commitment to democracy. More specifically, the *democratic ethos* consolidated and disseminated by the Occupy demonstrations is a flexible set of rhetorical tactics by which collectives (organizations, campaigns, and other groups) go about presenting themselves as being "authentically" committed to democracy because their commitment to democracy is performatively consistent; they don't just talk the talk but also "walk the walk." The *democratic ethos* is not a simple cultural ethic, attitude, or character trait. It is a flexible, repeatable set of tactics by which a collective discloses its own habits of self-composition as it simultaneously pursues persuasive goals. Unlike many conceptualizations of ethos, the democratic ethos is most fundamentally an ethos of a collective rather than an individual.

The democratic ethos is not new. Rather than generating something truly novel, Occupy consolidated a set of political tactics with long histories in radical leftism and made them more instrumentally effective than they had been before. The result has been a shift in the possibilities for cooperation and collaboration between left radicalism and left reformism. The democratic ethos that now appears in a variety of left and progressive organizations committed to democracy reforms is the result of an innovation in the longer history of what has been called "prefigurative" politics. The performance of the democratic ethos is derived from a radical intellectual and political tradition that rejects reformist compromises based on their problematic instrumental engagement with corrupt institutions. Unlike other strands of this tradition, however, the democratic ethos is visible in public persuasion and so incorporates a certain degree of instrumentalism wherein the *means* of political tactics and radical goals are distinct. The democratic ethos is an approach that responds to and departs from conventional liberal and neoliberal political rationalities but continues to negotiate with them.

The democratic ethos establishes a certain kind of radical credibility in the context of seeking reforms in compromised, corrupt, hierarchical political institutions. A strong democratic ethos invigorates the assumption that if a group is committed to democratic principles, it will be able to tarry with instrumentalism and pursue an agenda of institutional reform without losing its radical credibility and character. Occupy's consolidation and invigoration of a democratic ethos was grounded in demonstrating something like "authenticity" through communication technologies and techniques. This democratic ethos is a political performance in which the processes of internally constituting an entity—its internal communicative practices—are put on display for an audience. For a collective entity, the process of performing a democratic ethos is necessarily also about how it *forms itself* and makes visible that process of self-formation.

In the process of mapping the diffusion of Occupy's tactics and ideals, I have been struck by how prominent rhetorical theories of democracy, nearly all of which are grounded in liberalism, cannot account for many of the transformations in the US "democracy movement" I have been following for the better part of the last decade. The more research I've done on the vision of "democracy" performed in the Occupy demonstrations—and derived from the anti- or alter-globalization protests a decade before—the more and more obvious it has become that the renaissance in "democracy" we are witnessing in the United States is one that is substantially inspired, structured, and defined by the democratic practices and ideals of *horizontalidad, Zapatismo,* and their *encuentros,* cooperatives, and philosophies. For researchers of "democratic rhetoric," it is no longer tenable to rely exclusively on thinkers such as John Dewey, Jürgen Habermas, Chantal Mouffe, or Jacques Rancière to theorize the rhetorical manifestations of democracy. Some rhetorical scholars have been justifiably skeptical of the status of "democracy" as what Kenneth Burke might call a "god term" that implies and justifies continued adherence to liberal (and even neoliberal) norms of citizenship, deliberation, and political action.[4] This is particularly true when "democracy" is practiced by movement actors with obvious and avowed commitments to antiracist, queer, Indigenous, and decolonial knowledges, communicative practices, and values. Contemporary movements show us, however, that democracy is a concept and practice more than flexible enough to be reshaped and reinvigorated by illiberal or even antiliberal political traditions.

The chapters that follow map some of the specific theories and practices of democracy consolidated by Occupy and how they have disseminated into more reformist political rhetoric. Because of how these rhetorics are already deeply influenced by political theories of their own, it has been important to not "impose" an external theory (and particularly not a liberal theory) of those practices as an explanatory framework from the outset. As Darryl Wanzer-Serrano argues, theories of democracy must be decolonized in rhetorical studies—not only as a matter of principle but also because "democracy" is often conducted precisely by those groups who act outside of liberal democratic philosophical and political traditions.[5] Although I cannot claim to have responded fully to this decolonial imperative, I have tried to let the performed sense of "democracy" appear as fully as possible rather than confine it to a pre-existing theoretical frame. It is widely accepted that the Occupy demonstrations were expressions of anarchist and autonomous Marxist understandings of democracy as an antistatist refusal of institutionalized representation and liberal governance.[6] This was the assumption that I began my research with: that the diffusion of Occupy's tactics and ethos was more or less the demonstration of the influence of a Marxist and anarchist "radicalism" that was nonetheless fundamentally modern and Western. This assumption was not wrong, exactly, but it has certainly turned out to be in need of serious revision. The democratic ethos of the Occupy demonstrations is not simply an extension of leftist radicalism as practiced in the United States and Europe over the last century. It is also, fundamentally, the performance of a conceptualization of "democracy" inspired by Indigenous and worker collectives in Latin America.

Conceptualizing the democratic ethos of the Occupy demonstrations is a theoretical process in the sense that it integrates other primarily speculative and abstract accounts of instrumentalism, democracy, rhetoric, and ethos. Theorizing the democratic ethos, however, also requires fidelity to what has emerged out of the movement rhetoric itself. Rather than "applying" any particular theory to explain the phenomena of the movement rhetoric, this book attempts to develop a theoretical account based on the self-understandings and activities of the movement actors. My aim is to perform a commitment to elevating and prioritizing the actually existing movement rhetoric and tactics above consistency and fidelity to any unified theoretical perspective on rhetoric or democracy. My hope is that the result will be a conceptualization of the "democratic ethos" faithful to the thrust of political actors who consolidate, disseminate, and adapt it in a variety of impure contexts and through a historic moment of great change.

The significance of the 2011 demonstrations in US politics has been affected by the emergence and ascendance of right nationalism, the election of Donald Trump to the presidency in 2016, the COVID-19 pandemic, and the protests following the murders of George Floyd and Breonna Taylor in 2020. Even before these events, however, the force of the right-wing nationalist political coalition created compelling, urgent incentives for liberals, progressives, antiracist activists, and radical leftists to seek out common ground and learn more about how to act together. This pressure has led to more complex and frequent encounters between horizontalism and more reformist, institutionalized forms of progressive politics. As we will see, these encounters have resulted in rapid mutations in the ways that organizations attempt to recruit and retain supporters, members, and organizers by acknowledging a greater diversity of left positions and communication tactics as they craft their collective ethos.

Occupy's way of conceptualizing democracy as a radical left endeavor has had reverberations in left movement culture and progressive campaign rhetoric. Analyzing these reverberations begs the question of what "the Left" actually might be. I make no claim as to the unity, coherence, or consistency of an entity that self-identifies as "the Left." Nonetheless, as Lawrence Grossberg has argued, in the United States the term still suggests a distance from procapitalist conservatives, moderates, and Democrats that is meaningful though indeterminate.[7]

The rise of right nationalism and the election of Trump has produced a second important dynamic in how the democratic ethos has been adapted by left, progressive, and even liberal actors. Trumpism represents and intersects with a deeply antiestablishment, libertarian strand in US right political culture.[8] The resonance between this strand and the radical Left's antiestablishment critique of plutocracy led a number of commentators to glibly refer to Occupy as the "Tea Party of the Left," a comparison vehemently rejected by Occupy supporters.[9] Nonetheless, the antiestablishment, antigovernmental rhetoric of Occupy is uncomfortably similar to Trump's calls to "drain the swamp" of Washington, DC. Just as Occupy rejected the instrumentalist common sense of electoral politics, Trumpism and some other strands of right nationalism advocate the heedless, chaotic destruction of the federal government, regardless of consequences.

It is not difficult to quickly outline major differences between the Trumpian version of "draining the swamp" and far-left support for innovative, critical forms of democratic organization. Wendy Brown has effectively argued, for instance, that many ascendant forms of right nationalism, emerging out of a mutated form of Hayekian neoliberalism, completely reject the ideal of democracy and envision traditional morality and markets as the organizing principles that will replace state institutions in the wake of their destruction.[10] The vehemence of right-nationalist antiestablishment rhetoric, however, has generated an urgent need for horizontalists (especially those of a more anarchist bent) to distinguish their advocacy from growing anti-immigrant, antifeminist, racist, procapitalist, and libertarian antiestablishment positions. Perhaps this has translated into higher tolerance for "establishment" and reformist leftism.

It also may be the case that emergent collaborations between horizontalist and liberal advocates of democracy are the result of how participants in the Occupy demonstrations witnessed firsthand some of the shortcomings of direct democracy. The potential problems with direct democracy, many of which are not necessarily *instrumental* failures, are voluminous and have been documented and theorized for decades. One of these failures, noted in some of the Occupy demonstrations, is what Jo Freeman called in the 1970s the "tyranny of structurelessness," or the tendency of directly democratic decision making to implicitly privilege those with the most privilege to begin with, sometimes even enabling demagoguery.[11] The Occupy assemblies tried valiantly to counteract this tendency with various kinds of training and consciousness-raising, but in the end it was a struggle in many of the camps to counteract inequalities between participants resulting from stratifications in ability, gender, race, and class.[12] For participants with certain circumstances, experiences, and abilities, sitting outside and making their voices heard in hours-long meetings was not a viable way to participate in democracy. In the end, the most enduring legacy of Occupy may be that it pushed some supporters sympathetic to horizontalism to reconsider liberalism's potential to foster equality of democratic participation through systems of representation.

The full spectrum of reasons why radicals and reformers find themselves increasingly making common cause is, in the end, unknowable. The best we can do is take note of the ways that coalitions are being formed and ask: What can we see and say about some of the ways that left reformism and radicalism have found common ground as a result of these lessons and pressures?

Democracy between Reformist Instrumentalism and Radical Prefiguration

Reformism and radicalism tend to differ in the way they approach *performative contradiction.* Reformist politics tolerate or even embrace performative contradictions between stated goals and tactics. When the disjunct between the means and ends of politics produce a performative contradiction, instrumentalism is ironic—but not all instrumentalism, as we will see, is ironic in this way. Radicalism, on the other hand, attempts to eschew such performative contradiction and even defines itself *against* the ironies that performative contradiction produces. Radical efforts to avoid performative contradiction are not always successful. Thomas Frank, for instance, dismisses radical perspectives based on the performative inconsistency between their commitment to inclusion, horizontality, and affective attachment and their willingness to exclude, marginalize, and hostilely reject would-be allies based on their lack of education in radical thinking and lifestyles.[13] Reformism openly embraces a distance between tactics and goals in a way that radicalism does not.

In spite of accusations to the contrary, Occupy was a loosening and evolution in a type of insular, isolated radical politics that avoids instrumentalism at all costs. Occupy is strongly associated with an anti-instrumental leftism that extends and adapts a commitment to radical "prefigurative" democratic tactics. One of the most well known of these tactics are participatory deliberative procedures, documented by sociologist Francesca Polletta in her research on twentieth-century left organizations, including the Student Nonviolent Coordinating Committee and Students for a Democratic Society.[14] The concept of prefiguration, however, extends well beyond participatory democratic decision making and encompasses a variety of ways in which leftist collectives self-organize according to political principles, relationships, and values. The origin of the concept of prefiguration is often traced to a 1977 article by Carl Boggs in which the author defines prefiguration as "the embodiment, within the ongoing political practice of a movement, of those forms of social relations, decision-making, culture, and human experience that are the ultimate goal."[15] For Boggs, and for many activists who embrace radical prefigurative politics, the radicalism of prefigurative tactics is precisely found in defining them *against* a more instrumental version of left politics in which the means and ends of politics are less closely aligned. Boggs claims, "The prefigurative dimension of revolutionary politics has repeatedly clashed with the instrumentalism of bureaucratic power struggles."[16] Boggs points out with some dismay that the "prefigurative strategy" has lacked a "external element" that would allow it to merge with more "statist strategies."[17] What is important to note about this claim is that here, in an early articulation of the concept, *prefiguration* is essentially presented as political strategy defined against "instrumentalism," understood as political strategy that adopts expedient tactics merely to pursue institutionalized power. The practices that movements use to foster a certain culture, make decisions, and embody their values are "prefigurative" in that they are seen as an alternative to pursuing change by more instrumental means.

The contrast between radical prefiguration and reformist instrumentalism has been reflected in the persistent contemporary reintroduction of the question: Should left politics employ conventional, instrumentalist political tactics associated with liberal democracy and neoliberal political rationality? Political actors on the most conventional, instrumentalist, or reformist side of this question would answer yes—they see the US government itself as a democracy that has political potential grounded in the past vibrancy of liberal principles and institutions. From this perspective, *Citizens United v. Federal Election Commission* and the deregulation of finance capital represent concrete problems that can be more or less effectively solved by passing laws, amending the Constitution, electing more responsible representatives, and so forth. For instrumentalist reformers, state institutions may have been corrupted by capital, but democracy requires politicians to defy corporate masters so as to accurately represent public opinion by passing legislation that re-enables government to serve the interests of "the people." Generally speaking, the reformist position is that liberal democracy should include fairer taxation policies, tighter and better funded regulations, and cleaner and better-informed elections. If certain radical principles have to be sacrificed along the way, so be it.

This instrumentalist and reformist position sees strategic value in strengthening communication that straightforwardly serves formal political equality and freedom from state interference, including opinion polling, checks and balances, rational legislative debate, truthful journalism, campaign donations, and voting. From this perspective, democracy is pursued by engineering better procedures of governance and decision making in hopes that they might one day become law. Within movement organizations, instrumentalist commitments lead collectives seeking change to identify concrete, achievable goals and use effective, efficient persuasive means to pursue them. What is essential to such approaches is that they accept and even celebrate a pragmatic division between the means of politics and the ends of politics. For such reformers, radical ends might require liberal or neoliberal persuasion.

Radical approaches to democracy attempt to theorize or create new, ideal forms of political practice that do not necessarily posit governmental reform and instrumental problem-solving as their telos. Departing from liberal common sense, left radicalism often assumes that no, conventional, instrumentalist, and institutionalized forms of liberal and neoliberal political persuasion are not genuinely democratic. For some strongly antistatist forms of radicalism, "democracy" would be communism or even anarchism. From this perspective, the modern state has few democratic qualities because it is organized as a vertical hierarchy dependent on instrumental logic and flawed processes of representation.[18] Procedures that strive to support formal equality and freedom through state mechanisms merely bolster undemocratic systems of governance. From the radical perspective, democracy is a type of political activity that must not only go beyond voting, donating to election campaigns, polling, and persuading the public, as such activities inevitably fail to reckon with neoliberal political rationality and the pervasive influence of wealth on the US sociopolitical life and constitutional foundation.

Left radicalism encompasses a variety of perspectives, but horizontalism is one of its most visible instantiations. Horizontalism conceptualizes *democracy* as resistance to the plutocratic state as well as the demonstration of the antihierarchical ideals that support dismantling federal and state government and corporations themselves.[19] Horizontal and egalitarian self-organizing processes that include all people and many nonhuman entities define democracy as a nonhierarchical form of social life. Horizontalism is an instance of a broader radical approach in which democracy is, by definition, a way of acting politically that strives to dissent against, transform, dismantle, or overthrow plutocratic governance while building egalitarian alternative communities.

Radical-left rejection of state institutions and instrumental approaches to politics that engage with such institutions is well known. What is trickier is the relationship between radical Leftism, including horizontalism, and the mass media—political and social institutions whose structure and messages are just as determined by capitalist logics as state institutions (and perhaps more so) but are far more difficult for activists to reject completely. If activists hope to project their vision and activities out to a broader audience, they must communicate instrumentally through the mass media, including global social media corporations. Without a toehold in corporate media, activists cannot *persuade* others.

Mass media, of course, are not the only form of communication roundly critiqued as instrumental; the act of persuasion itself has been critiqued for millennia. Bryan Garsten points out that persuasion has always been suspected of devolving into either pandering to an audience or manipulating them.[20] Feminist rhetorical scholars have defined persuasion as a problematic process of exercising communicative force over others.[21] Some rhetorical theorists have taken issue with the assumption of the primacy of "intention" in the concept of persuasion; these debates have pointed at how a rational, intentional, and individual human subject is the source of rhetorical agency and persuasion without considering the broader linguistic context.[22] All these concerns suggest that the very concept of persuasion assumes an instrumental division between means and ends. Persuasion is an inherently instrumentalist concept in the sense that communicative technics, as the means of politics, can and should be considered as being distinct from the goals they are employed to pursue. When activists select communication techniques with the goal of changing the minds of an audience or getting an audience to act in a particular way, they are engaging in instrumental persuasion, no matter how radical their goals. Pursuing this process through the mass media merely highlights the instrumental qualities of such forms of communication.

The Occupy demonstrations consolidated and innovated a certain leftist way of balancing radical prefiguration and instrumental persuasion. Prefigurative practices like participatory democracy have a long history in leftism in the United States.[23] However, prefigurative elements of left politics have largely been considered important for their capacity to shape internal movement decision making, relationships, and the values of participants.[24] Occupy, on the other hand, *broadcasted* its prefigurative democratic practices and made them visible to a wide audience in order to persuade that audience.

In doing so, it innovated in the repertoire of radical-left politics. The forms of political action consolidated and disseminated by Occupy have established ways of performing radical democratic values associated with participatory democracy and putting them on display for outsiders. The latter task establishes credibility, recruits new participants, gets media attention, and accomplishes a range of other persuasive tasks more instrumental than principled or merely prefigurative. The features of this continuing emergence and diffusion of *the democratic ethos*, strongly shaped by horizontalism but adapted to the context of liberal organizations and institutions, is what I hope to elucidate here.

Democratic Ethos: Prefiguration as Instrumental Persuasion

Occupy's version of prefiguration was not simply an effort to instill or affirm democratic values in the core organizers and assembly participants. It was also an outward-facing *persuasive* effort to boost the credibility of the message of the demonstrations, recruit new participants, acquire donations, critique other forms of organization, and facilitate coverage of the credibility of the demonstrations by news media. These were instrumentalist goals that differed from some of the ways that movement actors have performed prefiguration in the past.[25] This persuasive orientation of the Occupy demonstrations was central to how the organizing mechanisms of the demonstrations went beyond what I will call *internal prefiguration.* Internal prefiguration is a way of understanding the political value and importance of how collectives prefiguratively organize themselves as what Karma R. Chávez has called "protected enclaves" away from the spotlight and their public audiences.[26] *Persuasive prefiguration,* on the other hand, is prefigurative action that is directed at an audience external to the core activist organizers and existing participants. As a performance for an audience of potential supporters, critics, and future members, persuasive prefiguration has an instrumental dimension in the sense that it is more attuned than internal prefiguration to altering its methods to accomplish practical goals. Persuasive prefiguration is still, however, prefiguration in the sense that it is about how collectives self-organize to preserve and propagate radical values within themselves. When techniques of self-organization are then revealed and broadcasted to others in strategic ways to assist in the tasks of persuasion, prefigurative persuasion is a way of presenting the collective ethos of the group.

The variety of ways *ethos* has been theorized helps to shed light on the distinction between prefigurative politics that attempt to *transform participants* and prefigurative politics that attempt to *persuade others*—as well as how self-transformation and persuasion are linked. There are two basic understandings of the concept of ethos that have emerged across academic disciplines. The first is what I will call ethos as *doxa*—roughly meaning the presence and enactment of cultural values and ethics. The second is persuasive ethos—an element of an instrumental effort to accomplish the tasks of convincing others to take some type of action. For political and rhetorical theorists such as Michael J. Hyde or William Connolly, the concept of ethos is more closely tied to doxa: an underlying set of ethical or moral assumptions expressed in a political culture, political philosophy, or texts.[27] This understanding of ethos is both more philosophical and more colloquial than any other. It is something like zeitgeist, spirit, or ethic—sometimes all three simultaneously. This way of conceptualizing ethos is comparatively disconnected from the instrumental arts of persuasion. Hyde's approach to ethos attempts to bridge the gap between ethos as doxa and ethos as persuasive art by arguing that specific persuasive acts contribute to the process of building, consolidating, and affirming the doxa or dwelling place of communal ethos.[28]

In the Aristotelian rhetorical tradition Hyde references, however, ethos is a rhetorical tactic in which a speaker displays their habits of thought and action to demonstrate good will, trustworthiness, and good judgment. This tradition, which has profoundly influenced the study of rhetoric in the late twentieth and early twenty-first centuries, strongly emphasizes the instrumental tasks of persuasion as a technical art.[29] As a persuasive artistic proof, ethos is the enactment and practice of doxastic ethical commitments. But it is performed as part of rhetorical action that has an instrumental component in which means and ends are divided, sometimes ironically so. Conceptualizations of ethos that hew closely to the classical tradition often emphasize how ethos is built and defended through *hexis,* or habits. Isocrates's assumption, adopted by Cicero and Quintilian, was that the intentional cultivation of the ethical character of a student was an essential component of rhetorical education. For these educators, performed ethos would naturally result from the deliberate ongoing development of individual ethical habits that could then self-evidently shine through in rhetorical acts.

Some scholars have attempted to locate the Aristotelian concept of ethos in the context of the *Nichomachean Ethics,* but its association with persuasive artistry in the *Rhetoric* has led many scholars to identify ethos with a performative repertoire rather than merely with the conduct of an ethical life.[30] One's actual habits may be brought to bear in the task of performing one's good character, but they are not essential to the task. To treat ethos as *merely* instrumentally persuasive, however, would mean disregarding the paradoxical concern with authenticity that underwrites the concept of ethos. If "ethos" is merely tactics and rhetorical tricks, the concept of ethos gets divorced from any assumption of an authentic relationship between a speaker and their core values, principles, and habits of life. The potential gap between ethical living and persuasive ethos opens up space for accusations of irony and mere instrumentalism.

Feminist and antiracist unease with the cultural and political limits of classical Greek models of character and virtue has led to general calls to pluralize the concept of ethos (as *ethē*) and acknowledge how differing cultural contexts produce subject positions variously inhabited to produce a sense of a rhetor's ethos.[31] Even in the context of this call to pluralize ethos, however, we have not yet seen a description of the ethos of collective actors. Traditionally conceived, the relationship between individual speaker and collective ethos presumes that collectivity is the relatively static background that individual rhetors draw from and act against. The type of prefiguration consolidated by Occupy requires us to understand certain groups as themselves being collective political actors engaged in persuasive efforts. These collectives are not the cultural backdrop but the event and agent; they *are* the rhetors, if you will. Just as the habits of individuals provide resources for the projection of that individual's ethos, the techniques and technologies that constitute groups provide resources for the projection of a *collective* ethos. Political and social movements are projects conducted by collective actors that speak, write, march, create, and act in concert with one another. These forms of political action require techniques and technologies that go beyond the individualistic craft or techne of ethical cultivation and self-presentation. Techniques and technologies suggest what kind of values, traditions, political-intellectual influences, collaborations, and sense of unity a group cultivates together. The hexis by which self-reflexively radical groups organize themselves constitute internal prefiguration.

When a group acts together to influence others, however, it can also *persuasively* prefigure based on its collective ethos. A group with higher levels of decision-making transparency and accountability to its membership, for instance, can support a different kind of claim to a democratic ethos than a group that simply contacts its members for fundraising. Similarly, a political campaign that seeks support primarily through television advertisements cultivates a different kind of ethos than one that relies primarily on social media, live rallies, and door-to-door canvassing to convert new supporters.

This is not to say that these media technologies and persuasive techniques have an inherent political or ethical value. On the contrary, such technics are enmeshed in larger, deeper sets of assumptions and institutions that are culturally specific and historically contingent. Communication technologies have certain affordances but are also described in language and given meaning through associations, values, and narratives.[32] Techniques are practiced, encouraged by educational systems and corporations, and required by government. When integrated into systems that prioritize instrumental rationality, they then develop accordingly.

Ultimately, media technologies and persuasive techniques are enmeshed in the broader dynamics of doxa, the unexamined and taken-for-granted practices, values, objects, and languages that constitute the background of political practices. Just as there is no single ethos, there is no single, unified doxa; it would be more accurate to describe doxai that are geographically, temporarily, and institutionally specific. Doxai, one could argue, are the nonhuman elements of political action because they are "the cultural resources available to be enacted, critiqued, and reenacted in the course of generating political change and stabilization."[33] Many theorists of doxa, including myself, have written about doxa as a linguistic reservoir, but it might be more precise to take a cue from Bernard Stiegler and say that doxai enacted and critiqued during political actions are commonsense technics—of which language is only one.[34]

Connolly has theorized political ethos as itself being precisely such a cultural reservoir, while Sheila Jasanoff has focused attention on the way that technologies fit into doxa. William Connolly's more Deleuzian work on the ethos of pluralization suggests that ethos is an ontological "fund" or "subterranean connections from which responsiveness" might be cultivated, "and cultural continuities upon which new negotiations might be built."[35] He argues that a *democratic* ethos, especially one oriented toward pluralization, mobilizes subterranean cultural continuities against existing moral codes that have become unproductively ossified.[36] Jasanoff uses the terminology of "sociotechnical imaginaries" to describe how doxai are "collectively held, institutionally stabilized, and publicly performed visions of desirable futures, animated by shared understandings of forms of social life and social order attainable through, and supportive of, advances in science and technology."[37] According to Jasanoff, technologies are not simply doxa-delivery devices. They have complex narratives attached to them that encourage their affordances to mesh with beliefs and practices in specific, changeable ways. These approaches challenge us to think of *ethē* as cultural, environmental, technological, and linguistic reservoirs that shape our senses of what ethical action or character might be and how the reservoirs are themselves, in turn, shaped by the ongoing performance of their contents. Attributing cultural and political force to techniques and technologies encourages us to recognize the depth, complexity, and plurality of the specific technics involved in both internal and persuasive prefigurative performances.

Connolly and Jasanoff's approach to ethos presumes that one of the tasks of normative theory is to express and cultivate innovations in existing political ethē (or ethics) by forwarding a philosophical defense of the detailed premises of a preferred political ethos. In a sense, the description of the "democratic ethos" developed in this book participates in such a project in that it attempts to describe a political ethic that is enmeshed in political doxai, emerges out of a specific early twenty-first-century political conjuncture, and has an increasingly identifiable set of features that seem to have an existence apart from their instrumental "use" by any one political actor.

There are, however, two crucial differences between how this study of Occupy's democratic ethos differs from political-philosophical efforts like Connolly's. First, the features of the "democratic ethos" described in this book are distilled by describing the actually existing rhetorical techniques and technologies of political actors rather than by reading political theorists. I am attempting to describe the form of an ethos as it actually exists and is developed by the collective actors that perform it. This means that the second key difference between this study and a more political-philosophical approach is that it locates "ethos" in the performative and technological dimensions of politics rather than in beliefs, knowledge, or identity. The democratic ethos consolidated by the Occupy demonstrations is certainly a way of mobilizing a sort of leftist political reserve to contest a taken-for-granted set of instrumental political assumptions, but that reserve is not one of beliefs, narratives or imaginaries; it is more like what Diana Taylor has called a "repertoire."[38] The repertoire that lends itself to the performance of a democratic ethos includes, for instance, communication technologies, deliberative techniques, ways of expressing emotion, and signals of alliance and coalition. These techniques and technologies are not inherently democratic. In fact, as we will see, it is only when they are performed as part of authentically democratic dissent—or *dissensus,* as Jacques Rancière has argued—that they project a democratic ethos. What this means in practice is that an "authentic" democratic ethos is performed against and through the idea that politics are what I will be calling "ironically instrumental."

Understanding authenticity as a persuasive performance highlights a crucial dynamic of the democratic ethos in the context of political advocacy: the tension between performative consistency and performative contradiction. When a political performance happens, including the performance of persuasive prefiguration, certain techniques and technologies are taken up and acted out. These technics are not, however, value-neutral because they are already positioned in doxa, just as the proposals and assumptions of advocacy are not value-neutral. The question is whether and how a correspondence is achieved between the technics that constitute the advocate itself and the content of the changes or positions it advocates for.

Persuasive ethos is not *character itself* but the *appearance* of character generated to pursue some situational, rhetorical goal in a given time and place. An "authentic" ethos, in the context of a persuasive performance, requires a certain level of consistency between what has been *done* by the individual or collective in terms of self-fashioning (in their habits, actions, etc.) and what they *say* should be done by others (including their supporters) and institutions. It therefore requires on some level disclosure of the processes of self-formation that constitute a collective. Authenticity of various types has certainly been important in democratic politics before Occupy. But Occupy seems to have enacted, invigorated, and ultimately established a flexible, specific and repeatable reservoir of technics for the consistent performance of an authentic democratic ethos in left politics. Collective actors demonstrating their own version of an authentic democratic ethos strive for performative consistency between the means and ends of their action. In so doing, they claim that other institutions are *un*democratic, that they demonstrate too wide a division between the means and ends of politics, and that they are thus engaged in a performative contradiction.

Formulating the relationship between performative contradiction and performative consistency in the context of the Occupy demonstrations helps us see how the relationship between the two operates as derived from the tactics of radical prefiguration. The technics used to produce less radical collective political actors (such as nonprofit organizations, election campaigns, or legal-aid providers) are re-envisioned as sources of democratic authority, credibility, and character, as these groups strive to achieve goals of political and social change while simultaneously producing a sense that other (for instance, more neoliberal and instrumentalist) approaches to politics performatively contradict themselves. In the case of a democratic ethos, performative consistency must revolve around demonstrating how the composition of a collective entity has been habitually pursued through technics informed by democratic political principles consistent with the goals of advocacy. This is the case whether it be consistency in terms of the habits of an individual, the communicative structures of an organization, or the coordination tactics of a movement. A democratic ethos may be instrumental (because it is part of persuasion), but it also generates the sense of a collective democratic self that is authentic because its ways of self-constituting are consistent with its persuasive advocacy. The ethos of democratic subjects, collective or individual, pivots on the question of the verisimilitude of their democratic performance.

At the same time, however, establishing this sense of an authentic democratic ethos seems to require articulating a critique of the ironic "democratic" claims of other instances of politics. Given the emphasis on performative *consistency* in the democratic ethos, performative *contradiction* plays an important role in the identification of what it means to be merely or ironically instrumental rather than authentic. Because the foil of radicalism is excessive instrumentalism in reform efforts, the inauthenticity against which the democratic ethos of authenticity contrasts itself remains certain instrumentalisms that harbor performative contradiction. Ethos is not merely about the production of a sense of authenticity, credibility, authority, good judgment or any other culturally specific value or practice. It is about working against the appearance of tension, irony, and contradiction in the relationship between an enunciation and the entity it came from.

Plato seemed to consider the whole concept of ethos to be too closely tied to the corrupting influences of sophistry. Why would "ethos" even need to be named, after all, if not to learn how to instrumentally analyze and perform it? In the wake of Jacques Derrida's reading of the *Phaedrus,* Plato's text has become well known for its provocations on the technology of writing.[39] Even in the thought and writing of Plato, good character and the truth of integrity, nobility, and beauty were best explained by juxtaposing them with the instrumentality of writing and ethos. This dialectical tactic demonstrates how essential the idea of "merely persuasive" self-presentation is to developing any affirmative conceptualization of authentic character. Yet beyond this acknowledgment of how necessary the concept of instrumentality is to the production of a sense of authenticity, the *Phaedrus* lets us in on a habit of thought that persists in the democratic ethos until our very moment. This is the habit of associating inauthentic presentations of self with an instrumental communication technology.

Occupy's version of democracy reaffirmed and invigorated performances of democratic ethos that claim to be more "authentic," in part because of how prefigurative technics constitute instrumental persuasion. Occupy claimed an authentic democratic ethos that was inefficient, focused on embodied experiences and emotions, and based on principles rather than results. The consolidated democratic ethos identifies communicative technics with a range of values and principles quite distinct from rationality and efficiency. Instead, communication technologies and techniques can contribute to a democratic ethos for the ways they prefiguratively express, cultivate, and transmit non-instrumental values such as harmony, respect, equality, responsiveness, diversity, purity, integrity, rebelliousness, and thoughtfulness.

In its own way, however, Occupy was far more accommodating of instrumentalism than more "pure" prefiguration has been in the past. The demonstrations certainly strove for performative consistency. But they reoriented technics that had previously only been elements of the internal prefigurative communication within movements and made them visible to outsiders as part of persuasion. In so doing, the demonstrations followed even more closely in the footsteps of the Zapatistas, whose process of publicizing their internal operations have been well described.[40] Occupy's move to make its decision-making processes as public as possible was ultimately strategic in many ways and served the goal of building credibility for the demonstrations while promoting, recruiting, and justifying the demonstrations' values for the media and other onlookers.

Occupy may represent an innovation in the left democratic ethos in the United States, but if it has innovated it has done so in the context of a long-standing liberal-progressive democratic tradition fascinated with the need for "transparency" and superior technologies. James Carey and John Durham Peters have described how progressive theorists of democracy and communication, such as John Dewey and Charles Horton Cooley, grappled with the ethos of communication technologies that were new to them at the turn of the twentieth century.[41] Pure forms of horizontal democracy, however, are distinct from progressivism's consistent commitment to reforming, building, and strengthening state institutions. A less purely horizontal and more instrumental commitment to authentic democratic and oppositional techniques of communicating and organizing is what Occupy demonstrated, intersecting with progressivism's more accommodating radical elements. The result has been that Occupy has opposed the liberal and neoliberal visions of democracy in which efficient and effective capacities of persuasion are lauded based *solely* on whether they can instrumentally achieve specific electoral and policy goals through transparency and better technical knowledge.

The resulting horizontal democratic ethos is deeply earnest, strives for authenticity, pays homage to the past, and puts a premium on integrity and performative consistency—all within the context of attempting to effectively engage the media and push its message out as widely as possible. Even more specifically, the democratic ethos consolidated by Occupy carefully reveals its own organizing mechanisms and communication practices (or habits) in order to demonstrate its character and credibility. As both an individual and organizational practice, a democratic ethos relies on the disclosure and projection of structuring democratic values over and above instrumentalist calculations—to achieve the goal of presenting itself as more authentically democratic than some other more ironically instrumental ways of conceiving democracy. The Occupy demonstrations certainly didn't invent the democratic ethos, but they consolidated and projected a certain version of it that is compatible with the traditions of *horizontalidad*, anarchism, and autonomous Marxism while interfacing with instrumentalist liberal doxa far more thoroughly than forms of prefigurative politics have done in the past. The contrasting attribution of both authenticity and instrumentality to different communication technologies may itself be part of persuasion, but it nonetheless reproduces a version of the classical dynamic of ethos: the tension inherent in using instrumental techniques to perform the authentic integrity of a truly democratic self.

The broad features of the democratic ethos demonstrate a long-standing and influential set of radical tactics, but with some key changes in the persuasive performance of prefiguration. The democratic ethos has produced a set of technics that mainstream, reformist anticorporate politics can draw from, reference, and mobilize to build their own *ethē* as they advocate for political, economic, and social change. Mapping the presence of these tactics in Occupy and less radical types of movement politics demonstrates that while persuasive ethos may be fundamentally instrumental and goal-oriented, as a democratic performance it necessarily includes the gesture of communicating "more authentically" than antidemocratic entities. In the process of projecting a democratic ethos, an authentically democratic entity shows itself, marshaling communicative technics to support the fundamental claim that "*we are more democratic than that.*"

The democratic ethos, as a type of persuasive prefiguration, is proving to be flexible enough to be adapted to instrumental forms of anticorporate politics in spite of its genesis in the strongly antistatist and anti-instrumentalist Occupy demonstrations. By unabashedly promoting the internal organizing practices of the demonstrations as proof of an authentic commitment to democracy, the 2011 demonstrations consolidated an ethos that continues to serve as a viable alternative to the prevailing ethos of technocratic, instrumental liberalism. Because the democratic ethos is still instrumental in the sense that it is part of persuading a mass audience, however, it is more easily able to be combined with traditionally liberal forms of politics.

This book has been organized with the goal of showing how left radicalism and instrumental liberalism have contributed to the performance of the democratic ethos. The first two chapters, taken together, illustrate the sharp differences between Occupy and the prevailing liberal/neoliberal instrumentalism. The remaining three chapters look at cases where they have combined. The first chapter describes persuasive prefiguration in the Occupy Wall Street demonstrations of 2011, with a particular focus on the practices of the New York City encampment. The Occupy demonstrations consolidated a democratic ethos that draws heavily on traditions of prefigurative politics while integrating a more instrumentalist sensibility. In the United States, the hallmark of the Occupy demonstrations were the General Assemblies, a form of direct democracy that affected how the encampments organized themselves and projected a democratic ethos. Occupy managed to combine often divergent anarchist and autonomist tactics by turning prefigurative community building into a form of persuasion as it was projected outward. This combination consolidated and conveyed an earnest democratic ethos of authenticity based on the performative consistency of protesting economic inequality while modeling radical democratic practices. This performance of the democratic ethos refused the instrumentalism of liberal and neoliberal political doxa. It nonetheless was also an instrumentalist innovation in the existing technics of prefiguration that focused exclusively on democracy as an end in itself within radical movement culture.

To provide contrast with the democratic ethos of authenticity, the second chapter describes a reform effort that has *not* recognizably adopted the democratic ethos of Occupy. The Seattle "Democracy Vouchers" project illustrates how liberal reforms are pursued in a climate of greater attention to the issues of political corruption since the 2011 demonstrations but have not taken up the democratic ethos of Occupy itself. The Honest Elections Seattle initiative campaign employed a well-worn set of liberal political technics that produced an ironic instrumentalist ethos of performative contradiction. The "voucher" financing strategy has long been advocated by liberal intellectuals such as Lawrence Lessig. The most high-profile city to implement this type of campaign finance solution is Seattle, Washington, which tried it for the first time in the 2017 municipal elections. The campaign to implement the voucher program, however, was itself funded by wealthy supporters who described their large donations as a sort of undemocratic means to pursue democratic ends. This instrumentalist logic of pursuing democratic results through undemocratic means—as well as a strong reliance on measurable, data-heavy, technologically-dependent tactics—exemplify a type of ironic instrumentalism that has not attempted to incorporate and project a democratic ethos. The Democracy Vouchers project in Seattle illustrates how concern about the role of money in politics can generate support for election reforms but without a substantial transformation in the form of political action. The result is a continuation of the ironic instrumental ethos.

Each subsequent chapter describes how the consolidated democratic ethos of authenticity has been adapted by collective actors in the context of contemporary liberal forms of political action—amending the Constitution, running for elected office, and legal aid to municipalities fighting corporate incursions. Together, they suggest that the democratic ethos lives on in the political technics of instrumentalist reformers. These reform efforts are attuned to the need for an infusion of radical values via a democratic ethos to counteract the tired instrumental rationality of liberalism.

The third chapter describes how the 2016 Bernie Sanders campaign for the Democratic presidential nomination adopted elements of the democratic ethos, especially in the context of digital communication and fundraising.

The 2016 Sanders campaign relied in part on a version of the "netroots" narrative, in which progressive digital campaigning is rhetorically pitted against conservative television advertising driven by political action committee (PAC) funding. The Sanders campaign constructed a narrative about the inherently authentic and democratic qualities of its own internal data management and communication practices while simultaneously enhancing its democratic ethos with a commitment to refusing PAC money and seeking support only through small donations. The result was a shift away from valuing campaign tactics merely for their efficiency and effectiveness and toward projecting them outward as evidence of the democratic ethos of the campaign and the candidate. The controversy over the fate of the personal data of the Sanders donors and volunteers, which received great attention from news media, illustrates how the campaign's internal digital organizing tactics were performed to defend its decision not to support Hillary Clinton and the Democratic National Committee.

The fourth chapter describes a conflict between radical and reformist advocates of a constitutional amendment to address corporate influence on the political process. Since the Supreme Court's 2010 decision in *Citizens United v. Federal Election Commission,* momentum has grown substantially for passing an amendment to the Constitution that would limit the political influence of corporations. The democratic ethos has been adopted by some parts of the movement but not others, leading to tensions and clashes around "transparency" and deliberative norms. A series of mass conference calls between movement leaders led to a breakdown that reveals how varying types of commitment to instrumentalism and authenticity cause fissures even among advocates with similar goals.

The fifth chapter describes the work of the Community Environmental Legal Defense Fund (CELDF), an environmentalist legal-aid nonprofit founded in 1995.[42] CELDF's tactics have evolved substantially over the decades and its narrative about its own history works to produce a sense of authentic radicalism as it increasingly refuses instrumental strategies. It now attempts to pass municipal laws codifying the rights of nature, including those pertaining to rivers, ecosystems, animals, and communities. CELDF argues for the inclusion of a new class of entities as legal persons with rights while simultaneously attempting to dismantle the institution of corporate limited liability and the sovereign authority of state and federal government, including regulatory agencies such as the US Environmental Protection Agency. This radical rethinking of the basis of democratic sovereignty includes a new role for the material world while reinforcing an image of rural democratic purity. In the years after the Occupy demonstrations, CELDF began referencing Occupy and pursued collaborations on urban houselessness with horizontal organizations. It also began framing its legal-aid work as a type of confrontational direct action that uses failures in the courts as a source of mobilizing energy to draw attention to state-based injustice.

All the types of politics described in the final three chapters—a presidential election campaign, lobbying for a constitutional amendment, and the advocacy of a legal-aid nonprofit—are concerned with issues closely related to Occupy and have absorbed some of the democratic rhetorical culture of horizontalism. The changes in these democratic rhetorics are not purely caused by the Occupy demonstrations. Occupy itself, after all, was a mobilization and recombination of long-standing approaches to democratic politics. Nonetheless, features of Occupy's persuasively prefigurative ethos appear in reformist, instrumentalist political rhetorics that previously had a much smaller resemblance to radical-left politics. Occupy seems to have established or consolidated the parameters of a left-democratic ethos based on the revival of authentic persuasive communication as an important democratic value that includes sincerity, integrity, performative consistency between mission and organization, and a broadly anti-ironic ethic. Additionally, these ways of integrating horizontalism into more established and instrumental political strategies show how the democratic ethos, while associated with an antihierarchical politics of purity, has actually been flexible enough to be meaningfully incorporated into relatively "vertical" and reformist politics. As we will see, Occupy was more instrumental in its orientation than prefigurative radical politics have generally been in the past. By moving from internal prefiguration to the consolidation of a persuasively prefigurative democratic ethos, Occupy provided a flexible set of rhetorical options for political collectives to perform their commitments to radical-left values.

Accounting for these evolving practices, especially in the middle of a substantial realignment in US politics, is challenging. As one scholar put it, "Writing with movements is like taking a photo of the human body in rapid motion."[43] I refer to political actors in this work as demonstrating certain techniques and technologies, but it is always with the caveat that various individuals and collectives are constantly in the process of evaluating, improving, changing, and consolidating their conceptualizations and practices of democracy and the tactics that flow from them. Additionally, this book has been written in the middle of what seems to be an invigorated right-nationalism fomented in part by the failure of liberal democratic institutions and grotesque economic inequality, upheaval and fracturing in the two major political parties in the United States, and the beginning of a tidal shift in public opinion against certain social media companies. It has been completed in the middle of a global pandemic that promises to alter political landscapes in unforeseen ways. I nonetheless hope to provide a sense of what is emerging from the efforts of movements to adapt to these circumstances and integrate horizontal values while effecting important change.

ONE

The Democratic Ethos of Authenticity in the Occupy Wall Street Demonstrations

In the fall of 2011, activists camped out in Manhattan's Zuccotti Park, renamed it Liberty Plaza, inspired similar demonstrations across the United States, and conducted one of the most visible anticorporate political performances of the decade. Although the demonstrations famously refused to make specific policy demands, they generated provocative critiques of plutocracy and inequalities in wealth. Building on the momentum of mass protests against austerity and debt in Spain, Egypt, and elsewhere, Occupy drew critical attention to the many ways in which governments enable economic inequality. Part of Occupy's critique of plutocracy involved exposing the lip service paid by politicians to liberal values and forms of political to organization that have since been gutted by neoliberal markets. This critique of the ironic performative contradictions of liberalism was accompanied by the performance of a democratic ethos built out of consistency between the messages of the demonstrations and communicative technics by which they were conducted.

In the years immediately after the 2011 demonstrations, hundreds of interdisciplinary scholarly articles celebrated Occupy in ways that were enthusiastic but often narrowly focused on its relationship to live and in-person politics, embodiment, public space, or new communication technologies, all of which resonate in critical, cultural and rhetorical scholarship on social movements.[1] Much of this research on Occupy was based solely on participant-observation methods in which *being present* at the live demonstrations enabled a scholarly perspective that was itself of a piece with the stated focus of the demonstrations themselves, especially vis-à-vis the physical occupation of space and the politics of presence.[2] Poetic reflections like Michael Taussig's certainly capture a sense of the experience of *being there.*[3] Todd Gitlin's occasionally critical description of Occupy benefited from detailed analysis of how the demonstrations worked on the ground but was limited by its proximity to the moment in time it documented.[4] More recent,

Judith Butler has attempted to broaden this focus to develop an account of embodied and emplaced revival of civilly disobedient public assembly as an activist tactic.[5]

In-the-moment and ethnographic sensibilities have left a lot of questions about Occupy unanswered, while a focus on embodiment and public space sometimes fails to capture something about Occupy that sets it apart from other street protests. The tendency of this scholarship to simply celebrate Occupy is often underwritten by the acceptance at face value of Occupy's refusal to make specific policy demands or engage elected officials. These works focus on further developing an account of public protest in the context of radical democratic thought, performance studies, and cultural critique, which certainly captures an important dimension of Occupy and established its significance in the multiple overlapping traditions of radical-left scholarship, especially in its concern with the centrality of the body in performance and protest.

Occupy and other "movements of the squares" in 2011 have also been described as inaugurating a new political era grounded in more democratic communication technologies.[6] Manuel Castells is a widely cited example of a thinker who sees a certain kind of horizontal political meaning in the new communication technologies so central to the 2011 demonstrations.[7] Although these technologies were important to Occupy and continue to play a role in both movement and electoral politics, rapid changes in the political environment since 2011 have made it difficult to accept analyses of communication technology that do not take into account, for instance, the rise of bots, trolls, white nationalism, Trump, microtargeted advertising surveillance, disinformation campaigns, and a host of other ways in which the democratic potential of new communication technology has been complicated or even poisoned.[8] Some of Occupy's rhetorical appropriations of new technologies, including livestreaming assembly meetings, were initially interpreted by researchers as evidence of radical, liberatory resistance to the confining frames of legacy news media.[9] Livestreaming and extensive video documentation of movement actions have grown since Occupy and have substantially changed in connotation in the pandemic era. Protestors have been attempting to document police brutality in public space for decades before Occupy, but we are now seeing the extensive use of video to share a variety of events, including planning meetings, updates, debates, member testimonials, workshops, and other forms of movement rhetoric. In an era when giant multinational media corporations such as Facebook provide such livestreaming capabilities and video meetings are persistent elements of certain workplaces, livestreaming protest events doesn't seem to carry the same kind of "radical" rhetorical charge.

These issues and others suggest the need to revisit the task of explaining the unfolding significance of the rhetoric of Occupy—both in the terms of the academic leftisms and horizontalisms that shaped it and a more reformist, instrumentalist progressivism that has simultaneously rebuked it and absorbed it. Many of Occupy's organizers and participants have since moved on to other projects closely tied to the concerns and methods of Occupy but are no longer called "Occupy."[10] Some of them have even rejected Occupy's antistatist tactics in favor of electoral politics.[11] Others have joined advocacy and lobbying organizations.[12] Occupy participants in New York City turned out to Sanders rallies and organized for his campaign.[13] They supported constitutional amendments and campaign finance reform.[14] Their tactics spread to organizing and protesting on other issues. This suggests that Occupy was an event whose relevance for democratic movement rhetoric continues to unfold in ways that are complex, long-term, and uneven.[15] In other words, after the initial deluge of celebratory and critical writings about Occupy, we are now in a more effective position to unpack the significance of the demonstrations for movement rhetoric and performance, as well as the political significance of new communication technologies and the evolution of twenty-first-century democratic values.

Occupy strove to cultivate an ethos different from the focus on manipulating institutional levers effectively and efficiently. Instead, Occupy celebrated technics and technologies that were performatively consistent with its critical refusal to engage with governmental institutions and dominant logics of market competition, political efficiency, and effectiveness. The result was a democratic ethos that strove to unify means and ends by adopting and adapting technics that affirmed the values that the demonstrations sought to broadly manifest in the long term. Occupy rejected irony and performative contradiction. In news coverage of the Occupy demonstrations, much was made of the question of Occupy's goals, demands, and purpose, an emphasis that ended up highlighting Occupy's refusal of instrumental logics alongside its refusal to make demands of state institutions that, as demonstrations both assumed and argued, operated according to the same instrumental logics.[16]

Pursuit of such news coverage, however, was a key goal of the Occupy demonstrations.[17] While Occupy may have largely eschewed direct engagement with governmental institutions, it wholeheartedly attempted to engage the media. Scholars writing about news coverage of Occupy have rightly pointed out that traditional news outlets were slow to recognize and cover the demonstrations and in some cases were persistently hostile. In the end, however, press coverage did convey Occupy's critique of plutocracy and its alternative vision of cooperative resource-sharing and decision making.[18]

News outlets were fascinated by the General Assembly (GA), especially left-leaning publications that generally reflect more traditionally liberal and progressive values. The *Nation,* the *Atlantic,* and *DailyKos* all published reflections on the people's mic, the innovative mass repetition and amplification of the words of speakers in the General Assembly.[19] *Rolling Stone's* in-depth analysis of Occupy took the GA and the people's mic as the central captivating feature of the demonstrations.[20] National Public Radio followed up with a reflection on the wide and ongoing importance of the assembly process in December 2011.[21] The assembly process was interesting because it was novel, but it was also interesting because it was rich, complicated, and provided a compelling and multilayered performative conceptualization of democracy that captured attention and support from those who didn't necessarily already agree with the message. The demonstrations worked hard to capture the attention of outsiders and cultivate a specific, effective, and persuasive set of messages for that audience. One of the core demands of Occupy was to pay attention, "buy in," and circulate its message.

That message, however, was often translated as an avoidance of making demands on governmental institutions. Far-left analyses of Occupy, both academic and journalistic, embraced the "demandlessness" (or utopian demands) of the encampments as a key strength that fostered inclusion, raised awareness of many issues, and supported the emergence of a vision of democratic values.[22] These analyses highlighted how the lack of specific policy proposals enhanced Occupy's democratic ethos by presenting an internally consistent, righteous refusal to engage corrupt, self-contradictory institutions.[23] Some analysts argue that this refusal had an inadvertent instrumental value in the sense that the extensiveness and generality of Occupy's grievances have allowed left-leaning policy makers the flexibility to deploy the force of Occupy's intervention in the name of policy demands they believe to be realistic.[24] Campaign finance reform and "overturning" *Citizens United v. FEC* were among the demands discussed and sidelined in the early planning stages of Occupy.[25] These issues were just a starting point for the way Occupy raised awareness about how many aspects of most people's lives are structured by predatory finance capital and its influence on government. Foreclosures, student debt, bank bailouts, for-profit prisons, gutted labor protections, outsourced and contingent employment, deregulation of dangerous consumer goods, environmental devastation, the list went on and on, multiplying to produce the sense of a broad umbrella of grievances that impact 99% of the residents of the United States and the world.[26]

Occupy organizers and participants often claimed that demandlessness was important because it fostered prefiguration and inclusion. According to this logic, Occupy was most important as a display of unironic, anti-neoliberal politics and governance. The demonstrations critiqued the policies and practices of plutocracy, but many participants valued the demonstrations because of how they performed a vision of what democracy can be. As Todd Gitlin concludes with some skepticism, "Demandlessness, in other words, was the movement's culture, its identity."[27] This sense was articulated in a cluster of slogans such as "'The movement is its own demand,'" "This is what democracy looks like," or "Be the change you want to see." A more specific way of putting this was to say that Occupy demonstrated the political values it wanted to see actualized in the world.[28] The argument, which is essential to a "horizontalist" orientation toward democracy, is that vertical, hierarchical, and organization-based left politics have failed to bring about change because they have too often bought into instrumental logics that justify problematic liberal and neoliberal technics and ultimately change nothing even when they succeed by conventional political metrics.

The political values Occupy demonstrated have increasingly required more institutionally engaged forms of political action to demonstrate *their* democratic ethos, or their ways of cultivating trust in their "authentic" performative consistency between the reforms they seek and their methods for seeking them. The performance of authenticity is central to the democratic ethos. It is important to note that conceptualizing "authenticity" as performative consistency is a departure from some of the ways that authenticity has been theorized in other contexts.[29] Charles Taylor, for instance, describes a strand of the modern conceptualization of authenticity as something like acting out one's own personal telos as an original, unique being.[30] The problems associated with this conceptualization of authenticity as ethic are voluminous; not only is it deeply individualistic, it also seems complicit in a neoliberal ethic of competitive self-fashioning ("you do you") that is ethically thin at best and, at worst, complicit in systems of privilege and oppression. We hear in Thomas Frank's critique of "the occupiers" a distaste for those who saw the demonstrations as an opportunity for mere self-actualization vis-à-vis their "personal journeys."[31] The possibility of this turn inward toward the pursuit of an authentic self for its own sake, divorced from a sense of responsibility to others, seems to be an inevitable risk of the democratic ethos of authenticity.

The authenticity of the democratic ethos is also not authenticity in the sense that Diana Taylor disavows as she theorizes the concept of performance, which is authenticity as "the real" or "original" creative expression.[32] This is not to say that generating some sense of a difference between what is real and what is not isn't crucial to the performance of "authenticity," as Shane Vogel has argued.[33] Demonstrating a distinction between authenticity and irony is essential to the performance of the democratic ethos. But because authenticity *is* the performance of this distinction, it cannot be, as Taylor would say, something original or real in itself.

The type of authenticity that correlates most closely with collective action is a *performative consistency* rather than an interior authenticity of actualizing oneself or the expression of originality. The performance of authenticity, with the understanding that such a performance is yet on some level instrumental, also opens the door for identifying ironic performative contradiction and critique based on such contradiction. Consistency between the performative and constative dimensions of collective advocacy for democracy—and criticism of performative inconsistency—is the central feature of the democratic ethos consolidated by Occupy.

In various political actions, including amending the Constitution, campaigning for the presidency, and passing local laws (all described in subsequent chapters), consistently integrating liberal and horizontal methods can be challenging. This is because of Occupy's performative consistency is rooted in a strong opposition to state-based politics, which reflects a deeply seated, long-term commitment of the radical-global Left in the wake of what is often called "alter-globalization."[34] Political collectives such as the Zapatistas and demonstrations such as the 1999 World Trade Organization protests in Seattle (to name only two well-known instances in Central and North America) show how the radical Left is governed by loosely anarchist principles often associated with the politics of "exodus" critiqued by Chantal Mouffe, Ernesto Laclau, and others who see more promise in pursuing a left hegemony that shapes political institutions. More recent, radical leftists worldwide have embraced the ethos of Argentinian *horizontalidad* with its refusal of the state and its embrace of worker cooperatives.[35] The ideological and practical continuity between Occupy Wall Street (OWS) and such global neo-anarchisms and horizontalisms have been well established.[36] Horizontalism currently exists less as a theory of politics and more as a strategic vision of how resistance to liberal and neoliberal political technics can happen in a way that refuses the state, its hierarchical structures, and the ironies and performative contradictions of liberal representation.[37] In fact, the refusal of traditional sources of governmental authority leads horizontalism to locate authority in political technics themselves rather than in any validating theory of good politics.

The centerpieces of Occupy's specific demonstration of horizontalism were the directly democratic General Assemblies, the ostensible decision-making bodies of the encampments. These well-known assemblies provided some of the most highly recognized technics of Occupy, including the people's mic, participatory hand signals, trained facilitators, consensus-based decisions, a "progressive stack" of speakers (explained later in the chapter), and a specific way of structuring the order of business. Occupy's assemblies made important decisions (especially in the early days of the encampments), trained new participants in the values and methods of horizontal decision making, and provided a dramatic focal point for external onlookers, including the media and supporters.

The Occupy demonstrations were not necessarily an example of "pure" horizontalism in the sense that they rejected any and all forms of instrumentalism. In various global movements and demonstrations, horizontal governing technics have been developed in conversation with a variety of political-philosophical resources. These political philosophies most prominently include post-Marxisms and anarchisms. So, although horizontalism has an emerging unity as a political-philosophical position in its own right, it continues to act out certain tensions within and between the political philosophies that inspire its technics.

The next section of this chapter describes the mutually imbricated legacies of prefiguration and persuasion in left politics. Both prefigurative community and instrumental persuasion were central to establishing Occupy's critiques of economic inequality and ironic performative contradiction. Rather than being an ironic instrumentalism premised on the clever manipulation of doxa to undermine itself, Occupy attempted to prefiguratively perform inclusion, equal participation, and deliberation. The Occupy demonstrations were also instrumental, however, in the sense that they attempted to persuade an audience by cultivating media attention. The result of the Occupy demonstrations was not the passage of a specific policy; it was the successful acquisition of this attention. The result was the production of a democratic ethos that blended prefigurative community with instrumental persuasion to model performatively consistent instrumentalism in which distinct means and ends coexist but agree with one another. Although there are tensions between prefigurative and persuasive approaches, they each proved indispensable in the vision of democracy demonstrated in the OWS New York City General Assembly in late 2011 and how it ultimately produced a democratic ethos subsequently adopted and adapted by more reformist forms of political action, such as efforts to amend the US Constitution, the 2016 Bernie Sanders campaign for president, and providing legal for local communities combatting corporate incursions.

Prefigurative Community and Instrumental Persuasion in Occupy Wall Street

The original New York City Occupy encampment was initiated by a coalition of experienced political actors with long-standing commitments to horizontal democratic tactics.[38] Occupy demonstrated a type of horizontal democracy that reflected the influence of several important strands of political thought and action. The first of these was "participatory" democracy as it has been practiced historically in progressive left politics in the United States Some theorists of horizontalism cite the history of prefigurative forms of US activist organization that includes feminist, antiwar, and antinuclear activism in the mid-twentieth century, as well as Quaker meetings.[39] Second, Occupy's version of horizontalism was clearly connected to Latin American *autonomía* or autonomous politics, most notably as it has emerged out of the democratic practices of the Zapatistas and Argentinian cooperatives. Third, anarchist-inspired leaderless organization as it has evolved out of the alter-globalization movement in conversation with other demonstrations of the "squares" in Europe and elsewhere.

To make a distinction between these influences is primarily a schematic gesture because many individuals and organizations embrace all these traditions and consider them conjoined, overlapping, and in solidarity with one another. Certainly, in the Occupy demonstrations they seemed closely aligned or even indistinguishable, especially in their commitment to horizontal democracy. Historically, geographically, and theoretically, however, there are important distinctions to be made between how different manifestations of horizontal democracy emphasize both prefigurative and persuasive techniques.

Francesca Polletta has identified these two emphases emerging out of mid-twentieth-century US movement politics as "organizing" and "activism."[40] The division between these two ways of conceptualizing radical-left political technics is imperfect and analytic, but it captures an important and persistent dynamic between two processes. The first focuses internally on techniques and values for building community. The second focuses outward on persuading audiences external to the collectives and organizations themselves. Rhetorical scholars of movements, including Karma R. Chávez, have attempted to describe the relationship between enclaved or internal communication within movements and their outward-facing messages; Chávez's work illustrates how communicative practices reflect some aspects of how organizing and activism relate to one another.[41] Donatella della Porta has described how globally many movement organizations embrace multiple strategies (promoting alternative models of social life along with taking to the streets and spreading information to a broader audience) that include both "organizing" and "activism."[42] While clearly connected, internal and outward-facing communicative activities remain conceptually and often practically distinct or even contradict each other in movement groups.[43]

Building specifically *prefigurative* community is also, of course, distinct from most traditions of community organizing, including the well-known and oft-critiqued approach of Saul Alinsky.[44] While community organizers tend to have very specific goals and work with communities that have geographic and identity-based cohesion prior to organization, prefigurative community is generally formed on the basis of shared ideological and political commitments and the internal demonstration of those commitments is an end in itself. Because "community organizing" has more clearly defined persuasive goals, it is more instrumentally oriented than purely "prefigurative" communities. In practice, however, this schematic difference is blurred. Organizing prefigurative community building according to democratic values is a way of encouraging the construction of economic, social, and political independence, so collectives can better make decisions about how to meet the needs of their members, combat racism and economic oppression, and generally withstand or oppose the political forces that threaten them.

Prefiguration has been largely understood as a process in which activists and demonstrators envision new (often horizontal) political forms within their own internal organizations but not necessarily while publicizing them. When horizontal democracy is practiced in quasi-permanent cooperative communities, it is far easier to theorize its prefigurative potential in terms of the future self-administering processes of that community. When horizontal democracy is practiced as part of activist groups taking direct action or planning protests, on the other hand, it is easier to understand its prefigurative potential in the effects it has on participants. In both instances, as Marina Sitrin and Polletta describe, prefiguring a horizontal democratic future is an activity that happens with or without making the horizontally democratic processes visible to the outside public.[45]

Persuasion of outsiders, on the other hand, encompasses more instrumental actions such as protests, marches, rallies, and sit-ins that directly attempt to garner media attention and draw an audience's attention to operations of powerful and oppressive political and economic forces.[46] It is, of course, not uncommon for a set of prefigurative techniques to be operationalized in collectives (or affinity groups) that are planning persuasive political actions that may be, like the 1999 alter-globalization movement protests in Seattle, relatively short-lived or long-distanced. Community organizing also embraces persuasive technics such as protests when they are needed or effective.

Persuasive protest is, of course, much more concerned with making a rhetorical impact on outsiders and political institutions. The attention that protest and direct action draw, however, has rarely been focused on making transparent the internal processes of affinity groups that plan, organize, and coordinate horizontally. In fact, direct-action groups involved in civil disobedience (notably Anonymous) go to great lengths to hide the identities of members and the inner workings of the group out of concerns about reprisal from law enforcement. Although such direct-action groups might arise spontaneously and persist over time, their primary function is not to meet the everyday material needs of the members. Instead, the goal is to allow for the political development of the individual participants and draw attention to (and perhaps stymie) the operations of state and corporate power.

This means that prefigurative community and persuasive protest are closely related while also often understood as being in tension on the basis of their differing relationship to instrumentalism. In fact, one of the most notable dimensions of Argentinian cooperatives and the Zapatistas is the remarkably strong confluence of prefigurative communities and more instrumental, persuasive activism.[47] Chris Dixon, a scholar-activist, argues that North American urban and cosmopolitan politics should rededicate themselves to working more in the middle ground between organizing "beyond" and "against" existing frameworks; Dixon's work represents an important example of thinking through the relation of these two aspects of radical politics and how they can and should relate to one another.[48]

Polletta's work on movement democracy in the United States in the mid-twentieth century is centrally concerned with exploring the relationship between prefiguration and instrumentalism in those movement organizations. She argues that participatory democratic organizing practices actually had substantial instrumental value.[49] Participatory democracy, while justified on prefigurative grounds, was historically able to do things such as diversify leadership, solidify bonds between activists, and encourage creative problem-solving.

Contemporary prefigurative politics, however, differ in some ways. Because the value of contemporary prefiguration has been primarily understood in terms of its potential to shape those who participate in direct actions, its potential to build other worlds and alternative forms of political organization has been somewhat confined to people who already have existing commitments to horizontalism. This has led to criticism of prefigurative politics on the grounds that it is a form of preaching to the converted. Lawrence Grossberg argues:

> In political terms, that would seem to presume that people, left to their own devices, naturally as it were, will necessarily come to see the rightness and righteousness of the left's—or, more specifically, the horizontalist left's—commitments. Unlikely at best. The answer must then be that one controls those allowed into the community, limiting it to those already committed to the values and visions—and ignoring the question of the conditions (economic and temporal, for example) that

> enable only some to participate—guaranteeing that such communities remain small and local. It is as if, unable to find ways of changing the world, people shrink the space of struggle to something more manageable. In practice, radical democracy seems to mean that those who already accept the validity of the process (as well as its larger political vision) are empowered to work out the details.[50]

Prior to Occupy, horizontal democracy in the United States was most strongly embraced behind the scenes of direct actions or was often limited to self-contained autonomous communities such as the ones Grossberg alludes to. Contemporary prefigurative democracy is a way of organizing opposition and follows a set of deliberative procedures that are agreed upon by participants as part of a commitment to horizontal ethico-political ideals. These often include decision making by consensus and the absence of a formal, representational leadership structure. Since the 1960s, most prefigurative communities and direct-action affinity groups celebrate the direct democracy of their decision-making process and hope to draw more people into such practices, but the process of propagating such practices has been understood as happening mostly by involving people in the prefigurative organization rather than publicizing internal communication practices through the media.[51] Outsiders often see bodies in the street, broken windows, circulating petitions, opposition to commercial activity, or some other type of creative civil disobedience. The structure of the group might occasionally be described for outsiders, but the details of the internal democratic process are not generally visible or explicitly mobilized in persuasive projects. This means that prefigurative effects of internal democratic commitments seem to be produced primarily in and through the individual participants and the capacities of the collective to grow, innovate, and build its own potential.

Occupy demonstrations, however, provided a specific way of combining prefigurative community and persuasive protest that is notable. In the Occupy demonstrations, prefigurative practices were covered intensively by the media. This coverage was not always sympathetic, but sometimes it was. The 2011 demonstrations famously included General Assemblies that coordinated both the self-sustaining prefigurative community functions of the fragile encampments (such as providing food, laundry, security, and libraries) as well as their associated persuasive actions (protests, marches, declarations, bailing people out of jail, etc.). Of course, the capacities of these temporary camps paled in comparison to the vibrant, permanent autonomous communities of the Zapatistas, Argentinian cooperatives, or faith communities of color in the urban centers of US metropolises. They nonetheless attempted to cultivate a similar vision of freedom, self-sufficiency, mutual care, equality, and loving attachment. The Occupy camps seemed to try to make up for what they lacked in durability with high levels of intensity. Additionally, the New York City Occupy camp was a hotbed of planning, teaching, and coordinating persuasive activism. Some of their greatest successes happened in the form of making the coercive force of the state starkly visible while clashing with police and other authorities over the course of months.

The General Assemblies (GAs) were the deliberating bodies of Occupy encampments. In New York City, the GA met daily or twice daily from the time just before the occupation of the park began until just after the occupiers were evicted from Zuccotti Park. From the beginning, the GAs were able to address only a certain amount of the occupations' activities and participants. Working groups made many decisions separately, some of which were ultimately approved by the GAs and others of which were not.[52] In fact, frustration and disappointment with the GAs as decision-making bodies was expressed by participants and organizers from early on, which led to attempts to establish the Spokes Council model in late October of 2011.[53] The Spokes Council was designed to supplement and bolster the New York GA's weaknesses but ended up devolving into infighting.[54] While the GA in Liberty Plaza convened, it was one of the centrally visible, if not defining, features of what we now call Occupy. Amid what sometimes looked like chaotic demandless diversity of perspectives, tactics, and positions, the assemblies appeared to be the heart of Occupy and its defining demonstration of horizontal democracy. The procedures of the assemblies and their techniques of organizing political speech formed the backdrop for the collective statements and critiques attributed to Occupy.

The New York GAs occurred in an open-air location that could potentially be viewed by law enforcement, journalists, tourists, and other onlookers. The assemblies were a synthesis of consensus-based procedures and the amplification techniques of the people's mic, all of which have been extensively discussed and described by participants and analysts alike. To establish a sense of the GA's interpretation of democracy, I've consulted the incomplete yet extensive NYCGA minutes that were taken each day and posted online.[55] I have supplemented these minutes and notes with several other kinds of texts. The first are books containing the narrative and analyses of Occupy participants and organizers. These include *Thank You, Anarchy* by Nathan Schneider, *Translating Anarchy* by Mark Bray, *Occupy Nation* by Todd Gitlin, and the multiauthored *Occupy!: Scenes From Occupied America*.[56] Most of these materials refer specifically to the GA in Zuccotti Park in New York City, the first and most visible encampment. Various audio-visual and written instructions circulated widely about how to facilitate and participate in democratic assemblies such as the GA; these instructions (and debates in the forums of occupywallst.org and www.nycga.net about modifying the GA procedures) provide crucial insight into how Occupy built and enacted its sense of democracy in a way that blended prefiguration and persuasive instrumentalism.

The relationship between prefigurative community and persuasion constituted a relatively new approach to prefigurative politics in which prefiguration was conceptualized as something more than a "behind-the-scenes" element of organizing that worked primarily on and through activists and horizontal community members themselves. Instead, persuasive prefiguration was also the ethos of the demonstrations in the sense that it was happening as transparently as possible for an audience of outsiders. Attention was paid to the persuasive prefigurative potentials of the communicative technics by which horizontal democracy was at the center of the demonstrations produced that visibility.

The next several sections will describe the *persuasive prefiguration* of the Occupy demonstrations and how some of the prefigurative processes on display in the demonstrations were put to instrumental uses. After describing what was innovative about Occupy's approach to the combination of prefiguration and persuasion, I will argue that a persuasive and instrumental approach to prefiguration such as Occupy's has enabled horizontal democracy to build bridges with more conventional types of organizations such as governmental agencies, nonprofit organizations, and election campaigns. When prefiguration is part of a collective ethos built in part to persuade outsiders, it can be persuasive if its means and ends are performatively consistent. Three typically prefigurative types of activity were instrumentalized through wide exposure and eventual media coverage: mutual aid, participatory decision making, and direct action.

Democratic Decision Making as Prefigurative Persuasion

Over the course of its life in the park, the New York City GA enacted persuasive prefiguration in several ways that garnered extension media attention. These included teaching the skills of democratic participation, recognizing and appreciating difference, providing for basic bodily needs, fostering affective attachments to other participants and the community itself, maintaining the community's infrastructure and decision-making abilities, and coordinating protests. These activities constituted a regularized, consistent set of techniques that were made transparent and ultimately projected outward to build the democratic ethos of the demonstrations. These concerns, however, were conducted with strict attention to the way that horizontal values could be demonstrated for an audience in the process of accomplishing the broad goals of the camp, which included projecting those values to outsiders as part of the ethos of the demonstration.[57]

Occupy in many ways succeeded in blending prefigurative politics with instrumental priorities by innovating a compelling new tactic: the processes of horizontal decision making were made visible for a wider audience. This process, in which the inner workings of the collective as it self-organizes are projected outward as part of persuasive goals, is a crucial dimension of the democratic ethos of "authenticity" consolidated in the Occupy demonstrations. The horizontal democracy of the General Assemblies was a way of organizing incendiary direct actions traditionally embraced by anarchists (marching over the Brooklyn Bridge without a permit and disrupting traffic, for instance).[58] But the locations of the GAs and their high levels of accessibility and commitment made them quite visible in ways that internal activist processes of horizontal democracy have rarely been.

From the beginning of the occupation of Zuccotti Park in mid-September of 2011, the minutes of the GA reflect a gentle and mutually supportive bifurcation of Occupy into two overlapping sets of activities. First, there were activities that turned inward to secure and organize the space of the park as a community. Second, there were activities oriented outward by organizing marches, protests, and other forms of persuasion that would draw attention to the message and existence of Occupy throughout the city.[59] In some of the earliest available GA minutes, for instance, it is noted that in the closing moments of the newborn assembly "consensus was reached that one group will do direct action on Wall Street, and another group will stay here and maintain the square."[60] This simple sense of two primary sets of activities persisted all the way into late October when the proposals for the new Spokes Council continued the distinction by suggesting a division between "working/operations" groups and "thematic/movements" groups.[61] These two sets of activities roughly correspond to the division between traditional prefiguration and public-facing persuasion.

Traditionally prefigurative activities of the GAs included deliberation about how to sustain, nourish, and distribute the resources of the camp, including affective bonds and relational identities. The GA also demonstrated its internal commitment (expressed through deliberative form) to the horizontal principles of inclusivity and equality. Community-building techniques included leaderless facilitation, consensus-based decision making, and a broad commitment to affectively engage with coparticipants across differences.

Compared with the more sustained horizontal approaches to popular power, *autogestión,* and territory described by Sitrin and Dario Azzellini, Occupy was fundamentally a transitory and temporary set of events and practices. Horizontal democratic processes were how the short-lived encampments met their needs and self-organized to accomplish daily tasks. Occupy involved some people who shared prior bonds, but it also involved mass numbers of strangers who were not necessarily members of a shared place or community before or after the demonstrations. As a result, Occupy's version of prefigurative deliberation did not operate in the same way as, for instance, the worker cooperatives or neighborhood councils described by Sitrin or various types of community organizing.[62] GAs were a form of horizontal decision making that was prefiguratively meaningful for the participants. Also, however, they were *a performance for others,* and awareness of this dimension of the GAs was quite high among the participants, who often acknowledged the role of the GAs as a type of political theater.[63] As they practiced prefigurative deliberation, the assemblies demonstrated the potential for a rhetoric of prefiguration to operate not just for participants but for observers, sympathizers, and even opposition.

The most abstract and visible of these communication practices were the deliberative guidelines for the assembly, repeated at every meeting. These elements of what the assembly called its "process" were the frame that structured the order and content of the assembly. But they also imparted a set of prefigurative values that were practiced, disseminated, and repeated in smaller working groups responsible for maintaining the horizontal camp community. This is an essential element of consensus-based horizontal decision making as practiced prefiguratively. Not only does the community build its capacity to share material resources among its members, but the deliberative process is one in which the values of the community are established and maintained through techniques of internal organization.[64] In the Occupy assemblies, these values included decision making by consensus, constant participation of everyone, sharing leadership skills and roles, maintaining a distinction between facts and opinions, encouraging diverse voices, and transparency and accountability. At the beginning of each assembly, facilitators reviewed these priorities as they instructed the assembly participants in the details of the process they were about to enter into. Many assemblies included newcomers who would be hearing the instructions for the first time. Assemblies also inevitably included many participants who had heard the affirmation of horizontal democratic values repeated many times before.

Some commentators have argued that Occupy assemblies reflected a certain commitment to traditional models of deliberative democracy or social democracy.[65] Although these similarities were certainly present, the Occupy assemblies put far less emphasis on evidence and reason than traditional "deliberative democratic" procedures. Instead, they were more committed to the pursuit of self-reflexive equality and reflected a commitment to nurturing affective bonds and creative, spontaneous inclinations—priorities clearly associated with prefigurative politics.

Speaking and listening in such a large crowd could often be very slow, and occasionally facilitators took it upon themselves to encourage the assembly to stick with the process and one another. For instance, at the beginning of the October 4th assembly, a facilitator added this comment to the typical instructions in the deliberative process: "So I've been hearing a lot of frustrations, and a lot of concerns about what we can do as individuals, acting in solidarity. But I think it's important to pat all ourselves on the back and remember how hard this is, and that we are making something beautiful. I would like to say a quote from a poet, Andrew Gibson, who says: 'We must create. It is the only thing louder than destruction!' So keep that in mind when things get hard, because this is how a democracy works!"[66]

Participants frequently stood up to declare their affection for the assembly and Occupy in general. While these moments sometimes involved speaking out of turn or off topic, they generally seemed to be handled by facilitators with a type of firm good humor that attempted to keep things on track while acknowledging the value of the sentiment. For instance, the minutes of the October 25th assembly record a visitor announcing (in the middle of a deliberation about whether to provide funds for a direct action in Queens): "I am from PA, it's my first day here, I would just like to comment. Our country was founded in the spirit of opposition to despotism. My soul is overjoyed to see this movement resonate with the greatest men and women in history. Congratulations (clapping). PoP [Point of Process]: 'That was beautiful but not related.'"[67]

The distracted tangents represented by such comments (as well as overly detailed questions about simple routine proposals) frustrated many organizers and led to deep ambivalence about the GA, especially among veteran organizers who had extensive experience with the pitfalls of prefiguration and participatory governance.[68] Moments of affectionate appreciation, however, illustrate the way the assembly set a tone and fostered emotional bonds in addition to operating as the ostensible decision-making body of the camp.

One of the most important ways that the GA demonstrated the prefigurative commitments of horizontal democracy was foregrounding its efforts to be inclusive of diverse voices. This was done in two primary ways. First, GA facilitators openly practiced and defended what was called a "progressive stack," in which speakers from disadvantaged backgrounds were placed further ahead in the line than, for instance, cisgender white men, who would be placed toward the end of the queue of speakers. Additionally, facilitators would regularly remind those attending the GA to follow the principle of "step up, step back," which encouraged them to "step back" if they were from an identity group that has traditionally had access to political participation and social privilege and "step up" if they were from an identity group that has historically been marginalized. Although these practices were imperfect (and white cisgender men generally seemed to be the majority of speakers), diversification was widely supported and came to be understood as essential to the GA's process. The "progressive stack" incorporated the values of prefigurative community at the level of the GA structure, while the "step up, step back" reminder asked the individual participants to internalize the values of horizontal community as a moral imperative. In recent research about prefigurative decision making in movement organizations, Polletta and Hoban found that adherents of prefigurative democracy say that encouraging commitments to equality among differently privileged group members is one of the most common justifications for using participatory processes such as the ones use in Occupy's GAs.[69] The intense focus on these techniques, as well as the attribution of democratic values to their shape and consistency, was one of the core elements of the democratic ethos that the demonstrations projected outward for persuasive purposes. Unlike the ironic instrumentalism of some liberal democratic politics, the more horizontal democratic ethos strove for consistency between these technics and the content of its advocacy.

Participants in the NYC assemblies cite the revision the Declaration of the Occupation of New York City as one of the best examples of how the "process" of the GA was able to meaningfully foster inclusion of diverse voices.[70] Much of the Declaration was written by a working group (and so "behind the scenes" of the GA), but significant revisions to the Declaration resulted from deliberations in the GA itself. Perhaps the most important among these was a change in the language of the opening paragraph. An early draft began by implying that social divisions in "the people" were a thing of the past; the language attempted to prefigure a future in which the "formerly divided" people had been unified. Certain participants in the GA objected to this overly idealistic framing and successfully pushed for changes to the document to prevent it from coming across as naïve or overly idealistic, especially when it came to the existence of racialized hierarchies.[71]

The practices of the "progressive stack" and "step up, step back," guided the assembly toward listening to the perspective of people of color who objected to the initial "color-blind" language. The Declaration was, in the end, shaped by the priority placed on equality and inclusion, and these elements of the process built the ethos of the demonstrations.[72] Because the Declaration was circulated widely as a statement of Occupy's grievances, purpose, and demands, it drew attention back to the participatory processes of the camp that produced the declaration in the first place.

The result of the publication of the prefigurative decision-making processes in the assemblies was that they became part of a process of persuasion with instrumental goal of convincing a broader audience to buy into the critique of economic inequality and corporate political influence.

Persuasively Prefiguring Mutual Aid as Donation

The Occupy demonstrations acknowledged that the process of cultivating horizontal democratic capacities requires a number of intensive, highly deliberate skills, emotional responses, and problem-solving proclivities that capitalist political culture does not necessarily foster.[73] Deliberative skills such as step up, step back and prioritizing marginalized voices were some of these. The prefigurative emphasis on mutual aid, however, was also a central, widely publicized component of the demonstrations that facilitated binding people together and encouraged resistance to the individualism, instrumentalism, self-interest, and greed of capitalist political culture. The Occupy camps were built on practices of mutual aid that quickly and flexibly adapted to blend with more mainstream progressive practices of donation as a means of demonstrating solidarity, participation, and even collective membership.

The very personal, emotional, and educational work of fostering the affective attachments that underwrite mutual aid must be done by participants in horizontal politics as they simultaneously strive to acknowledge and counteract differences in their own privilege. This means that the value of practically supporting one another resides not only in instrumental effectivity (helping to define agendas, select strategies, forge flexible strong working relationships, and accomplish specific policy changes) but also in the potential to internally prefigure and hence create the social and political values activists embrace.

Thinkers of prefigurative community closely associated with Argentinian cooperatives have described horizontal community as being constituted by a number of interrelated elements.[74] These include concrete projects related to sustenance and survival, the occupation of physical space, self-management, self-reflection about the ongoing process, and changing social relationships between political actors to further enhance love, trust, and self-reflection.[75] These elements of community are considered ends in themselves; they are both the means and the goal of political organization. Elements such as these shaped the prefigurative activities and processes of the New York City GA to some extent. They were strongly present, however, in the ways the GA addressed and cultivated the dynamics of the camp itself. The NYCGA took up issues related to the material needs of the people in the camp and the social relationships between participants in ways that expressed a strong commitment to building a camp community that could persuasively model radical values for an audience.

Various hardworking and dedicated people banded together in working groups with names such as Comfort (sleeping, staying dry, etc.), Kitchen (cooking and managing food donations), Sanitation (cleanliness, garbage, and eventually recycling), Safer Spaces (language use, interpersonal relations, inclusiveness, and boundaries), Security (managing disruptions, potential violence, and ignorance about camp practices), Medical, Facilitation (training new people in the techniques of running assemblies and discussions), and many others. With important exceptions such as the Press Working Group, these groups were largely inward-facing and primarily concerned with the quality, safety, and harmony of camp life and the activities that took place within the physical spaces of the camp.

These working groups sent representatives to the GA to describe their activities, ask for cooperation with their goals, and seek feedback, funds, and volunteers for various projects and ideas. In mid-September, before the donations started rolling in, announcements from working groups frequently consisted of things such as showing others how "to dumpster [dive]," offering to teach languages, requesting maps of the park space, and coordinating the shared use of bedding.[76] Over time, as donations became larger and the occupation became more complex, working groups began to make decisions more independently from the GA. By the end of October, as donations grew, the process of the GA had evolved to streamline formal allocations of funds and announcements. By this point, working-group presentations to the GA, when they were attempted, were often colored by exhaustion with the tendency of the enthusiastic but chaotic GA (often populated by visitors and newcomers) to second-guess carefully planned and routine minor requests about things such as printing flyers, installing fire extinguishers, and purchasing computers and walkie-talkies.[77]

Beyond redistributing bedding, food, books, and information, the community-oriented working groups also attempted to cultivate certain sensibilities. The assembly reminded itself to stay hydrated, use electrical outlets (at the McDonald's in the men's room under the sink), check its internalized oppressive behaviors, look out for the symptoms of hypothermia, submit work to the art exhibit, read the good-neighbor policy, and "not pee or poop in public doorways!"[78] Prefigurative internal organizing techniques were reproduced in each of the alternative social institutions, including the free distribution of food, shared possessions, open access to medical care, and continuous advocacy of communication practices that included recognition of existing inequalities.[79]

In addition to the ways the assembly broadcast its process at the start of the meetings themselves, the deliberative process was also discussed visibly and at length online. This extension of the self-organizing tasks of the GA into digital forums multiplied its capacity to demonstrate its values well beyond the space of the camps themselves. As many commentators have noted, this multiplication of deliberative technics also amplified narratives about the authenticity of Occupy's purpose and activities.[80] The www.occupywallstreet.org website, for instance, hosted lengthy discussions about consensus decision making. Additionally, assemblies and camp life were sometimes streamed live, though such streams seemed to have happened somewhat erratically; the minutes of the assemblies posted online are followed by occasional comments requesting reliable livestreams of the GA.[81] In a historical moment prior to the livestreaming capacities of Facebook and other social media platforms, these streams represented organizational techniques that were, like the procedures of the assemblies themselves, unmediated by corporate filters and narratives. This freedom from corporatized media platforms further enhanced the sense that the demonstrations were embracing self-disclosure in a deeply authentic way that built their democratic ethos.

Early commentary on Occupy's use of digital tools, including social media, visual imagery, and livestreaming, expressed high hopes for the possibility that such media might enable the fuller expression of theatricality, populism, and horizontal ideals.[82] Part of this optimism is the hope expressed by "netroots" advocates—the hope that grassroots political actors might bypass the filters of centralized news production to reach one another, supporters, and the public more directly.[83] A closer look, however, reveals that the Occupy demonstrations deliberately cultivated the support of legacy media networks and applauded themselves when the national press gave them positive coverage.[84] The New York City GA (NYCGA) celebrated when the *New York Times* and others covered demonstrations, marches, and protests and actively analyzed how the coverage related to the GA process.[85] So while grassroots or citizen media were important to the movement, Occupiers certainly recognized the instrumental value of more traditional coverage.

Not all participants and organizers were ready to instrumentally embrace powerful profit-driven social media platforms such as Facebook, Instagram, and Twitter, and these platforms did not necessarily lend themselves to the needs of the demonstrations. Posting meeting minutes online, for instance, meant posting lengthy written texts as an accessible archive. Comments on the meeting minutes were not extensive or consistently present, but long-distance readers did occasionally weigh in on aspects of camp life.[86] Readers of the GA minutes online occasionally pleaded with the GA to post minutes more promptly and provide more comprehensive notes.[87]

The digital extension and preservation of the GA accomplished an instrumental purpose that was very important to the organizers and participants of the autonomous camp community: cultivating material support for the encampment. One of the central and regular features of GA was the time it spent enabling announcements and requests from various working groups, some of which were requests for material goods needed in the camp. Sleeping bags, food, storage bins, medical supplies, and communication technologies were just some of the many items requested during the GA. These requests were largely made via an expansive mode of address that recognized that the audience for the request extended far beyond the immediate collection of people in the park. For instance, the GA minutes reflect an announcement from the Comfort Working Group on September 28, 2011, addressed primarily to those outside the park: "First of all, they need a lot of sweatshirts, sweatpants, and socks [editor: how to donate]. The way we're going to get that is please donate them and drop them off at comfort! This is mainly addressed to people who are not here. So everyone reading this, please donate sweatshirts, sweatpants, and socks!"[88]

Requests to meet the needs of the demonstrators were extended geographically and temporally to a wide swath of people in various places who considered themselves part of the demonstrations and contributed to the camp community as it made its requests. Certain requests were distilled and reposted on the nycga.net website within the list of meeting minutes to highlight urgent needs.[89] The vitality and strength of the camp was very much dependent on the way its digital platform extended announcements made in the GA about how to materially support those present in the park.

News coverage of the NYCGA and Zuccotti Park occupation regularly mentioned how donations of food and money were being made to support the demonstrations.[90] Some of this coverage focused on the spirit of goodwill and generosity, while some of it focused on the problems that arose out of the need to effectively manage the funds.[91] Donating, especially from a distance, became an important way to participate in the collective mission, the ideals of mutual aid, and constitution of the demonstrations. Although the donations created administrative tasks for the GA and the working groups, they also created an important opportunity to model something like "transparency" in the decision-making processes necessary to handle the funds. This, in turn, bolstered the ethos of the demonstrations' critical persuasive message about the corrupting influence of money on government.

Working groups used the GA to announce their best ideas about how camp life should be conducted. For instance, the minutes of the September 21st assembly report that a member of the Comfort Working Group announced: "speaking of abandoned bedding I would like to request that as soon as you get up from sleeping, please bundle your sleeping gear and place it in a nearby pile with other peoples' bedding unless you are okay with your bedding becoming someone else's."[92] The ideas and suggestions of the working groups changed quickly in response to changing conditions. By the time the campers were evicted in November, for instance, tents had sprung up to provide privacy, a sense of relief from the constant activity, and shelter from the increasingly harsh weather. But throughout the duration of Zuccotti Park's occupation, clusters of participants worked hard (if not always successfully) to maintain the camp community as a safe, healthy, lively, and comforting space full of resources for those who spent time there.

The projection outward of requests for donations was an instrumental extension of the more communal practices of mutual aid organized within the camp itself. As the GA extended itself spatially and temporally and the practices of mutual aid prefigured within the camp were broadcast through social media, the left press, and the news media, the more instrumental, individual act of donating money, food, and other useful items became part of how mutual aid was supported. The result was a recasting of donation as a type of persuasive prefiguration, with extensive press coverage of the financial balance of the Occupy movement. This narrative frame—fundraising totals—was a familiar and intelligible one for news media and facilitated the process of framing donation as an authentic act of left politics.

Persuasively Prefiguring an Antiplutocratic Ethos

General Assemblies helped to coordinate and publicize protests, marches and written statements about economic inequality oriented toward persuading an audience of the existence and parameters of economic injustice. In some ways the GA in the NYC camp was a form of persuasive protest that demonstrated a commitment to anarchist-inspired contemporary techniques of direct action through civil disobedience, which dramatized the monopoly on force underwriting policing and the law.[93]

Outward-facing anarchist-influenced persuasion tends to be more focused on presenting arguments about the illegitimacy of modern state institutions and their corporate backers. This type of radical protest encompasses a vision of prefigurative community but invests more of its energy in addressing tensions in practices of persuasive confrontation and critique and the instrumental potential of such actions. David Graeber, a staunch anarchist defender of high-profile direct action, for instance, includes in his description of Occupy two pages describing the kitchens and libraries and sixteen pages detailing how and why clashes with police were handled in a certain way.[94] In practice, this means planning direct actions that prefiguratively practice the freedom to demonstrate the pervasive unfreedom wrought by violent tactics of corporatized state rule. Graeber and others claim that direct action goes beyond civil disobedience in the sense that it questions the political order itself rather than any specific laws.[95] Direct action proceeds without asking for permits, damages property, evades the law, and demands space to pursue and perform nonsanctioned political activities. It performatively declares its independence.

Protest is not merely prefigurative, of course. What sometimes remains unacknowledged in anarchist discussions of direct action is the instrumental quality of such activity when it is not considered to be merely an expression of freedom from oppressive state rule. All protest is a means to various political ends, including passing legislation, rallying new members, changing people's beliefs, or excoriating the enemy. But even radical antistatist protest seeks one important outcome: drawing attention to an issue or cause in such a way as to cultivate media attention and convince an audience to become activated about a cause. In other words, protest is an attempt at persuasion that generally attempts to engage the structures of mass media, be it legacy news or social media. In the case of Occupy, legacy news media was essential to its persuasive successes. As Bray, a member of the Press Working Group in NYC, argues: "As much as we would love to be able to circumvent their prominence, OWS became an international phenomenon because of the corporate media."[96]

The idea that horizontal prefiguration is a "process" and not a "final end" places it in a certain kind of tension with persuasive protest, which is inherently more instrumental. Graeber, for instance, argues against ironically instrumentalist approaches, claiming "you will never achieve the ends at all unless the means are themselves a model for the world you wish to create."[97] Sitrin similarly argues that horizontalism is both a tool and a goal; the thorough implementation of the tool is the goal, and horizontalism should in some ways be best understood as a gerund rather than a noun. This means that using the "corporate media" to project a message such as Occupy's is a tactic that strays from the sort of purely prefigurative politics most often associated with horizontalism.

John Holloway delineates the difference between horizontalism and what he calls the Marxist parameters of the Bernstein-Luxemburg debate precisely on the basis of their differing approaches to instrumentalism, especially as it relates to the state. Holloway argues that such Marxists "have typically seen the state as being the instrument of the capitalist class" in such a way as to imagine that "the relation between the state and the capitalist class is an external one: like a hammer, the state and the capitalist class is an external one: like a hammer, the state is now wielded by the capitalist class in their own interests, while after the revolution it will be wielded by the working class in their interests."[98] Instead, Holloway argues, democracy must be built from the bottom up, because the state and its mechanisms are not actually separable from the social and economic conditions that gave rise to them and that they are enmeshed in. Governmental institutions wrought by capitalism are not appropriately democratic tools; they are expressions of foundational social and economic processes.

In these ways of thinking, representative democracy justified on the basis of its efficiency and effectiveness is merely an excuse to re-entrench vertical power and economic inequality. Political representation, as a shortcut to faster meetings and streamlined decision making, bypasses the essential components of genuinely democratic slower processes that actively attempt to reshape social life. Because representative democracy is so often justified on instrumentalist grounds, it is difficult to separate the horizontalist critique of representative democracy from its critique of the state in general. The rejection of representation and working to overthrow or reform the state is the horizontalist alternative that rejects instrumental thinking and a division between political means and political ends. Occupy was notoriously associated with this rejection of state institutions.

Some scholars have pointed out that the Occupy demonstrations were, however, not purely horizontal and prefigurative in this way.[99] In fact, there were extensive debates among the participants of the NYC camp about the purpose, methods, and tactics of protest. One of the largest working groups of the NYCGA was the Direct Action Working Group, in which ideas, tactics, and resources were shared, debated, and supported.[100] If the GA had not also been coordinating such efforts, the prefigurative community may have remained known primarily to the ranks of those who attended the GA and lived in the camp. Because various marches, protests, and other kinds of creative, highly visible protest were coordinated through the GA and claimed the slogans associated with the camp, the camp itself and its prefigurative communal aspects were projected outward and made visible to a broader constituency through legacy news media.

This was not necessarily the primary goal of the protests and other actions, however. In fact, most of them were organized to persuade audiences of the importance of political and economic inequalities, the set of issues we have come to associate with Occupy. Horizontal democracy (or historically, participatory or direct democracy) has been a long-standing component of how far-left collectives self-organize to plan persuasive direct actions.[101] As noted, this has been partially for practical reasons, such as the ones Polletta cites, and partially for the prefigurative reasons anarchists embraced.[102] Regardless of the reasons, horizontal decision making has happened largely behind the scenes when planning direct action and has not generally been a visible central feature of the actions themselves in North America. The relationship between the GA and Occupy's direct action went far beyond this traditional relationship and did so very quickly and creatively. The result was that the prefigurative technics of self-organization that shaped camp life were disclosed and projected outward to bolster the ethos of the protests and other direct actions associated with the camps.

Variations on anarchist-inspired direct action were closely tied to the GA in more specific ways that demonstrate how the very nature of direct action within Occupy made visible the internal communication practices of prefigurative democracy. The march over the Brooklyn Bridge, as one of the direct actions associated with Occupy that garnered the most media attention, illustrates the broad outlines of persuasive protest in Occupy and how it related to the prefigurative practices of both community building and civil disobedience.

Direct action inspired by anarchist traditions is centrally concerned with drawing attention to politico-economic violence and power by acting out freedom from that power.[103] To that end, a core element of direct action is breaking the law in highly visible ways. Contemporary "little a" anarchists often take inspiration from the thought of Mikhail Bakunin, who wrote of such actions: "we must spread our principles, not with words but with deeds. For this is the most popular, the most potent, and the most irresistible form of propaganda."[104] The acting out of freedom to subvert power was, of course, used to tremendous effect by US civil rights activists in the mid-twentieth century, albeit with the goal of using arrest to push for specific changes in what anarchists might call "the system." Contemporary forms of left direct action such as those used in Occupy also attempt to persuade an audience of the injustice of the state, corporations, and police by acting in a way that dramatizes the tremendous power and force of these institutions—for instance, when protestors intentionally draw physical force onto themselves from law enforcement agents.

Confronting police can be frightening and intimidating, especially for newer activists, but anarchists believe it to be important (and sometimes even effective) if it results in a situation in which the police use unreasonable force that paints protesters in a sympathetic light.[105] In such an instance, the injustice of institutional violence can be clearly demonstrated. A peaceful but illegal street protest that results in the use of police violence, especially if the violence is recorded, illustrates larger inequalities and the misuse of power.[106] This standard approach to direct action is typified by documentaries on Occupy that contain large amounts of footage of peaceful protesters clashing with violent police.[107] In fact, when the occupiers were evicted from Zuccotti Park, one of the laments that rose from observers was that the media and supporters were not allowed to video record the event.[108]

Advocates of inciting and recording conflict with police are not concerned only with the prefigurative potential of such conflicts; police violence is also instrumentally effective in the search for media attention and coverage. On the level of prefigurative politics, direct actions that lead to violent clashes with police can build community and affective attachment as recordings of that violence are circulated among protestors.[109] Action premised on the acting out of freedom from state oppression is also a form of prefigurative politics in the sense that it is the performance of an attitude of living and being something other than a subject of state power.[110] As a form of persuasion, however, actions that draw police violence are more likely to make headlines and accomplish the task of painting protestors in a sympathetic light for a wider audience.[111] The October 1, 2011, Brooklyn Bridge march was precisely such an event. During the September 30th assembly in the camp, pacers for the march were requested, and the Legal Working Group reminded those present of their availability to help with arrests.[112] The march across the bridge ended up splitting into two groups; one that took the pedestrian walkway and one that marched onto the part of the bridge generally reserved for automobile traffic. The group stopping traffic was confined by the police, leading to approximately seven hundred arrests.[113]

The march and its accompanying arrests were covered by a number of legacy news outlets, some of which had not been covering Occupy at all up until that point. This coverage drew attention to not only the critique of economic injustices made by Occupy generally but also the prefigurative practices of mutual aid and self-governance appearing in Zuccotti Park. Articles about the Brooklyn Bridge march in legacy news outlets focused on the question of whether the police had misled and trapped the protesters, contributing to the familiar anarchist dramatization of the conflict between an oppressive state and a peaceful group demonstrating.[114] This sympathetic dramatization was significantly enhanced by the figure of the GA and the encampment, the GA and encampment being clear exercises in nonviolent democratic self-organization.

The news coverage of both the Brooklyn Bridge march and the eventual eviction of the campers emphasized the injustice of the police treatment. Such sympathetic coverage did two things simultaneously: it portrayed the demonstrations in a sympathetic light while also making more visible the actions of a governmental institution (the police) already the target of the protest's critique. The failure of the protest and the encampments to go off without a hitch (i.e., the successful halt of the Brooklyn Bridge march and the eventual eviction from Zuccotti Park) ended up encouraging sympathetic coverage from the news media that was instrumental in cultivating support for the demonstrations.

This relationship to failure is a uniquely prefigurative one; a drive for prefigurative consistency and purity is sometimes only achieved by rejecting traditional markers of instrumental success. In other words, a permissive and cooperative relationship with police management of a protest would be a sign of ideological co-option. The heavy-handed police tactics, on the other hand, are a sign of the righteousness and authenticity of both the message and the tactics of the demonstrators. Whether or not organizers deliberately embraced this philosophy of prefiguration as instrumental failure, the result of the arrests and evictions of Occupy demonstrators was wider and more sympathetic coverage that framed the protestors as standing up for authentic democracy and legitimizing their ethos while doing so.

Conclusion

In its role as publicity engine, recruiting tool, political theater, and basic primer on horizontal decision-making processes, the NYC GA was a source of frustration and compromise among dedicated organizers. As we have seen, however, these inefficiencies were in part the result of a commitment to technics of visibility, inclusiveness, and physical care that were part of an attempt to persuade horizontalism's harshest critics as well as its most committed supporters.

Long-standing critics of horizontal politics, prefiguration, and radicalism didn't necessarily see the difference between Occupy and previous instantiations of prefigurative politics. Thomas Frank argues, for instance, "As long as demands and the rest of the logocentric requirements were postponed, Occupy could never graduate to the next level. It would remain captive to [. . .] the 'cult of participation,' in which the experience of protesting is what protesting is all about."[115] The value placed on the "experience of protesting" that Frank and other liberals have been so skeptical of was very important to the Occupy participants; Frank and others are not wrong on this account.[116] This is one of the most important dimensions of prefigurative politics described by Polletta and, later, Holloway, Graeber, Sitrin, and others.[117] Among Occupy participants who have also written about the demonstrations, a premium is often placed on the transformative personal effects of chanting with the people's mic, sleeping in the camp, meeting new people, and generally developing new moral-affective attachments and sensibilities. The difference is that personal self-development was not the only important result of such activities and values; they were also the techniques for demonstrating the ethos that backed the collective enunciation of a strong, persuasive critique of state and capitalism picked up on by the media. Reveling in democratic values among sympathetic coparticipants was far from the endgame of Occupy's prefigurative politics.

Not all the news coverage of camp life was positive, but the details of the camp community found their way to an audience less concerned with some of the more abstract dimensions of horizontalism.[118] Camp life was also a vision of horizontal democracy that was projected outward and, as some commentators like to argue, that projection"changed the discourse" about economic inequality and corporate politics.[119] This is something that prefigurative politics have often aspired to, but such politics have often been easily bracketed off as unproductive, overly critical, or absurdly committed to lifestyle politics. The fragile prefigurative community established in the Occupy demonstrations, however, displayed a willingness to tarry with instrumentalism that generated an ethos that departed from ironic instrumentalism's market logics and performative contradiction between political means and ends.

This is not to say that Occupy was completely new or innovative; the demonstrations certainly operated out of the tactical and rhetorical legacy of place-based nonviolent direct actions such as sit-ins and peaceful appropriations of private and public space.[120] But Occupy also made relatively accessible and visible some prefigurative decision-making processes that have been used behind the scenes by radical-left activists for decades. In so doing, it was able to carve out new territory for horizontal democracy as a project with the potential to simultaneously channel both critical antiplutocratic protest and cooperative, consensus-based mutual aid—while doing so for an audience of outsiders by mobilizing prefiguration to build the ethos for instrumentally enunciating a persuasive critical message. The result is a prefigurative politics that publicly embraces something more than criticizing or fleeing from plutocracy. What was prefigured was a relationship between collective self-composition and persuasion that has established a model for demonstrating the ethos of democracy.

Radical protest has often aspired to draw attention to liberal political structures and systems that are destructive, violent, and antidemocratic. What Occupy did differently was attempt to persuasively communicate with and educate the broadest possible swath of people about their conceptualization of the democratic alternative to such structures and systems. In doing so, it dovetailed with the priorities of liberal and progressive democratic opposition to plutocracy.

As the internal processes of self-organization were made visible to build the ethos of the collective voicing of the message of the demonstrations, the Occupy demonstrations consolidated prefiguration as a *persuasive* set of activities. This innovation was accomplished by broadcasting the inner workings of the demonstrations to a wider audience. The result was that the internal organization of the camps was tantamount to the set of autonomous community *hexis* or habits that validated the authenticity of the anti-instrumental critique projected in the direct actions. These rhetorical effects, while far from being measurable or specific, were produced in and through a democratic ethos that strove for performative consistency between method and message as it confronted and engaged the instrumentalism underwriting liberal conceptualizations of democracy. As a performative democratic persuasive *ethos,* rather than simple *prefiguration,* the demonstrations reached outward toward possible allies, opponents, potential converts, and the uninitiated to present a vision of democratic authenticity.

TWO

The Seattle Democracy Voucher Campaign and Ironic Instrumentalism

In 2015, the city of Seattle voted to pass I-122, the Honest Elections Seattle (HES) ballot initiative. The initiative included a number of anti-corruption measures and also authorized a substantial new program for funding municipal election campaigns with a property tax. The result has been Seattle's "Democracy Voucher" program, in which all eligible voters in Seattle receive four twenty-five dollar vouchers they can donate to candidates of their choice in city council and city attorney elections. Seattle's form of public campaign funding departed somewhat from other public campaign finance programs across the United States. Other initiatives work by matching and multiplying small donations of voters' own money, sometimes at a ratio as high as six to one.[1] The Seattle voucher program differs from this approach in that it does not require voters to use any of their own money; they simply donate the vouchers, which campaigns then redeem for cash. The voucher approach to public campaign funding has been advocated by Lawrence Lessig and Bruce Ackerman, who argue that its market-based mechanisms are more constitutionally defensible than some other forms of public financing for election campaigns.[2] Since Seattle's voucher program was implemented, similar programs have been considered in Austin, South Dakota, Washington State, Albuquerque, and elsewhere.[3]

The underlying concept of the voucher program is supported by a group of influential national-level reform organizations. These organizations lobby, organize, and fundraise for electoral reforms such as ranked-choice voting, mandatory voter registration, open primaries, donor transparency, voting rights for felons, and other related initiatives.[4] Many of these efforts describe themselves as responses to the Supreme Court's 2010 *Citizens United* decision and the issue of "money in politics." Many of them claim to be "bipartisan" or "cross-partisan." In the wake of the 2016 election cycle, these groups often attempt to articulate an ethos of respectful, "moderate" and civil political discourse in response to what they describe as an overheated, polarized political environment.

Some versions of the election reforms sought by these groups are changes that have been pursued on and off for decades. The voucher-based system for publicly funding elections, however, is a relatively new twist. Its reliance on a market logic demonstrates adherence to what Wendy Brown calls neoliberal political rationality, but most advocates of the voucher funding system argue that its purpose is, in the end, to increase equality in the political process.[5] In Seattle, voucher advocates repeatedly explained that the goal of the program was to increase political participation of the poor, the homeless, and people of color living far from the "view neighborhoods" that traditionally provide most of the donations to Seattle's municipal election campaigns.[6] This goal mixes liberal ideals and neoliberal political rationality in a way that has become somewhat familiar since the 1990s.

As a political endeavor that strives to strengthen liberal democracy, the voucher program attempts to establish an electoral mechanism for guaranteeing (or at least increasing) political equality. The campaign to pass the voucher program, however, was conceptualized by those who designed it as a means to an end. The program was not designed by Seattle residents (though some community organizations were consulted and provided input).[7] A significant portion of the campaign to pass the program was funded by out-of-state donations, some of them quite large. The voucher program was implemented with the ostensible goal of amplifying the voices of the people of the city and reducing the impact of wealth on politics. The passage of the initiative, however, was achieved by leveraging imported wealth to generate a program that could serve as a sort of test case or experiment for campaign finance reform in other places.

This chapter describes the rhetoric of the 2015 campaign to pass the HES initiative, how the campaign was covered in the local and national news, and how the initial years of the voucher program were then reported on by interested organizations. Analysis of the HES rhetoric shows how it exemplifies the broad rhetorical features of ironic instrumentalism, an approach to political action that has been critiqued by horizontalism and the Occupy demonstrations. The HES campaign demonstrates how liberal and neoliberal political rationalities operated in tandem to produce a sense of performative contradiction, specifically through the large-donor funding mechanisms of the campaign and the voucher program's status as a national "test case." Outlining the ironic, instrumental features of Seattle's 2015 HES campaign helps to establish an understanding of the baseline political rationality against which the democratic ethos of authenticity can be compared and into which it has been integrated.

The HES campaign's dissociation of the means of politics (large donations from wealthy special interests) from the ends of politics (greater political equality for poor and disenfranchised residents) reflects a classically liberal approach to democracy as a matter of instrumental rationality. Because the program remains enmeshed in neoliberal and liberal rationalities, Seattle's democracy voucher program reflects attention to Occupy's *issues* without also reflecting a commitment to Occupy's *methods*. Rather than demonstrating the more horizontal democratic ethos of performative consistency consolidated by Occupy, the HES initiative showed how the liberal democratic engineering ethos embraced irony and performative contradiction as instrumentally necessary steps on the way to a greater good. This liberal engineering ethos, with its commitment to a sharp division between tactics and goals, expresses an ironic instrumentalism that produces the sense that political techniques are necessary and important in their own right even if the values that structure them contradict the very goals they are employed to serve. Lewis Mumford, an early thinker of the relationship between technics (inclusive of both technologies and techniques) and political forms, argued that oppressive authoritarian technics have for some time been exercised under the auspices of basic democratic principles, producing an ironic degeneration of genuinely democratic technics.[8] Although we may want to bracket Mumford's narrow sense of what is included in "democratic technics," the sense of irony that accompanies the exaltation of antidemocratic technics in the name of democracy is certainly still with us. Political technics generate the ethos of collectives in part through the connotative associations and narratives that circulate around the technics themselves.[9]

The clever, effective, and knowledgeable engineering ethos is compatible with neoliberal approaches to democracy. As we will see, however, the liberal engineering ethos cannot be reduced to neoliberalism. The HES initiative advocated the use of neoliberal tactics in its approach to managing the behaviors of political candidates, but its articulation of the goal of political equality was more straightforwardly liberal. HES pursued liberal goals through tactics that didn't at all perform the liberal values they sought to realize, producing a deep sense of irony and performative contradiction, which is a fundamental component of democratic action that evinces an ethos of ironic instrumentalism. This ethos stands in sharp contrast to the more horizontal democratic ethos of Occupy, which has been disseminated into political action in part as a strong commitment to an ethos of performative consistency and democratic "authenticity."

The HES campaign helps demonstrate the forms of instrumental liberal and neoliberal political reason that Occupy initially criticized and reacted against. As we saw in chapter 1, the democratic ethos consolidated by Occupy reacted against and critiqued political irony and instrumentalism with an ethos that attempts to retain a performative consistency between the means and ends of political action. This means, as liberals such as Thomas Frank have noted, the rejection efficiency and effectiveness.[10] It also means developing technics that clearly articulate the possibility of performing an unironic consistency or authenticity. This does not necessarily mean that the technologies are inherently "authentically" democratic, merely that they have the possibility of being performed as such and in being performed that way they project such an ethos. The result is a democratic ethos that departs from the instrumental and ironic calculations of the engineering ethos. This unironic democratic ethos has been a strong component of efforts to amend the US Constitution, the 2016 Bernie Sanders campaign, and enacting community rights ordinances that codify the rights of nature and right to housing. The HES initiative shows how the issue of "money in politics" is being addressed in the context of a neoliberal and liberal political rationality that has bypassed the political influence of Occupy and maintained an ironic form of instrumentalism as part of its engineering ethos.

Occupying Campaign Finance Reform?

The Occupy demonstrations of 2011 have a strong association with electoral reform. One of Occupy's working groups, the Politics and Electoral Reform Working Group, labored to address issues of campaign finance and political corruption.[11] The efforts of this working group, however, were not widely embraced during the demonstrations.[12] Because of the strongly horizontal organizational priorities of the demonstrations, specific election reforms tended to be bracketed off and sidelined in the interest of asking more fundamental questions about the relationship between capitalism and liberal democracy. Occupy's general critique of economic inequality and the impact of the financial sector on political institutions made it relatively easy for observers (and some participants) to lament the rejection of campaign finance reform as a central "demand" of the demonstrations. The resonance between Occupy's general message and the issue of campaign finance reform was strong enough, however, for liberal commentators such as Lawrence Lessig and Robert Reich to claim that Occupy was fundamentally *about* something like the corruption of politicians with donations and super PACs.[13] Participants and observers of Occupy in this vein argued that the problem of "corruption" was the key issue that the demonstrations should focus more intently on to demand reforms related to campaign finance, overturning

Citizens United, protecting voting rights, and establishing other anticorruption measures that would repair representational democratic institutions.

Both of these perspectives—that Occupy was about electoral reform, especially campaign finance, or that Occupy should have made demands related to those issues—tend to either bypass or dismiss the deeper transformation in the concept of democracy that Occupy seemed to strive for. From these perspectives, the antistatism, horizontal decision making, and communal demonstration camps of Occupy were at best incidental elements (sort of "2011 flavors") of a fairly standard street protest and, at worst, substantial impediments to getting anything done. Because both of these perspectives dismiss or criticize the ways that Occupy was internally organized, they tend to see the value of the 2011 demonstrations primarily in terms of how they were able to "get the word out" or "change the conversation" about the problem of political corruption. From this perspective, Occupy drew attention to an important issue but did little after that.

In the case of the Seattle "Democracy Vouchers" campaign, this assessment—that Occupy drew some attention to the problem of money in politics but subsequently had little impact on efforts to create change—is entirely accurate. The 2015 HES initiative, as well as the campaign to pass it and its implementation, bear almost no traces of the antistatist, horizontal, direct democratic ethos of the Occupy demonstrations. The Honest Elections Seattle initiative is therefore instructive as an example of what Nancy Fraser calls a "progressive neoliberalism" that celebrates diversity and inclusion without engaging in a more substantial assessment of the deep roots of economic inequality.[14] While Fraser argues that we have entered a new era of more populist (and less neoliberal) politics, the HES initiative suggests that the texture of left politics continues to be more complex than a narrative of historical transformation might allow. The ethos of the HES initiative also helps to clarify the stakes of Occupy's attempted intervention in progressive movement culture and tactics. Pushing progressivism away from liberalism and neoliberalism has happened not only at the level of identifying problems but also by establishing and enacting values by which to assess the democratic qualities of the alternative organizations and movement structures.

The voucher program implemented in Seattle reproduces a pale shadow of progressive democratic politics, with an ethos grounded in technical expertise, a shallow conceptualization of diversity, and an overriding commitment to instrumentalism as the basis for designing democratic structures. HES provides a rich example of the type of progressive instrumentalism that more complex forms of liberal politics build on, integrate, and revise. The examples of post-Occupy political action discussed in the final three chapters of this book all integrate but attempt to de-ironize and radicalize the type of instrumentalism demonstrated by the HES initiative. To that extent, describing the liberal conceptualization of democracy that shaped the HES initiative and its campaign lays the groundwork for then seeing how Occupy's democratic ethos has intervened in an already-existing set of instrumentalist tactics and values. The fact that the Seattle voucher program was implemented four years after the Occupy demonstrations shows how the dispersion of Occupy's democratic ethos has been uneven, piecemeal, and contingent. In fact, the voucher program itself may soon fall victim to its own distance from Occupy's democratic ethos; one of Seattle's most controversial and socialist City Council members decided to opt out of the voucher program in the 2019 election because of its strict limits on how much funding candidates can seek. Claiming that the deep pockets of Amazon, Microsoft, and others were lined up against her, she argued that the program was "not designed for a race like ours where Amazon and the whole big business establishment is united against us. It does not prevent corporate PACs from overnight dumping hundreds of thousands of dollars into the race to try to buy the election."[15] If the existence of the program and its implementation are justified entirely within the boundaries of an ironic instrumentalism, candidates will always be free to calculate that it is not to their advantage to participate.

Ironic Instrumentalism

The ethos of the campaign to pass Seattle's democracy voucher program is an example of *ironic instrumentalism* in the sense that it articulates a deep attachment to the capacity of technologies—including governmental technologies, communication technologies, and the economic power produced by profitable technologies—to solve political problems that they have played a role in causing. This approach stands in contrast to Occupy, which in a decidedly unironic way cultivated a democratic ethos that eschews instrumentalism in favor of performative consistency. The campaign to pass the 2015 HES initiative, on the other hand, was rife with self-conscious ironic performative contradiction based in a division between political techniques and democratic goals. The ironic performance of democratic values in the campaign cultivated an ethos grounded in instrumental rationality, prioritizing efficiency and effectivity above the liberal values of political equality that were ostensibly its goal. The result was an ironic ethos of cleverness and technical know-how grounded in political and technological expertise.

One of the central components of ironic instrumentalism is a technocratic fascination with and valorization of technical know-how that is not limited to any specific technology. Critiques of instrumental rationality have been a persistent theme throughout the twentieth and twenty-first centuries in thinkers as diverse as Herbert Marcuse, Michel Foucault, and Wendy Brown. This broad strand of thought effectively identifies a sort of technocratic ethos based on instrumental calculations, efficiency, and effectiveness. More recent, an interdisciplinary swath of critical scholars has adopted Foucault's analytical methods to trace how calculations of efficiency, effectiveness, self-capitalization, and market competition have been adapted to shape the formation a neoliberal ethos.[16] The neoliberal ethos is one in which individual and collective subjects build credibility through their capacity to demonstrate measurable and effective self-capitalization according to the logics of neoliberal technics. If "character" is a contingent expression of specific cultural values and reservoirs of doxa, this type of neoliberal ethos is just as much a form of persuasive "character" as the traditional Aristotelian criteria of judgment, goodwill, and virtue. The neoliberal ethos prompts us to remember the limits of equating ethos with any one type of technics or set of cultural values. For instance, a city might perform a neoliberal ethos as it demonstrates its suitability for a new corporate headquarters by describing how its institutions of higher education have been bent toward the production of industry-friendly workers. As long as no one questions the assumption that it is the job of a city to attract such investment, the neoliberal ethos of the city is consistently performed.

The communication technologies that help to make up such a collective also have an ethos of their own that contributes to the ethos of collectives that regularly compose themselves in and through such technologies. These communication technologies are increasingly diverse, and they generate ethos in different ways. Twentieth-century critiques of bureaucratic rationality, instrumentalism and efficiency-obsessed ethos of technology are still important today. But in an era when we have multiple technologies of communication and innovation operating alongside one another and according to competing political rationalities and narratives, it is most precise to speak of the *ethē* of communication technologies in the plural rather than one dominant, overriding "neoliberal technological rationality" that is true of all communication technologies or even all digital technologies. It is especially important to pluralize our senses of the ethos of communication technologies when the differences between them play an important role in the performance of a democratic ethos that explicitly attempts to offer an alternative to neoliberal political technics. The ethos of the efficiently self-capitalizing subject is not the only type of ethos generated by technology. Reformist liberal and neoliberal democratic politics continue to prize communication technologies and candidates based primarily on their effectiveness, efficiency, and capacity to work in and through the complex closed systems of policy making.

Although twentieth-century thinkers of technology have tended to conflate technology with instrumental rationality, the attribution of "reason" to the process of dividing means from ends is far from a purely technological endeavor. The liberal democratic thought of figures such as J. S. Mill and John Locke has been shaped by the concept of utility, for instance, which suggests a distance between the means and ends of politics. Ironic instrumentalism, however, is not simply instrumental rationality or technology itself. Other versions of instrumentalism don't necessarily demonstrate irony in a self-conscious or deliberate way; in fact, as we will see in the next few chapters, when the democratic ethos cultivated in the Occupy demonstrations has begun to be enacted in concert with more instrumental efforts, it emphasizes equality, integrity, and performative consistency. This doesn't mean that irony is absent from such efforts (we could certainly accuse them of irony if we had a reason to do so), merely that they are not self-consciously or overtly ironic.

Ironic instrumentalism operates within an instrumental rationality without embracing it fully; the irony is that efficiency and effectiveness are *supposedly* being made to serve loftier political ideals but somehow come to be embraced as values in themselves. Carolyn Miller describes the figure of the engineer as the character of purely instrumental rationality and ascribes such rationality to technology itself.[17] An exclusively instrumental approach to democratic technics operates within what Miller calls a "closed system" in which desirable goals and a range of technics for pursuing those goals have been predetermined. Ironic instrumentalism, however, is not a "closed system" in the way that Miller describes. Ironic instrumentalism prizes various technics according to existing metrics of success and their capacity to push toward something that contradicts the underlying assumptions of those metrics; this contradiction is precisely what makes it ironic. The ethos of ironically instrumental democratic action is that of leveraging engineering ability or know-how against the system that generated the metrics of the effectiveness of that know-how—gaming the system or beating it at its own game. In spite of attempting to reach beyond existing technics, however, such an effort is difficult to evaluate outside of the systemic logics that allowed a problem to be defined as "solvable" in the first place. The result is ironic in the sense that it might claim to (or even hope to) eventually move beyond an instrumentalist set of technics while remaining mired within them.

Because ironic instrumentalism simultaneously employs and critiques a set of admittedly undemocratic political techniques and technologies, it wholeheartedly embraces communicative and political artifice. The artifice of ironic instrumentalism is not necessarily a falseness in the sense of being something that is not true or real. Rather, it is artifice in the sense of something that proclaims itself as having been made or done by design, something expedient and clever that embraces the tension between its means and ends. Ironic instrumentalism is a committed *celebration* of artifice as a demonstration of superior logic and skilled manipulation of a complex and open-ended environment to achieve desired ends. Skill in manipulation (or persuasive effectiveness) is valued in a way that competes with liberal political values such as equality, inclusion, transparency, and freedom.

Ironic instrumentalism divides the technics by which politics is pursued from the vision of democracy at the end of the road, generating a sense of a disjunct between means and ends. Marcuse, a careful thinker of instrumental rationality, argues that liberal democratic values and closed-system instrumental thinking have been interpreted as having a certain compatibility: "For example, the proposition that every individual is equipped with certain inalienable rights is a critical proposition but it was frequently interpreted in favor of efficiency and concentration of power."[18] The "irony" of such a confluence, however, is available primarily only to the thoughtful, critical observer rather than being a necessarily self-evident tension arising from the juxtaposition of political statement and context. The ironism of such observations has been characterized by Richard Rorty as a properly private set of critical perspectives rather than an element of public action itself.[19] However, the tension between liberal values and technics are the primary source of performative contradiction in the ironic instrumental ethos that validates attempts to engineer more democratic structures through means that are not necessarily in line with the values associated with political equality.

In the case of the HES campaign, the ironic qualities of this performative contradiction were an element of the public discourse about the campaign and shaped the ethos of the campaign. This is what has been called by scholars of Socratic rhetoric the complex irony of performative contradiction rather than the simple irony of sarcasm or mockery.[20] Complex irony requires some level of awareness or recognition of a disjunction between what speech-act theorist J. L. Austin called the performative and constative levels of speech and discourse.[21] Rorty argues that ironism is the power of redescription, in which taken-for-granted assumptions and ways of speaking about things are cast in a new light by calling those assumptions into question, using relatively unfamiliar language, and shedding new light on what such discourse *does*.[22] Irony casts doubt on doxa, the taken-for granted sense of things that everyday languages reflect, a sense that has ossified in the wake of its repetition. But irony is impossible without doxa; it feeds off of doxa as it asserts the falseness or contradictions of doxa, leading Kenneth Burke to argue that "true irony, humble irony, is based upon a sense of fundamental kinship with the enemy, as one needs him, is indebted to him, is not merely outside him as an observer but contains him within, being consubstantial with him."[23] Robert Hariman has argued that this is the weakness of irony for contemporary politics; it must always rely on the assumption that there is an "a-rhetorical" position from which to identify the artifices of doxa.[24] Nonetheless, Hariman asserts, "Irony remains the master trope of liberalism."[25] The persistent affinity between liberalism and irony is precisely the result of political liberalism's willingness to separate means and ends and acknowledge the provisional and instrumental character of political techniques. Embracing the possibility or necessity of performative contradiction generates space for any mode of political action to acknowledge its own ironic qualities, inserting the role of the observer *into* the process of pursuing political goals.

In the case of Seattle's HES initiative, the liberal value of political equality was a central dimension of the constative level of the campaign's rhetoric; political equality was what the campaign declared that it was attempting to achieve. At the performative level, however, the campaign ironically contradicted this stated goal by pursuing victory through all means necessary, including large donations and expensive media buys. These conventional tactics are precisely those that the campaign called "corrupt" and attempted to legislate against. The ironies of this performative contradiction emerged in news coverage of the campaign as national (rather than local) supporters of the campaign attempted to justify and defend the performative contradictions of the campaign while local news coverage condemned the initiative on the same basis—that the campaign represented a form of "corruption" of local politics by out-of-state big money interests.

Legal scholars have identified "corruption" as the key problem that electoral reforms should seek to address.[26] One of the most vocal and active of these has been law professor and Creative Commons advocate Lawrence Lessig. As a public intellectual, Lessig is well known for both his critique of campaign finance corruption and his contributions as a legal scholar to envisioning creative and open digital systems. In his work on campaign finance in books such as *Republic, Lost, The USA Is Lesterland*, and *America, Compromised*, Lessig has argued that electoral politics in the contemporary US are deeply corrupt.[27] The concept of "corruption" developed by Lessig and other scholars is an essential component of how liberal advocates of campaign finance reform pose the problem of "money in politics" as a matter of the breakdown of otherwise effective and appropriate governing structures.[28] Campaign finance vouchers are not the only electoral reform that Lessig advocates; in addition to a brief run for the Democratic Party presidential nomination in the 2016 election cycle, he has also been an active supporter of ending gerrymandering, increasing ranked-choice voting, expanding automatic voter registration, and other related reforms. Lessig's popular writing on democracy vouchers was cited in press coverage of the HES campaign as the origin of the democracy voucher program.[29]

Lessig's concept of corruption is explicitly amoral and functionalist. He compares the role of money in politics to the role of alcohol in the health of an alcoholic individual.[30] Lessig argues that "corruption," in the sense of how alcohol corrupts the body, is not a moral failing; it is rather a form of dependance that makes moral decision making impossible.[31] Politicians acting in the interests of their wealthy campaign funders are not behaving in an immoral way, argues Lessig; they are simply symptoms of a diseased government that has come to rely too much on corporate cash. Lessig openly embraces the underlying assumption that corruption is not an ethical issue; it is an engineering problem. He argues that we should not target individual politicians, we simply need to move forward with finding the most effective possible solution to the problem of our failing governmental structures by reforming them and returning them to health. This position reflects a commitment to the idea that good politics are essentially a matter of well-designed, functioning institutions rather than ethical action or values.

Lessig represents a broader commitment among liberal advocates and thinkers to the continuous re-invigoration of a vision of the constitutional democracy of the United States based on founding principles, expert legal and economic knowledge, and high-quality informed deliberation. These efforts tend to favor capacious use of any and all existing organizational forms and funding mechanisms for campaigns as long as they serve the ultimate goal of effectively enacting new anticorruption laws. Thus, they demonstrate a clear commitment to the type of ironic instrumentalism that valorizes the pursuit of any and all communicative technics on the basis of their effectiveness—even if those technics are part of the problem they seek to solve. For instance, in 2014 Lessig spearheaded the creation of the "Mayday PAC," a political action committee with the intention of funneling large donations from wealthy individuals and corporations to political candidates who supported campaign finance and anticorruption reforms.[32] Lessig argues that the ironies and performative contradictions of projects such as the Mayday PAC are justified by the nobility of their ultimate goals.[33] He openly and wholeheartedly argues for the embrace of the performative contradiction, stating baldly, "Call it 'Project Irony.'"[34]

The ironic instrumentalism demonstrated by the anticorruption politics of Lessig and others can be critiqued on some of the same bases that critical scholars critique neoliberal political rationality.[35] This is because ironic instrumentalism resorts to market-based logics and "astroturf" political advertising in its pursuit of political goals. Neoliberalism, in the sense that theorists like Brown have developed the term, "involves extending and disseminating market values to all institutions and social action" so that "the state must not simply concern itself with the market but think and behave like a market actor across all its functions, including law."[36] Ironic instrumentalism is also, however, an expression of more traditional political liberalism; this is why it is ironic and not simply neoliberal. The ironic instrumentalist ethos is based not only on a clever and efficient embrace of market mechanisms in state institutions; such efforts are juxtaposed with full-throated advocacy of liberal values, including freedom, equality, democracy, and justice. In the ironic instrumentalist ethos of the HES initiative, these liberal values included political equality and popular sovereignty.

The neoliberal drive for the expansion of market values to any and all aspects of human existence is decidedly unironic; it is an entirely performatively consistent commitment to the broad utility of market values in all aspects of human life. This performative consistency is not necessarily based on true rationality, of course; it is merely a logic in which the values of efficiency and effectiveness are prioritized while market competition is the ur-technic for performing those values. Catherine Chaput argues that it is a mistake to differentiate neoliberalism and liberalism based on some imagined difference in their rationalism; neither is more or less rational than the other.[37] Liberalism, however, can rely on market technics to work toward equality without market competition itself enacting that equality. Bradford Vivian identifies the ironic juxtaposition of neoliberal values and tactics with a liberal ethos as an essential component in neoliberal rhetoric, but this understanding of neoliberalism as ironic simply collapses neoliberalism and liberalism into one another.[38] Neoliberal technics can be entirely unironic. It is only when neoliberal technics and values are combined with liberal technics and values (and they are not always) that an ironic performative contradiction in the ethos of political action begins to take shape.

Nonetheless, as Vivian argues, ethos is accrued to the *form* of various political technics and a liberal ethos of ironic performative contradiction between neoliberal means and liberal ends persistently signals a clever, pragmatic effectiveness.[39] Ironic instrumentalism fully embraces a performative contradiction between political means and ends, following a more liberal path toward inherent irony. As a result, it embraces liberal values, including equality or liberty, as principles in the sense of the ultimate goals of politics but not what can or should necessarily guide the means of political action. In the case of the HES initiative, the means employed in the campaign to pass the initiative were certainly neoliberal, but the campaign also demonstrated goals and values that were strongly liberal. The distinction between the technics and the values of politics leaves the door open to embrace market logics as the political means to pursue the ends of greater equality in instrumentalism that is strongly ironic. This is precisely what we see in Seattle's democracy voucher program, in which a campaign to publicly finance election campaigns has been engineered with a heavy reliance on market mechanisms, expensive advertising, and extensive funding from wealthy donors.

Ironic instrumentalism also preserves another strand of progressivism that sees political advancement as, in part, driven by economic and technological change *itself* rather than the tasks of imbuing market logics with political institutions.[40] This means the enthusiastic embrace of one of the fruits of such historical change: new communication technologies and the wealth that has accumulated from their production. These new technologies, along with the economic and organizational structures that have developed to support them, offer hope for the revitalization of democracy outside of state-based mechanisms of representation. At the same time, however, the projection of an instrumentalist ethos requires distancing state-based representational mechanisms from the "corruption" of actual economic and financial markets. Public-intellectual advocates of democracy rooted in ironic instrumentalism claim a great affection for capitalism and free markets, but they argue that mechanisms of state-based representation should be guarded against the corrupting influence of capital more actively and effectively.[41]

This is why pursuing democratic values through ironic instrumentalism involves the maintenance of a classical political liberalism that rests on the assumption that government can be a "neutral" arbiter of political and economic disagreements and differences. If properly designed, built, and maintained (in this way of thinking), technologies of government can produce freedom and equality by virtue of their structural integrity and capacity for mediating conflicts resulting from differences of identity, wealth, and opinion. New communication technologies and the methods of engineering them, however, have provided a fresh range of ways to imagine the process of engineering democracy. The content of the advocacy around specific issues matters less, in this perspective, than the extent to which the machinery capitalizing on advances in technology allows robust disagreement and the inclusion of rationally competing perspectives.

In the case of Seattle's democracy voucher program, the result of integrating the techniques of engineering developed for new communication technologies has been a strong drive to conceptualize the voucher program itself as a sort of "beta test," an experimental trial run that will reveal the design strengths and weaknesses of a new platform. The telos of the Seattle voucher program is its expansion and implementation nationwide, as we will see in the press coverage, reports, and campaign rhetoric of the initiative. This goal of expansive implementation of a refined model of the voucher program, underwritten by a campaign paid for in part by the profits of the large, new communication technology companies themselves, seeks to operationalize the economic and technological advantages of new communication technologies and their engineering practices for the larger benefit of liberal democratic government. The performative contradictions in how the voucher program was pitched—as an effort to counteract the wealth produced by new communication technologies—only highlights the features of the ethos of ironic instrumentalism more vividly.

Between Campaign Rhetoric and News Coverage

The campaign to pass the I-122 "Honest Elections Seattle" ballot initiative was waged through the dissemination of mailers, targeted digital advertisements, paid signature gatherers, television advertising, and volunteer canvassers. These efforts, along with the salaries of the campaign staff, were paid for by the most well-funded bankroll in Seattle's 2015 municipal election cycle; the second most well-funded campaign was that of socialist candidate Kshama Sawant, whose successful run for municipal office cost less than half a million dollars.[42] At approximately $1.5 million, the HES initiative was one of the most expensive municipal campaigns in recent history.

The Seattle Ethics and Election Commission makes records of all donations and vendor payments for municipal campaigns since 2003 available online, including the 2015 HES initiative.[43] Developing a picture of the campaign's ethos includes mapping its activities through these records as well as describing the accumulated news coverage of both the campaign to pass the initiative and its subsequent implementation in Seattle's 2017 city council races. Additionally, several nonprofit organizations sponsored research reports on the role of the vouchers in the 2017 election and these reports have been cited in the press and have contributed to retrospectively developing the ethos of the initiative.

The campaign itself, much of the news coverage of the campaign, and the research about the initiative's implementation all reflect the assumption that democracy is well served by increasing the number and diversity of donors in municipal elections. Some critics, most notably the editorial board of the *Seattle Times,* argued that the measure was an unnecessary form of outsiders imposing legislation on the city. The general goal of increasing diversity of donors and decreasing the influence of large corporate donors, however, remained unquestioned.[44]

The research reports, news coverage, and campaign tactics are all important to understanding how irony emerged out of the tension between the constative and performative dimensions of the ethos of the ballot initiative. Certain elements of the ethos of the ballot initiative campaign were produced through a wider dialogue about the significance of the initiative rather than in the rhetoric produced by the campaign itself. For instance, the initiative's mailers, television advertisements, and digital advertisements didn't declare the initiative to be a sort of test case of a program that could be implemented elsewhere. Instead, this was a framing of the program that was largely constructed by national news coverage and dissemination of research on the initiative. The tactics of the campaign itself, however, reveal how the flush coffers of the campaign were produced and utilized as part of precisely such an effort to engineer a nationally exportable test case. The relationship between the initiative's stated values and underlying technics, especially as those technics were noted by observers, is crucial to describing how the ironic instrumentalism of the campaign's liberalism allowed ample room for integrating neoliberal mechanisms.

The ethos of the initiative was ultimately a celebration of instrumentalism with two central aspects that combined to produce a strong sense of performative contradiction and irony. First, the campaign trumpeted the values of political equality and popular sovereignty as central justifications for the initiative. The campaign and research on the implementation of the program presented its immediate goals—the expansion of political equality through the diversification of donor demographics—as an important expression of democratic values.

At the same time, the campaign presented the specific "voucher" funding mechanism as an efficient and effective method for achieving that goal rather than being a form of political equality in itself. The voucher program was broadly conceptualized as an experimental project that was gravely needed—not necessarily to combat corruption in Seattle but rather to be refined and exported to other places. The ethos of the campaign was produced in part based on the clever, unique, and innovative qualities of the voucher mechanism, an effective way of managing the behavior of political candidates through market-based incentives.

The irony of this contradiction had some negative connotations in local news coverage; the expansive funding of the campaign to pass the initiative tapped into a broader narrative about the role of wealthy carpetbaggers in US politics while expanding it to include young new tech millionaires and the nonprofit political reform organizations most interested in the results of the test case. At the same time, national electoral reform advocates embraced the performative contradictions of the voucher program, touting the cleverness and innovation of attempting to use existing political technics against themselves. In these instances, the ironies of the HEC initiative have been embraced in a celebration of artifice that clearly marks the ethos of ironic instrumentalism.

The Liberal Values of Honest Elections Seattle

The campaign to pass the HES initiative began after an earlier public financing proposal, "Fair Elections," narrowly failed to pass in 2013.[45] The 2013 Fair Elections initiative would have established a "super match" program for financing elections similar to New York City's, in which small donations are matched in larger proportions with public funds.[46] The HES campaign shifted to a voucher-type program advocated by Lessig and others and brought on additional support from a variety of national nonprofit reform advocacy groups, including Every Voice, Represent.Us, Public Citizen, Common Cause, and others.

Leading up to the November 2015 election in which HES was on the ballot, two research reports about election funding in Seattle were produced and circulated to the local and national press. Both local and national news coverage of the initiative cited these reports and their authors regularly.[47] The Sightline Institute, a Pacific Northwest advocacy organization that had also supported the 2013 initiative, generated a report that consisted largely of a series of maps of the city, arguing that the majority of Seattle's municipal election donations were coming from wealthy, white people living in "view neighborhoods."[48] The other report, published by WashPIRG (Washington Public Interest Research Group) but funded by the HES campaign itself, broke down donations by voting district and described how a large percentage of the funding for municipal election campaigns came from a small group of wealthy people.[49] The WashPIRG report also argued that nearly one third of the donations in 2015 were coming from outside of Seattle and fourteen percent were from out-of-state donors.[50] These reports described the general outsized influence of wealthy donors as a problem in itself, arguing in relatively vague terms that big money had too much influence on politics.

As an antidote, the HES initiative sought to encourage voters to more equally distribute participation in politics. The Sightline report speculated, "That's what Honest Elections Seattle might do to the political map of Seattle: spread participation from the rich, white, expensive neighborhoods with view homes to the whole city."[51] Both the Sightline and WashPIRG reports seemed to assume that the increase and diversification of voter participation would result from already-existing voter motivations rather than carefully engineered incentives. Participation among voters, they suggested, would be the result of their natural inclinations to seek influence, power, and political self-expression, none of which needed to be engineered because those motivations and interests preexisted the implementation of the voucher program. The executive director of the Seattle Ethics and Elections Commission was quoted as saying that the initiative would "get more people into the process,"[52] while other news articles argued that the vouchers would have or had amplified the "voices" of voters.[53] In fact, the "voices" of voters were often referred to in both research reports and news coverage of the voucher program, suggesting that enhancing or amplifying authentic democratic speech of individual citizens was the goal of the program.[54] This way of describing how vouchers might more equally distribute political participation comports smoothly with the assumptions of classical liberalism, in which political participation is assumed to be the result of preexisting interests in various individual and collective goods and merely needs to be formally included in electoral structures. Such interests do not need to be engineered or "incentivized" because they are already the result of a general competitive self-interest that governmental structures should fairly arbitrate.

In the absence of a unified and clear-cut set of preexisting "interests" among the voters of Seattle, however, a research report published directly by Every Voice, an advocacy group that had been the largest single donor to the campaign to pass the program in the first place, argued that the patterns of voucher use better reflected the demographics of the city than prior donation patterns.[55] The demographic composition of the city stood in for any specific policy preferences when defining the "interests" of voters. The report argued that "Seattle's Democracy Voucher Program achieves its intended goals by generating historic numbers of new and small donors, diversifying the makeup of campaign supporters to better reflect the people of Seattle, and limiting the reliance on big money in local elections."[56] The report, cited by a number of national news outlets in their coverage of the program's implementation, argued that everyday people had more of a voice and were better represented because the program had "made measurable strides toward altering the pool of donors to be more reflective of the city's population as a whole" and that "Democracy Voucher donors better reflected Seattle's population of young people, women, people of color, and less affluent residents."[57] Although only a small percentage of residents used the vouchers, this small percentage was, the report claimed, a far better representation of the general population of the city than the donors had been up until that point. An independent analysis of the voucher program, also cited in the press, argued that the diversification of the donor pool was present but quite small, demonstrating much room for improvement in the voucher program's implementation.[58]

In both reports, however, the goal of diversification of the donor pool is the measurable dimension of enacting the values of political equality and popular sovereignty. A *Seattle Times* article about the Every Voice study interviewed individual voters who had used the vouchers, quoting them as "feeling great" and more a "part of the system."[59] Other articles and press releases quoted campaign finance advocates arguing that campaign finance reforms mean that "people will get more power,"[60] that the vouchers were "empowering,"[61] and that the vouchers would "give every voter some influence."[62] One left-leaning liberal publication went further, describing the voucher program as "populist and deeply egalitarian."[63] These claims were bolstered by general references to the voucher program as restoring government to the people. In sum, the democracy voucher program generated an ethos that was in part built on its adherence to the liberal values of individual freedom to participate in politics, equality among citizens as they did so, and the pursuit of uncorrupted political representation.

The articulations and pursuit of these political values, however, was conducted through mechanisms that affirmed both neoliberal market-based techniques and a liberal anticorruption stance. The doxastic technics of neoliberal management—incentivizing behaviors by generating an artificial market—were freely employed in ways that comported relatively seamlessly with the liberal values of political equality and popular sovereignty. In treating political action as behavior to be managed rather than grounded in values to be cultivated, however, the HES initiative opened the door to abandoning those values in all but the most shallow declarative statements. The performative contradictions—and the appearance of ironic celebration of instrumentalism—emerged in the local and national news coverage of the campaign's own technics.

Market Competition for Donations: Neoliberal Mechanisms Serving Liberal Values

While the liberal values of political equality and popular sovereignty were articulated in vague ways by the initial reports from Sightline and WashPIRG, the reports, campaign advertisements, and campaign staff tended to focus more on changing candidate behaviors than articulating those values. According to both reports produced for the campaign, the goal of the democracy voucher program was to reorient politicians toward their larger constituencies and achieve a stronger and more transparent relationship of political representation. Because superior "representation" was conceptualized as demographic rather than ideological, however, the discourse and self-measurement techniques of the campaign drifted away from the values and toward market-based management. The Sightline report speculated about how the initiative could work: "Democracy Vouchers will upend the incentives for candidates: they'll make every voter in the city an easy prospect for $100 in contributions. It will probably be easier to collect vouchers than to dial for dollars from the donor class. Candidates may instead call on their supporters mostly to assemble their friends and neighbors to meet the candidate and let the candidate ask for vouchers."[64] Even more specifically, the Sightline report described the candidate behaviors that the vouchers strove to incentivize: "Doorbelling, house parties, receptions, fundraisers of many types, community forums, debates, street markets, and outdoor festivals—all the places candidates go to meet voters in person will become fundraising venues. Grassroots campaigning may expand markedly."[65] The WashPIRG report, funded by the campaign itself, argued that "democracy works best when our elected officials are focused on their constituents, rather than dialing for dollars from out-of-district contributors or focusing on an elite set of donors who can afford to give more than the average voter."[66]

This focus on using market incentives to influence candidate behavior expresses faith in the democratizing potential of a neoliberal political rationality. In this model, democratic behaviors are a clear (and measurable) set of goals to be engineered. Producing this set of behaviors doesn't necessarily require anyone to believe, think, or value ideals such as equality, much less think critically about their absence. As long as measurable behaviors are increased, it is only important that the market logics guide the behaviors of the target population.

News coverage of the initiative's goals was also squarely centered on the actions, behaviors, identities, and attention of the political candidates themselves. In the wake of the campaign's implementation, these articles interviewed Seattle political figures, candidates who used the vouchers, and national-level advocates to paint a picture of how the voucher program might lead candidates to campaign differently and how different types of candidates might take the leap into running for office. Some journalists expressed skepticism about various aspects of the program, including the hope that the voucher program would inspire an already sluggish electorate to participate more in politics.[67] But many of them reiterated and expounded on one of the core stated goals of the voucher program: getting candidates to change the way they campaign and pay more attention to a diverse range of constituents.[68] This would happen, the news coverage suggested, because candidates would "refocus" their attention, and make the candidates "more dependent on their constituents."[69]

One of the campaign's most expensive advertisements, filmed for television, dramatized this desired change in candidate behavior. The advertisement shows two different situations in which a white male candidate is speaking to a long table of potential supporters. In the first situation, the long wooden table has about dozen late-middle-aged white people seated around it. Heavy wood paneling, dark suits, leather chairs, formal place settings, and gold jewelry suggest a certain vision of a corporate boardroom that may actually be difficult to find in the offices of Seattle's most lucrative business ventures (some of which are more strongly associated with a corporate aesthetic that involves things such as designer cereals, luxury beanbag chairs, and ping-pong tables). The camera looks down the table from just behind the candidate's head, giving his point of view while the voice-over says, "Big monied interests dominate political campaigns nationally. It means candidates focus more on donors than on voters. That's wrong." A jump cut shifts the scene in which the same candidate is speaking to a table of similar length and a group of about the same number of people. In this scene, however, the demographics of the group are far more diverse, and it is evenly populated by men and women perched on folding chairs. The table has a red and white gingham tablecloth and is located in a sunny backyard with grass, trees, fencing, yard signs, and a grill. The voice-over narration continues, "Yes on 122 is a different approach. It keeps big monied interests out of our local elections. Yes on 122 gives ordinary people a stronger voice in government and keeps big money away." The general message is clear: the HES initiative will increase political equality by causing candidates to talk to different people and talk in different ways. The advertisement suggests that candidates will cultivate a more authentic, neighborly form of communication if they are properly incentivized to do so. This set of goals related to candidate behaviors employs a neoliberal logic of market incentives to produce more political equality among a diverse range of constituents.

After vouchers were first implemented in the 2017 city council races, the candidates who participated in the process extolled their virtues, arguing their own campaigns were evidence of the vouchers' capacity to diversify and democratize politics. For instance, Teresa Mosqueda, one of the first candidates who funded a successful campaign with democracy vouchers, argued in a number of interviews that as a renter with student loans and a full-time job she would never have been able to run for office without democracy vouchers.[70] Another candidate campaigned in low-income and homeless communities.[71] The advocacy of these candidates in the early stages of the initiative's implementation helped to solidify the position that the market-based mechanism of the voucher program was an effective way to "incentivize" diversity and democracy in candidate behaviors. The result was a coherent narrative that included the performance of neoliberal technics in the pursuit of more democratic liberal values.

What was missing from these efforts, however, was the affirmation of a broad-based commitment to an expanded and deepened political equality that went beyond a model of politics in which donation is an essentially important political act. The campaign relied less on arguing that political equality should be more important to the voters, candidates, and communities of Seattle but simply presented itself as having invented a clever device to make people *behave as though it were.*

Behavioral Experimentation in a Liberal Bastion

This emphasis on expertly managing the behavior of candidates (and to a lesser extent, voters), emphasized how the HES initiative itself was a clever, efficient, carefully planned electoral instrument rather than a demonstration of political equality. This emphasis on the measurable effectiveness of the initiative's impact on behavior contributed to the general ethos of the initiative as a sort of clever social-scientific experiment in political behavior with broader ramifications for managing political behavior nationwide. The goal of modeling and exporting the voucher program was explicated most fully in national press coverage of the campaign program implementation. Campaign staff and supporters from national advocacy groups explained to national news outlets more fully their hopes that the Seattle program would serve as a model for others. This press coverage of the voucher program focused far more intensely on the possibility of effectively "testing" the experimental program in Seattle to see if it could be effectively implemented in other city, state, and even national elections. By some accounts, including a critical and unsupportive editorial board at the *Seattle Times,* this was actually the primary purpose of the initiative.[72] The *Times,* as the major metropolitan newspaper of the city with the initiative on the ballot, had some cause to see the experimental measure as an unjustified incursion into the city's budget and practices. National news publications, on the other hand, trumpeted the status of the initiative as "first in the nation" while arguing that it was an important, groundbreaking test of a measure that might have potential as an antidote to *Citizens United.*

The two research reports initially produced by WashPIRG and Sightline to support the initiative did not discuss democracy vouchers as a model for the rest of the country.[73] The WashPIRG report alluded to this goal only in its final sentences, positing that the voucher program might "help build the movement for reform both in Seattle and beyond."[74] The mailers and television advertisements for the initiative also didn't specifically talk about the reform as a model. A television advertisement mentioned that "big monied interests dominate political campaigns nationally," before going on to described HES as a "different approach."[75] But this was the closest that the campaign's television and mailed advertisements got to referencing the goal of modeling a reform for the rest of the country.

In the national press, however, the goal of testing the voucher approach remained front and center. Before, during and after the 2017 election cycle, when the vouchers were first implemented, national news coverage of the voucher program described its status as a test case of an innovative new public financing program that might be implemented elsewhere. Supporters of the initiative from national advocacy organizations such as Free Speech for People, Represent.US, and Common Cause were interviewed about the exportability of the voucher program.[76] News articles trumpeted "the chance to create and test a novel approach to democratizing the financing of political campaigns"[77] while describing how supporters hoped that the initiative was "the first step forward in a wide-ranging reform effort spreading to other cities and states in the coming year."[78] A number of these articles referred to the vouchers as an "experiment"[79] and mentioned other cities and states that were considering their own version of a democracy voucher program.[80] Bruce Ackerman, the political theorist credited with coming up with the idea for democracy vouchers, wrote a lengthy piece for the *Washington Post* on the options for implementing the program at the national level.[81] The *Seattle Times,* which had firmly opposed the initiative, still acknowledged that the city took pride in being the "guinea pig" for the first-of-its-kind voucher program.[82]

The voucher program, as an "experiment" on the willing guinea pig of Seattle, was justified in the national press primarily in terms of the goal of finding a nationwide solution to the problems of money in politics. Ackerman's and Lessig's writings on democracy vouchers demonstrate how this is precisely the broad problem that the vouchers were conceptualized to address, so it is no surprise that their initial implementation would be framed that way. The city of Seattle was a reliably fertile ground for testing a mildly progressive policy reform that could be then extended to other, potentially larger, governmental bodies.

The primacy of the goal of testing the voucher program demonstrates how the goals of managing candidate behavior and expanding voter influence were relatively minor in the broader articulation of the purpose of the vouchers. Although the voucher program was initially presented by the Sightline and WashPIRG reports and the advertising campaign of the initiative as a specific solution to unequal political participation in the city, press coverage quickly shifted the presentation of the goals to the more expansive possibilities of testing and expanding the program to other places.

This focus on the Seattle program as a "test" or "experiment" reflects a way of understanding democracy as itself a type of technology that must be carefully tinkered with. In the United States, this approach has sometimes referred to the states and cities as "laboratories of democracy," with policy makers as the scientists or engineers hard at work on innovating better representative practices. Although the HES initiative pursued the goals of increasing voter influence and changing the campaign practices of candidates for elected office, its supporters also cultivated the ethos of the democratic engineering team intent on producing the correctly designed structure to address the taken-for-granted problem of "money in politics." This sense of democratic government as itself a technology compounded the ironic celebration of clever political artifice that contributed to the passage and implementation of the voucher program.

The campaign to pass the initiative pursued the goal of conducting the test in a way that could claim success based on whether the test was conducted rather than whether the test had any particular results. In other words, the goal of testing the democracy vouchers could be achieved without necessarily demonstrating that the vouchers enhanced political equality, substantially empowered diverse voters, or changed the behavior of candidates for office. If the *test itself* was the goal, a failed program would still constitute a successful test in the sense that it provided data for future decision making about what types of campaign finance reforms to implement in other places.

One of the key elements of the Seattle "test case" for democracy vouchers has been the production and dissemination of data about the voucher usage and voting patterns that have followed it. In the wake of the initiative's implementation, the Seattle Ethics and Elections Commission (SEEC) has gathered large amounts of data about the voucher program and made it widely available on their website.[83] For instance, the general public is able to access a complete list of all Seattle residents who contributed their democracy vouchers, including data about which candidate they sent them to and the date they were given.[84] Subsequent reports from Every Voice and the University of Washington Center for Studies in Democracy and Ecology matched this data with demographic data on voters purchased from Catalist, a progressive-brand national-voter data firm, to draw conclusions about how the program was able to attain its goals of increasing and diversifying voter participation in 2017.[85] The SEEC also produced its own internal reports and commissioned an independent consulting firm to produce a report about the implementation of the voucher program in the 2017 election cycle.[86] Each of these reports evaluates the success of the voucher program in terms of candidate buy-in, usage of the vouchers, and diversification of the donor pool. The availability of the data about the donors and the reports, however, constitutes the achievement of one of the goals that the democracy program sought to attain in the first place; the experimental trial run of a program for the purposes of evaluating its potential for implementation elsewhere.

The emphasis on the goal of beta testing the voucher idea expands the goal of more transparency in election funding itself to include more transparency in the production and evaluation of data about the reform effort.

The ironically instrumental ethos of the initiative, including its implementation, is served by the accessibility of this data and its use as part of the research reports about the voucher program. The reports provided insights about whether the voucher program succeeded in its other two goals—modifying candidate behavior and increasing and diversifying voter participation. But the provisions for producing the reports and the impression of transparency they contributed were the culmination of the pursuit of the goal of conducting an effective test of the voucher program.

In general, these goals were clearly derived from a conceptualization of democracy as a type of mechanical structure to be carefully designed and improved upon. In the push to produce certain candidate behaviors through market mechanisms, we can clearly see the outlines of a neoliberal political rationality. In the discourse about increasing voter participation and influence, however, a broader set of liberal political values become evident as a form of political reason distinct from how efforts to manipulate candidate behaviors were pursued with neoliberal market-based logics. In the goal of experimenting with and expanding the usage of vouchers nationally, the liberal and the neoliberal elements of the voucher campaign combined under the auspices of an ironic instrumentalism, which conceived of the process of tinkering with electoral reforms as part of demonstrating a knowledgeable engineering ethos by manipulating political technics against themselves. The goals of experimentation and incentivizing candidate behavior demonstrated a neoliberal commitment to market mechanisms and an instrumental rationality that justified the pursuit of values such as political equality and popular sovereignty by abandoning them in practice. The result, almost inevitably, was the failure of the initiative itself to meet its own criteria for democratic politics.

Carpetbagging by Ballot Initiative

The implementation of the HES initiative was covered, often with great approval, in the national press in 2017. In Seattle, however, the editorial board of the *Times* published two different statements of opposition to the initiative.[87] The *Times* argued that the initiative campaign was funded by outsiders and contradicted its own stated goals, arguing that "what's most shocking is that the core message of the I-122 campaign asserts that type of intervention is bad for local politics. Vote as I say, not as I do? No thank you, I-122."[88] It is perhaps an extra layer of irony that the local newspaper would fail to support a measure designed to enhance local democracy while nationwide the measure would be supported by the liberal Left.

Other newspapers also described how the campaign to pass I-122 was funded but passed over the issue more lightly. The SEEC published complete records of donors to the initiative campaign, making it clear even before the initiative passed who was bankrolling it. One of the largest donors was actually the Washington Community Action Network, a membership organization active in grassroots politics. The rest of the major donors, however, were from out of state. The top donor, coming in at $390,860.23, was the Washington, DC, lobbying group Every Voice. After that was the Washington Community Action Network with $351,962.06, New York political entrepreneur Sean Eldridge, who donated $200,000, a Seattle organization called Win/Win Action with $69,001.54, and Amalgamated Bank with $50,000.[89] The total amount of money donated to the campaign was a whopping $1,432,365.55, a figure more than twice the amount donated to any other Seattle municipal campaign during that election cycle.[90]

The HES campaign donor receiving the most attention was Sean Eldridge, the husband of Facebook cofounder and *New Republic* publisher Chris Hughes. Several news articles mentioned Eldridge's role in the campaign, one of them pointing out that he had recently lost a campaign for a US House seat in upstate New York.[91] Eldridge's reputation was affected by this high-profile defeat, with much of the press coverage mentioning how recently he had moved to the district and how much money he had spent on the election.[92] Eldridge's donations to the campaign were regularly mentioned in local news and opinion coverage of the campaign.[93] Right-leaning publications were especially pointed in their analysis of Eldridge's involvement, and the *Seattle Times* also made several critical mentions of how his financial support demonstrated the irony of the campaign's tactics.[94]

When the press mentioned Eldridge's $200,000 contribution to the campaign, there were important biographical elements that were usually added. The first was that he was described as a "venture capitalist" and the second was that his spouse was one of the cofounders of Facebook. While most of the articles failed to draw direct connections to Eldridge's failed House run, they almost never missed the opportunity to note the source of his spouse's wealth and Eldridge's own venture capital firm. The obvious conclusion that profits from new communication technologies were the source of the campaign donation funds (whether this was actually the case or not) added an important dimension to the campaign's ironic ethos by suggesting a very specific business model for developing new technology as well as a commitment to market values substantial enough to have garnered success and value by central neoliberal measures. The voucher program was not particularly dependent on new communication technologies; paper vouchers were initially mailed out to voters and had to be donated as paper objects. The VC model of dumping large amounts of cash into a new design to see if it could be rapidly scaled is certainly one that has come to be associated with new communication technology development. Referring to Eldridge, who has funded a range of progressive nonprofit organizations, being a "venture capitalist" suggests the potential of the VC business model to be exercised in the name of democracy. In fact, one of Eldridge's other nonprofit projects does precisely that: the Democracy Alliance is a network of donors that maintains an "investment portfolio "of "high-impact, progressive organizations that generate bold policy ideas, drive progressive messages, organize key constituencies, and support the next generation of leaders."[95] This model of pursuing progressive change describes nonprofit organizations as having a sort of market value that can be measured according to specific metrics of success and then invested in by capital.

The large campaign coffer of the HES initiative was spent in ways that have often been criticized by left-progressive anticorruption advocates as endemic to the dissolution of democratic institutions: namely, large, expensive media buys. Although "netroots" advocates have long argued that television is the medium most guilty of driving up the fundraising demands of contemporary political campaigns (and therefor justifying dependance on PACs and wealthy donors), much of the HES campaign fund was also spent on a range of targeted digital ads located in social media platforms.[96] The SEEC report on the expenditures of the HES campaign reveal that over 44% of the $1.4 million raised by the campaign went to the production and dissemination of advertisements. Another 10% was sent to a firm that provided paid petition signature gatherers and about 8% was spent on mailing flyers.[97] Included in advertising expenditures were large sums spent on predictively placing digital advertisements in addition to more traditional advertisements on cable television. This "slickly managed" political operation (as one article called it) carefully converted large amounts of money from wealthy private donors into effective political influence with limited need of grassroots support.[98]

In sum, the campaign operated in precisely the model that it itself sought to undercut. In fact, the WashPIRG report on the role of money in Seattle elections argued that it was large donors and out-of-state donors that generated some of the most important threats to the democratic integrity of Seattle's municipal elections.[99] The ironies that emerge from this "experimental" approach to democratic reforms were part of the basis of the *Seattle Times'* resistance to the HES initiative. The *Times* editorial board argued that the campaign to pass the HES initiative was an example of an attempt by national advocacy groups to "puppeteer local government" and that Seattle was not a place "where big corporate donors dominate local elections."[100] In effect, articles in the *Times* argued that the HES initiative was an example of "if it ain't broke, fix it 'til it is" and that the initiative was doomed to cause more problems than it solved. Arguing that the initiative was more or less an example of carpetbagging via ballot initiative, the *Times* took the position that Seattle's own homegrown tactics for improving municipal elections should be left alone to work without further interventions from outsiders.

This is not to say, however, that grassroots and community organizations didn't support the HES initiative—they did support it, some even going on the record to claim that they were the founding impetus for the program.[101] The *Seattle Times* editorial board and fringe libertarian groups notwithstanding, there has been little substantial critical pushback on the democracy voucher program from local community organizations at either the campaign or implementation stage. The irony of the program is genuine and can't be boiled down to a simple case of replacing liberal values with neoliberal markets. Ironic instrumentalism comes into focus when this performative contradiction is understood not just as something to be critically observed (as the *Seattle Times* editorial board did) but also as a demonstration of a forceful ethos through the knowledgeable manipulation of political skill in pursuit of more genuinely democratic institutions. Ironic instrumentalism is an ethos that is proudly claimed by national reform advocates who were interested in the capacity of HES to serve as an experiment and model for the nation. The ethos of ironic instrumentalism wears such contradictions as a badge of honor that proves the capacity to get things done in spite of the obstacles posed by political scruples.

Conclusion

The democracy voucher program both participates in and departs from a neoliberal rationality as Brown and others have articulated it. First, the HES campaign financing attempted to incorporate market-based mechanisms that encourage specific behavioral changes in candidates running for elected office. The production of self-capitalizing subjects is a central element of neoliberal political rationality, and the campaign openly attempted to engineer candidate behavior. Neoliberalism extends market logics and mechanisms into the production of subjects themselves, their behaviors and self-development.[102] In Seattle's voucher program, we see justification of the changes in how elections are financed in terms of how it will encourage the production of self-regulating, self-maximizing political candidates who will change problematic political behavior in response to the right market incentives.

However, justifications for the program also claimed that voters will become more involved in politics for reasons that do not as closely resemble neoliberal market logics. Instead, increased voter participation is framed as being a matter of strengthening popular sovereignty and political equality in the face of rapidly stratifying wealth. The vouchers were envisioned as enabling a transparent and (as much as possible) unedited representation of the demographic composition, public opinion, and interests of the population of individual eligible voters, including those who have been excluded from the political process altogether. The HES initiative also strove to increase engagement among voters by expanding their influence. So, while the voucher program operates according to an instrumental rationality that bears some resemblance to neoliberalism, the end goals it articulates are those of a more traditionally liberal (rather than neoliberal) democracy; freedom and equality of political participation for their own sake.

Beyond the tension between neoliberal mechanisms and liberal ideals, however, the more specific irony of the campaign is the performative contradiction between the fundraising and advertising tactics of the campaign and its strong anticorruption message. The tactics of the campaign were precisely those that it sought to eliminate, an irony that some commentators found off-putting but that more commentators found to be clever, effective, and ultimately justifiable. It may be that the irony of the HES campaign ultimately drew more attention to the corruption it sought to address than a more genuinely grassroots campaign might have. But the campaign celebrated its own cleverness enough along the way to cultivate a liberal democratic ethos of ironic instrumentalism inclusive of both the critique of corruption and the celebration of neoliberal engineering know-how as an appropriate vision of democracy.

As we saw in chapter 1, the Occupy demonstrations avoided the irony and instrumentalism of the voucher campaign in significant ways. The earnestness of the Occupy demonstrations and their constant striving for performative consistency marked an important shift in progressive politics that the HES campaign failed to register in spite of the fact that it occurred four years after the Occupy demonstrations took place. The emphasis on expertly designed technics that underwrite ironic instrumentalism has not vanished or been wholly replaced by a more horizontal democratic ethos. As we will see in the following chapters, Occupy's brand of horizontalism has infiltrated progressive reformism with a democratic ethos that continues to draw on the cultural force that comes with knowledge of political technics while moving away from the self-conscious contradictions of explicit irony. The dissemination of Occupy's democratic ethos has required it to be reincorporated in more reformist political efforts that strive to abandon irony while wrestling with instrumentalism's emphasis on efficiency and effectiveness. The next three chapters show us some of the ways that instrumentalism and authenticity have clashed and combined.

THREE

Bernie Sanders and Authentically Democratic Donations

Bernie Sanders's critique of how wealth influences electoral politics stands in contrast to the predominant instrumental logic guiding the campaigning practices of political candidates prior to the 2016 election cycle. The Sanders campaign famously cultivated small donors and refused super political action committee (PAC) support. Among Republicans, there has been little hesitation about accepting donations and unlimited super-sized PAC support. Democrats have also benefited from the support of super PACs—but they have done so while also attempting to criticize them. Democrats have argued that they can't "unilaterally disarm" by refusing PAC support and large donations while Republicans continue to accept such funding. This has led to a substantial ironic performative contradiction wherein, prior to 2016 and even beyond, many Democratic candidates accepted extensive funding from wealthy individuals and corporations while ostensibly advocating for legislation that would ban such support. This has made the ironic instrumentalist ethos of contemporary moderate-progressive politics quite pronounced. The goal of winning elections has clearly been prioritized over the very values that lead candidates to advocate for campaign finance reform. The means and the ends directly contradict one another.

From a more radically leftist perspective on democracy, voting and donating to election campaigns fail to surpass a limited, instrumentalist perspective on democratic participation. The liberal pursuit of cleaner voting and donating stands in stark contrast to the ways that donating and voting have been described on the radical left. Part of this is because of the contemporary ironies of low voter turnout and the decay of liberal political institutions. But even beyond these failures, most progressive and radical perspectives take the position that genuine democratic participation is something *more* than voting and donating. Real democracy, from radical and progressive perspectives, has a more dialogic, authentically communicative element in which everyday people exercise their capacity for self-governance through deliberative, values-based speech, writing, and embodied action. As nonverbal acts, donating and voting fall short of authentic democratic communication even without being warped by significant inequalities of wealth. Moreover, donating to an election campaign is the privilege of the wealthy.

There is an important connection, in some types of leftist thinking, between the shallow form of political engagement represented by voting and donating and the co-option of elections by wealthy interests. In the past few decades, donation-driven campaigns have come to be associated with expensive television advertising that consumes campaign budgets and justifies the use of super PACs. As electoral politics have become even more highly professionalized, obsessed with prediction, and ideologically narrow, leftism prior to 2016 had more or less given up on attempts to imagine radical versions of democratic elections.[1] In the wake of the 2016 election and the Sanders campaign's innovations, elections have become a renewed site of passionate engagement for left politics, particularly around voting rights for people of color.

The 2016 Sanders campaign was not a radical disruption in the general form of electoral politics, and it did not present nuanced and thoughtful (much less radical) positions on issues affecting people of color in the United States. As we know, the history of US "progressivism" is one of racial exclusion and unexamined whiteness.[2] Even the 2020 Sanders campaign took only small steps to overcome this legacy. The 2016 Sanders campaign, however, reinvigorated a certain model of progressive campaigning based on a democratic ethos of authentic communication. It did so by reinventing the significance of activities long dismissed by radicals as subservient to a mechanistic, antidemocratic liberalism: voting, campaign financing, data management, and campaign volunteer coordination. By framing these forms of participation within a broader commitment to live, face-to-face communication and dialogic engagement, the Sanders campaign described such instrumentalist forms of political action as potentially moral and cultural, as well as authentically democratic. The Sanders campaign's emphasis on connecting with voters live and through other "more authentic" means was only the beginning of how the 2016 Sanders campaign for president began the process of reinvigorating traditionally liberal mechanisms of campaigning and political representation. Liberal conceptualizations of democracy, long critiqued by radical leftists, were embraced in the Sanders campaign, adapted to the affordances of new communication technologies, and combined with an older vision of the democratic power of face-to-face communication. In doing so, liberal forms of action such as donating to an election campaign took on the mantel of authentic democratic communication. In certain ways, this allowed individualistic, transactional components of a presidential election campaign to be animated by a democratic ethos that reflected the types of prefigurative persuasion consolidated in the Occupy demonstrations.

The Sanders campaign strove to produce a sense of its democratic ethos by broadcasting certain details of its inner workings, much like the way Occupy's assembly-based democratic decision-making processes provided evidence of its authentic democratic character. Some Occupy participants became active Bernie Sanders supporters. Ultimately, however, the democratic ethos of the Sanders campaign seems to be the result of how it was able to perform consistency between its message and its own self-constitution—how it adopted the forms of prefigurative persuasion. A key element of this rhetorical performance was, of course, how it contrasted its own authenticity against the Democratic Party's ironically instrumental "no unilateral disarmament" logic of pursuing super PAC fundraising and television advertising. As we have seen, the Occupy demonstrations did not simply *internally* prefigure more radical forms of democratic community; they persuasively broadcast such democratic forms of organization in order to persuasively bolster their ethos, recruit participants, and perform consistent authenticity for a broader audience. The Sanders campaign combined elements of a persuasive radical critique of economic inequality with a presentation of its own internal democratic structure, including the integrity of the candidate himself, the refusal of super PAC support, and the careful management and protection of donor data. This combination of critique and performance of authenticity featured centrally in the persuasive prefigurative elements of the Sanders campaign's democratic ethos.

Long before Occupy, Sanders claimed affiliation with "democratic socialism." As we have seen in the years since the 2016 election, a strain of "progressivism" that animates liberal politics with advocacy for economic equality has been established in what Sanders has often called the "democratic wing of the Democratic Party." The existing blend of liberalism and quasi-socialism that has gone under the name of progressivism in twentieth-century US politics has appeared in a few other presidential campaigns, including those of Jesse Jackson, Howard Dean, and Barack Obama. These campaigns have been described as "progressive" for several different reasons (even though, of course, the resulting Obama presidency was criticized on the left for not being progressive enough). The Sanders campaign built on these features of past progressive campaigns while straying further left and claiming closer connections to socialist ideals.

The liberal and ironic instrumental ethos, in contrast, has celebrated virtuoso displays of technological competence, expert knowledge, and a deep commitment to the value of short-term effectiveness. The Sanders campaign's version of left progressivism differed substantially from the more deeply instrumental liberal progressivism that the Clinton campaign represented. As we saw in the example of the Seattle Democracy Voucher program, ironic instrumentalism can exist in progressive politics in a way relatively unresponsive to the left-democratic ethos consolidated by the Occupy demonstrations. The Sanders campaign was not civilly disobedient in the manner of the Occupy demonstrations; it did not break or even bend the law. It did, however, attempt to call critical attention to the illegitimacy of "establishment" institutions such as the Democratic National Committee and the media by bending and breaking long-standing instrumentalist presidential campaign traditions and by persuasively publicizing those deviations.

The result was the rhetorical recasting of the speechless, instrumental act of donating as both a form of authentic democratic communication and as proof of the campaign's democratic ethos and its commitment to radicalism. Just as the Occupy demonstrations used the public performance of participatory democratic processes and mutual aid to pursue donations, convert new participants, and cultivate news media support, the Sanders campaign performed its democratic ethos by trumpeting its internal organizing processes, including its cultivation of small donors and management of their data.

The wild success of the Sanders campaign's small-donor fundraising—both as a fundraising mechanism and as a publicity engine—prompts a question about whether it was a refusal of instrumentalism or just a better and more effective persuasive instrument. As campaigning through the cultivation of small donors grew, the Sanders campaign provided a lesson in the complexities of how persuasive prefiguration blends authenticity and instrumentalism in the form of the democratic ethos.

Authentic and Instrumentalist Campaign Communication

Contemporary progressivism includes elements of a well-established left critique of the media. This critical position holds that the media are an antidemocratic, impersonal, immoral, and biased set of technologies and social practices infamous for misrepresenting reality, fostering prejudice, sowing discord, prioritizing profits over truth, and giving voice to only a narrow range of privileged political perspectives.[3] For most left progressives, including Sanders, the media are a top-down, profit-driven form of instrumental mass communication and, as such, cannot hope to foster authentic, participatory, deliberative, democratic communication. Horizontalism, various Marxisms, critical theory, public sphere theory, anarchisms and other leftist political philosophies have underwritten this political perspective by developing trenchant critiques of the media as spectacle, misrepresentation, simulacra, ideology, doxa, biopower, and refeudalization.[4] There are innumerable ways that the media reinforce inequality and neoliberal instrumentalism in their content, technological affordances, and financial structures. These critiques resonate so readily that they have become banal and are increasingly extended to cover various social media corporations.

As the news media report on election campaigns, they often default to coverage of fundraising benchmarks, campaign strategies, polling results, and other supposedly value-neutral markers of instrumental success.[5] Focusing on such benchmarks, the core measures of professionalized political campaigning, have by some accounts helped to push both parties to spend ever-larger amounts on television advertisements that can only be funded by wealthy individual and corporate donors.[6] Liberal bipartisan campaign finance reform has been concerned with trumpeting the potential of electoral reforms and new digital technologies to liberate contemporary election campaigns from the albatross of television advertisements and their funders.[7] As increasingly sophisticated and expensive digital consultants emerge, it is less and less clear that television advertisements are actually more expensive than a robust and effective digital media operation.[8] Nonetheless, liberal and progressive political analyses have persistently associated digital communication with democracy and opposed it to reliance on television advertisements.[9] Part of this critique is that television advertising is a coercive, purely instrumental form of one-directional communication that affects voters mechanically through persuasive repetition.[10]

From the ironically instrumental "no unilateral disarmament" perspective, super PAC support and television advertising are necessary evils. Making the calculated decision to accept such financial support expresses the ironic ethos of supposedly savvy, effective campaigning. Ethos is not just about the trustworthiness and moral fiber of the candidate; it is about the campaign's ability to show that they can manage political necessity and prioritize winning.

As we have seen earlier, the concept of ethos has been developed in two primary ways: as a collective ethic or as a tool of instrumental persuasion. When "ethos" has been treated by scholars such as Michael J. Hyde as a broad-based collective ethic, it may be built and projected as part of practical problem-solving, but it is idealized and presumed to be performatively consistent with an underlying philosophical or spiritual ethic of a community.[11] Accounts such as Hyde's are a far cry from an instrumentalist perspective, on the other hand, that fosters and accepts a division between the means and ends of practical action. In fact, Hyde deliberately contrasts his Isocratean and Heideggerian theorization of ethos with a more vulgar Aristotelian concept of ethos as "mere" instrumental performance or persuasive tool.[12] This contrast reflects a long-standing classical distinction between conceptualizations of ethos as an authentic expression of the ethical collective knowledge of a community or a mere instrument of persuasion.

What is missing from accounts such as Hyde's is the acknowledgement of the extent to which any given performance of an "authentic" ethos based on the ethical commitments of a collective depends on contrasting itself with instrumental performances of merely persuasive ethos. The 2016 Sanders campaign demonstrates how the performance of a democratic ethos based on the "authentic" communication strategies of the campaign relied on declaring that other forms of communication (such as television advertising and the media in general) were instrumental, usually ironically so. In other words, the performance of an authentic ethos requires some other, more instrumentalist or ironic ethos as a foil.

To structure this conflict in terms of its own prefigurative persuasion, the Sanders campaign tapped into a long-standing leftist and progressive narrative about the battle between the ethos of authentic democratic communication and the instrumentalism of big media. Radical approaches to democracy, including those of horizontalism, have their own versions of the "authentic/instrumental communication" narrative that overlap with the progressive version.[13] The Occupy demonstrations, as we have seen, were also closely associated with the presumed political divide between progressive digital media and more conservative, monied legacy news.[14] This rhetorical frame of a battle between authentic democratic, dialogic communication and instrumentalist broadcast media has been complicated by a number of factors, but the frame was still strong enough in 2016 to shape the development of the ethos of the Sanders campaign in liberal and progressive news media.

Several writers, including John Judis, Michael Kazin, and Chantal Mouffe, have described the populist elements of the Sanders campaign and located it in the context of populisms emerging on the left and right across the globe.[15] Populist rhetoric sets up a division between "the establishment" and "the people" while demonizing the establishment and connecting as many unmet demands in the political environment as it can, claiming that they are all the result of the ineptitude and bad faith of those who are in power.[16] Existing analyses of the populist dimensions of the Sanders campaign (such as those of Judis, Kazin, and Mouffe) carefully note Sanders's critiques of the national government and how it has been captured by corporate interests and fails to represent the interests of "the people." This critique of plutocracy was, of course, a core element of Sanders's populism as well as the campaign's critique of the ironic instrumentalism of the "no unilateral disarmament" logic. What is less noted is how the Sanders campaign also framed "big media" as the establishment it was running against with a sort of small media of "the people." Plutocracy was not the only "establishment" figure of populist opposition—the media also played this role.

Describing the Sanders campaign's rhetoric as simply populist, however, makes it difficult to see how the specific claim to be more democratic than the establishment then shaped the campaign's choices about fundraising and communication. As Laclau and others argue, populism is a rhetorical form that works in the context of both left and right politics.[17] One of the things that distinguishes left and right populisms is their differing commitments to democracy as a set of tactics and values; the right is often populist without naming or enacting "democracy," whereas a figure such as Sanders was deeply committed to naming and enacting "democracy" in a performatively consistent way.

The use and performance of low-budget, social media, and conversational communication technics was a crucial part of this enactment of "democracy" in the Sanders campaign's version of populist opposition to the big media/government establishment. An important feature of the accusation that "big media" are grounded in political and economic instrumental rationality is the argument that campaigning via television requires campaigns to amass large amounts of cash by cultivating wealthy donors. New media, on the other hand, supposedly allow campaigns to maintain genuine progressive values by effectively and inexpensively cultivating small donors and spreading the word through organically established community relationships and social media networks that are more closely related to face-to-face personal ties and less tainted by financial interests.[18]

In the Sanders campaign, emphasis was put on a variety of forms of "authentic" communication rather than only on effective or efficient communication. As the Sanders campaign described its own self-organization, this "authentic communication" included digital communication, rallies, face-to-face conversation, social media, telephone networks, and other types of communication not reliant on funding from PACs or large donors. The hope articulated by the 2016 Sanders campaign was that face-to-face and digital communication could bring people together in more authentic ways and somehow re-establish the sense of shared destiny and common purpose that had been lost with the rise of PACs, mega-donors, and floods of money funding television advertising. New communication technologies and face-to-face communication, many progressives hoped, would enable political discourse that could revive more authentically democratic presidential campaigning. One of the most-discussed dimensions of this authentic communication was the relationship that the Sanders campaign had with its small donors, who contributed in record-breaking numbers.

Leftist thinkers sympathetic to horizontalism, however, have not traditionally conceptualized donating to a presidential election campaign as an authentically democratic form of communication. Michael Hardt and Antonio Negri, for instance, have argued clearly against any and all processes of political representation; the question of how a representative's campaigns are financed is utterly beside the point in their thinking.[19] Anarchisms that prioritize mutual aid and collective care encourage in-kind donations and practices of reuse as part of larger ethics of sharing and an effort to rethink economics and value.[20] Such practices are generally understood, however, as alternatives to governmental control over resources, the logic of markets, and reliance on state-issued currency as the basis for exchange. Ronald Walter Greene, a scholar of political rhetoric working in the traditions of autonomist Marxism and critical theory, has offered a trenchant critique of how campaign donations and expenditures have come to stand in for other forms of political speech under the current neoliberal legal and political logics.[21] Jodi Dean's robust critique of "communicative capitalism" followed a similar path.[22]

Even thinkers who are more tolerant of liberalism, such as Chantal Mouffe and Wendy Brown, tend to lump monetary donations into a category of political action that is shallow and relatively undemocratic. Mouffe has written incisively about the problems associated with what she calls an "aggregative" model of democracy that reduces political expression to numeric, measurable units such as polling results, donations, and votes.[23] Brown has argued that liberal emphasis on the issue of campaign finance participates in the neoliberalization of political speech via metaphors of the "marketplace."[24] Scholars such as Gerard A. Hauser and Mark Andrejevic, following the critical approach of Jürgen Habermas, have argued that shallow forms of political participation such as donating or responding to opinion polls represent the commodification of political participation and the reduction of genuine political speech to transactional, purely instrumental exchanges of personal data, money, and votes.[25]

For many such leftist-academic critics, authentic democratic participation seems to instead be a matter of producing engaged, thoughtful, passionate political speech and writing that is responsive to and critical of underlying material inequalities. Rather than the shallow, instrumental action of donating or voting, they argue, democratic participation is a matter of expressing, deliberating, and reasoning in ways that convey and produce the political emotions, thoughts, and deep-seated critical values of individuals and communities. Not all radical critics elaborate a positive vision of such democratic participation, but the assumption most of them make is clear: authentic political participation requires more verbally complex and critical forms of communication. Even scholars of movement rhetoric such as Phaedra Pezzullo and Kevin DeLuca who embrace nonverbal, embodied, or visual forms of communication do so on the basis of the expressive and affective complexity that is closely associated with visual rhetorics.[26]

On this general point, radical critics working in the wake of Marxism tend to agree with pragmatist theorists of democracy such as John Dewey and the general tenets of the progressive tradition.[27] Scholars of US political rhetoric have been deeply sympathetic to the values of the progressive tradition and have closely studied practices of such forms of democratic political communication.[28] Progressivism can be understood as a sort of "pragmatic" socialism (or democratic socialism) willing to negotiate with a hegemonic liberalism to gradually reform liberal institutions and make them more humane, increase economic equality, and moderate the effects of market competition and individualism. With this negotiation has come a willingness among progressives to acknowledge that a range of communication technologies might foster the same kind of democratic authenticity as face-to-face talk. James Carey argues that even Dewey, a well-known champion of a nostalgic notion of town-hall, face-to-face, socially intimate democracy, saw a range of communication technologies as essential to future progressive notions of democracy.[29] The challenge, for both Dewey and more recent and horizontal accounts of democratic communication, is for such technologically mediated exchanges to be authentic expressions of participants rather than being produced merely to legitimize the influence and claims of the powerful. Even by these relaxed standards of progressive (as opposed to more radical leftist) communication, cash donations have never approached the level of an authentically democratic form of communication—not for anarchists, autonomists, post-Marxists, critical theorists, or progressives.

The 2011 Occupy demonstrations were also, of course, expressions of the left-progressive intellectual traditions that have historically rejected the democratic significance of donating as a form of political action. Instead, that tradition has emphasized the importance of speech, embodied protest, and visual spectacle while also projecting such forms of action outward as part of an instrumentally persuasive process of ethos building. A disdain for instrumentalism has meant that many forms of leftism laud only democratic speech that separates itself from instrumentally seeking specific changes in government, media, and other large institutions. The result, evident in the influences on the Occupy demonstrations, has been a commitment to "internal prefiguration" as a matter of creating change primarily in and through the participants opting into radical politics themselves. The Occupy demonstrations, however, turned prefigurative democratic processes outward and performed them for a broader audience as part of persuasive prefiguration—an instrumental effort to persuade, draw financial support, and convey their message to the news media. As we saw, one of the results of this demonstration of the democratic ethos was a flood of donations from around the world to the New York encampment.[30] Additionally, however, the very act of donating itself was recast in the light of mutual aid processes prefigured in the camp life. This imbrication of "donation" within prefiguration seems to have shifted the set of connotations about donating and made it more authentically democratic.

The Sanders campaign's small-donor fundraising strategy highlights the extent to which cultivating small donors has subsequently been repurposed in left progressivism as part of a democratic ethos. In spite of the overwhelming historical consensus among progressive and leftist thinkers that campaign donations are not an authentically democratic form of communication, the Sanders campaign promoted its small donors as evidence of its grassroots democratic character and its departure from purely instrumentalist politics. Donations were central to its performance of authenticity. This adaptation was accomplished in part by contrasting the "authentic" communication of small donors with the purely—or even ironically—instrumentalist communication wrought by donations made by the very wealthy and corporations. The Sanders campaign did not entirely abandon television advertising as a tool.[31] But its emphasis on other types of communication affirmed the authenticity of its democratic ethos—or at least, affirmed that it was *more* authentic than advertising funded by super PAC support.

Refusing super PAC support and the trumpeting of the small average donation size (twenty-seven dollars) went hand in hand with Bernie Sanders's personal ethos as long-suffering socialist critic of mainstream politics, Wall Street, and capitalism. The Sanders campaign did what it could to generate a sense of how Sanders himself was an authentic radical. It emphasized how Sanders's class background differed from that of most presidential candidates.[32] Sanders was careful to reveal that his own upbringing was one of relative deprivation, thrift, and domestic conflicts over money.[33] He has spoken about the fact that his parents were immigrants without college degrees.[34] Additionally, however, he occasionally noted his privilege as a college-educated white man. He claimed that it was his intention to represent all voters lacking a voice in plutocracy, but especially the middle class, a shrinking group with less and less access to employment, health care, quality housing, childcare, education, and other social goods. Beyond Sanders's personal demographics and his stated commitments to issues of wealth inequality, however, his ethos relied on the fact that he had been vocally supporting such issues for decades before ever being elected to national office. The sheer persistent consistency of his message over time was an essential component of how his individual ethos was performed in the course of campaigning for president.

The implications of this refusal to accept super PAC support extended deep into the structure of the campaign as a whole and allowed for the expression of a *collective* campaign ethos. Just as donations to the Occupy demonstrations were encouraged as a form of participation, donations to the Sanders campaign were conceptualized and described by the campaign as a form of communication in themselves. The management of the personal data of donors became an essential component of how the campaign performed its commitment to democracy.

The campaign's democratic ethos fit into and, to a certain extent, altered the news coverage of the campaign. As the Sanders campaign refused PAC support and focused on cultivating small donors, it also claimed to have generated an internal "distributed" organizing structure that demonstrated a commitment to certain mild versions of prefigurative democratic principles.[35] The hallmark of the democratic organizing principles of the campaign, however, was clearly the funding structure and the critique of electoral instrumentalism that it signaled. Because the act of donating was so central to the democratic constitution of the campaign, news coverage of the campaign that was both leftist and centrist ended up projecting the ethos of the campaign as it covered a relatively standard dimension of the election "horse race"—the campaign's fundraising. As the 2016 campaign came to a close, the campaign's decision about how to manage the data produced by that act became a highly publicized, nuanced demonstration of how the campaign performed a democratic ethos based both on authentic performative consistency and the instrumental persuasion that presidential campaign politics entailed.

The Sanders Political Revolution

The 2016 presidential election was a watershed in many respects. As subsequent election cycles have demonstrated, the 2016 Sanders campaign for the Democratic Party nomination wrote a new playbook for left-progressive candidates running for elected office at all levels of political representation. When it comes to campaign finance, the 2016 Sanders campaign's tactics signal an emergent brand of left-progressive Democratic Party politics. This version of left-progressive politics maintains a skeptical distance from the Democratic Party "machine" and vigorously refuses super PAC support in favor of cultivating small donors. These campaigns, such as those of Alexandria Ocasio-Cortez, present themselves as striving for authentic democratic communication with supporters. Small-donor campaigns stand as an alternative to more ironically instrumental approaches to campaigning (which prioritize winning elections over true campaign finance reform) that have dominated party politics for some time. The performance of authenticity is conducted in part through the integrity, honesty, and trustworthiness of the candidates themselves. Just as important, however, is the performative disclosure of the internal structure and values of campaign organizations. Occupy's particular performance of horizontal democracy, wherein the prefigurative community was made transparent to bolster the ethos of more instrumental, persuasive communication, are appearing in progressive campaigns that are increasingly making their own campaign mechanics transparent in order to perform a democratic ethos.

Important research continues to be done about the internal workings of political campaigns, movement organizations, and other forms of democratic politics.[36] As we have seen, much of the initial spate of research on the Occupy demonstrations was conducted from precisely the vantage point of an "insider"; the researcher or writer who participated in the demonstrations in some capacity, visited the encampments, and translated a supportive, quasi-ethnographic perspective into a methodological justification that was strongly consonant with prefiguration itself.[37] Mapping the migration of a horizontalist democratic ethos, however, requires more than a description of the internal workings of collectives. It also requires analyzing how the inner workings of political collectives are persuasively performed for outsiders. For this reason, this chapter analyzes two connected sets of rhetorical texts: first, the outward-facing descriptions that the 2016 Sanders campaign produced of its own internal organizing principles, technologies, and funding practices; and second, the way that those elements of the campaign were described by sympathetic news publications. The combination of these two sets of texts demonstrates how the campaign was able to project its internal organization outward to persuasively perform a democratic ethos.

The individual ethos of Bernie Sanders himself was, of course, an important component of the campaign's collective ethos. The campaign's practices, however, were also vital. It is clear that within the campaign there were different approaches to how democracy might be enacted in the process of running a nationwide presidential primary campaign under the auspices of a major political party. Complicating the boundaries of "the campaign" were the important efforts of independent groups such as Coders for Bernie, the People for Bernie Sanders, and other volunteer groups that were not under the management of the 2016 campaign staff and yet took on many of the tasks that are traditionally performed or supervised by paid campaign staff.[38] This complex layer of volunteer and activist labor was another source of democratic ethos for the campaign. In general, the 2016 Sanders campaign worked tirelessly to perform a democratic ethos that set it apart from the instrumental qualities of "politics as usual" in the Clinton campaign, the Democratic National Committee (DNC), and the news media. Central to this effort was the cultivation and performance of "authentic communication" with the campaign's supporters. The campaign was, as an example of electoral politics, a type of instrumental effort in itself, but it nonetheless sought to adapt the democratic ethos of Occupy to foster an alternative to the ironically instrumentalist (no unilateral disarmament from PACs) campaigning that had become the norm in the Democratic Party. The core feature of this reinvention of the act of donating was to describe it as authentic communication that formed the basis of a long-term relationship between supporters and the campaign as the campaign took on the responsibility of managing and protecting the personal data of donors. As the campaign described its financing ethics and data management practices, it consolidated a form of electoral persuasive prefiguration that left-leaning news outlets enthusiastically embraced.

Performing Authentic Democratic Communication in the 2016 Sanders Campaign

Sanders's standard stump speech and the campaign's book-length publications reflect a strong effort to cast the campaign's communication style as one that was invested in authenticity and democratic dialogue while being critical of the instrumentalist politics of the media, Wall Street donors, special interests, Hillary Clinton, and super PACs. Some of these positions were also features of Donald Trump's 2016 campaign. Both Bernie Sanders and Donald Trump demonstrated a populist rhetorical style; one of the core features of populist rhetoric is a strong antiestablishment stance.[39] Additionally, however, both Trump and Sanders frequently criticized the media establishment and its coverage of politics. In the Sanders campaign's rhetoric, the media represented a form of instrumental communication against which its own performance of truth-telling and authenticity was contrasted.[40] Both the Trump and Sanders campaigns relied heavily on large rallies to energize supporters, spur media coverage, and inspire donations.[41] Also like Trump, Sanders embraced the opportunity to communicate with supporters through social media "without the filter of the [traditional news] media."[42]

Sanders argued that live events are essential to building progressive democratic movement because they foster an experience of democracy:

> One of the goals of our campaign was to "bring people together," not just metaphorically but in the flesh. The pundits and the establishment may not have thought so, but I have always felt that the ideas I was espousing were not radical or fringe. They were mainstream. The

> truth is that when people come into a room, or a gymnasium or an arena, and they look around them and see all the other people in that venue sharing those same views, they come away strengthened and energized. They are not alone. They are part of something bigger than themselves. They are part of a movement. This is especially true when the audience is of diverse backgrounds, which became increasingly true as our campaign progressed. A rally of thousands of people standing together—blacks, whites, Latinos, Native Americans, Asian-Americans, young and old, gay and straight, people who immigrated here and those born here. This is something unforgettable and extraordinarily powerful. It is not something that a television ad can accomplish.[43]

Electoral politics rest uneasily on deeply ingrained assumptions about the force of demographics in determining voting patterns. The claims in this quotation demonstrate how progressivism attempts to carve out a vision of democratic participation that does not presuppose behavior based merely on predetermined, instrumentally articulated "interests" of various demographics. Instead, Sanders offers a vision of political action that embraces a more authentic type of communication: live, in-person communication wherein people come together to talk and be *with* one another rather than being talked *at* by television advertisements that are carefully placed to hit atomized individuals in target demographics. In the passage above, Sanders paints a picture of the capacity of authentic, face-to-face communication to build a democratic coalition. In so doing, he describes the campaign's internal communication practices in order to bolster the credibility of the campaign's democratic ethos. A rally, Sanders seems to argue, is an opportunity to reach out to voters who may otherwise feel that the campaign was not really for them and build connections through live, synchronous communication in shared physical space. At the rallies themselves, Sanders spoke about a range of progressive issues in such a way as to emphasize how the campaign was a response to the concerns and issues of its supporters. For instance, while speaking in Phoenix, Sanders transitioned from one issue to the next with phrases such as "this campaign is listening to," senior citizens, disabled veterans, the American people, or young people.[44] Framing the campaign as a dialogue with constituents helped to figure the rally speech—a clear instance of one-to-many broadcast communication—as a more intimate conversation.

In this account, the media play several roles as the instrumentalist foil against which the campaign demonstrated its democratic ethos. Television news is, first of all, "the media establishment," the political biases of which the insurgent Sanders campaign was battling against. Second, it is the medium of the ironically instrumentalist strategy of campaigning (paid advertising) that requires huge influxes of cash donations that can only be acquired through large donors and super PACs. And finally, it is a form of communication that is undialogic, one-directional, manipulative, and inauthentic. Taken together, these three aspects of how the media relate to campaigning combine under an ironically instrumentalist logic according to which PAC support is needed to get favorable "horse race" coverage of fundraising benchmarks in the mainstream news and buy advertisements, which are necessary to win polls and votes. The entire operation is justified, most consultants argue, because it is a bad idea to "unilaterally disarm" by rejecting PAC funding when Republican campaigns follow the same formula with success.

Against this foil, the Sanders campaign described itself as speaking truth to the news media's power, operating on a small-dollar shoestring budget, and fostering more authentic, dialogic forms of communication. All these aspects of the campaign were closely connected to one another. In his own analysis of his campaign, Sanders writes, "I have never forgotten, however, that the most important political work that can be done is making door-to-door contact, speaking directly to your constituents and answering their questions."[45] The Sanders campaign emphasized, when possible, its dedication to a form of communication often used to evoke authenticity and truth: face-to-face political persuasion that happens locally. In his campaign announcement speech in Burlington, Vermont, Sanders promised, "We're going to take this campaign directly to the people—in town meetings, door to door conversations, on street corners and in social media."[46] Even in front of large rally-style audiences, Sanders worked to frame his campaign as a matter of being in proximate dialogue with supporters.

Sanders is not the first politician to strive for a sense of intimacy with an audience by emphasizing dialogue and authentic communication. However, these gestures play a more specific role in the way Sanders mobilized a democratic ethos while critiquing common fundraising tactics. For the Sanders campaign, authentic communication was also a counterpoint to how legacy news covers election campaigns as competitive spectacles without covering the issues and values candidates talk about. The Sanders campaign's emphasis on small donors was an important tactic for refocusing news coverage on the campaign's values and message even when most news coverage of election campaigns only describes the "horse-race" aspects of the election. In other words, political reporting focuses on the total amount campaigns have raised, the number of staffers they are employing, polling results, where the candidates are spending time and other "objective" or measurable aspects that supposedly predict a campaign's strength and likelihood of success.[47]

Because news media always cover presidential campaign fundraising benchmarks, the 2016 Sanders campaign's decision to refuse PAC support required news media coverage of the campaign's fundraising to simultaneously cover, to a small degree, the anticorruption, anti–Wall Street aspects of the campaign's message.

The Rise of the Donation as Democratic Communication

The Sanders campaign's framing of its practices as genuine, authentic democratic communication—including its exchanges and relationships with its donors—found even more fertile ground in the liberal and progressive press coverage of the nomination race. In spite of the fact that donating to election campaigns has often been dismissed as a relatively instrumental, shallow mode of political participation, progressive and left publication outlets covered the Sanders campaign's processes of donor cultivation as an instance of deeply authentic democratic communication. Progressive and moderate publications such as the *Huffington Post,* the *New Yorker,* and *Slate* described the financing strategy of the Sanders campaign in terms that blended instrumental reasoning with praise for the authenticity and the sincerity it demonstrated. John Cassidy, writing in the *New Yorker,* argued that the 2016 Sanders campaign's donation strategy was both inspirationally democratic and instrumentally effective: "By refusing to accept corporate money and basing his campaign on individual donations, he has reinvigorated American democracy. It is obvious that Sanders has, in the process, put a scare into Hillary Clinton's campaign. What is perhaps less widely acknowledged is how close he came to upending it."[48] In this analysis, the authenticity of the financing strategy is also what assisted the campaign's instrumental successes. Similarly, the *Atlantic* argued that the campaign's emphasis on small donations was vital to its ethos as well as its instrumental effectiveness: "Asking for small-dollar sums and renouncing super PACs is a way to telegraph sincerity. It has also been extremely effective. The campaign has set fundraising records and fostered a grassroots network of individuals now literally invested in the candidate's success."[49] The article went on to even more specifically claim that the Sanders campaign was framing donating as a way of developing a meaningful communicative relationship with voters: "When Sanders makes a fundraising pitch, it's a way to forge a connection with supporters. The requests themselves are typically framed as an invitation to take part in his populist crusade."[50] The attribution of good will and community spirit to the act of donating extended from the rhetoric of the campaign to the motivations of the donors themselves in some coverage; an analyst writing for the *Observer* claimed that he had "never seen a more public-spirited, idealistic and good-natured group of donors than the small donors who support Mr. Sanders. While many donors expect to get something in return for their donation [. . .] the Sanders small donor brigades give their average donation of $27 for one purpose and one purpose only: to make our country and world a better place."[51] The *Huffington Post* coverage of the finances of the Sanders campaign focused more on its instrumental successes and how it stacked up against Clinton fundraising.[52] A long *Slate* article that took a semihistorical perspective on political fundraising described the campaign as fundraising through "constant engagement" and "connection" with donors.[53] Various other articles, blog posts, and podcast episodes alternately emphasized either the instrumental or the ethical and democratic dimensions of the Sanders campaign's funding strategy.[54]

In much of this news coverage, the nature of the interchange between the donors, the candidate, and the campaign is described as something that is quite meaningful and that rises above a functional, effective instrumental exchange. The campaign's decision to cultivate small donors and refuse PAC support was actually sometimes framed in instrumental terms that emphasized how small donors advantaged the campaign's persuasive image. But the quality of the connection and communication between Sanders and his supporters was not described in instrumental terms. Instead, the authenticity of the relationship between the donors and their preferred candidate was described as a democratic triumph. The donations to the campaign were described as not only the *medium* of this communication but also its *content.* This understanding of the donations was facilitated by the fact that many Sanders supporters donated small amounts regularly and in response to campaign events; for instance, one supporter explained that he would donate when somebody or something "annoyed" him.[55] A punctual rhythm of donating established a back-and-forth between the campaign and supporters that was even more easily framed as a type of dialogic communication. An article in the *New York Times* described this dialog as a type of communication made possible by how the campaign prioritized digital media, but much news coverage of the communication between Sanders and his supporters was not so narrowly focused.[56] The result was that the donation itself was conceptualized as the communicative *medium*; the authentic democratic sentiments, ethics, and ideals, the *content* of the exchange.

The campaign's small-donor success story, enabled by digital media, played well in the news coverage that compared the Sanders campaign with the Clinton campaign. News coverage of campaign benchmarks allowed the Sanders campaign to use its funding strategy, an essential component of its internal structure and organization, to bolster its democratic ethos in some of the most traditional "horse-race" news coverage of all the campaigns.[57]

For instance, CNN and *Time* articles covering the amount that the campaign raised also mention, in passing, the campaign's focus on small donors or the differences between the Clinton and Sanders fundraising strategies.[58] In sum, the Sanders campaign's refusal of super PAC support was a principled stance based on a commitment to democratic values. It was also a shrewd, effective tactic for garnering and managing news media coverage. By refusing to adopt the more ironically instrumentalist logic that drove the Obama and Clinton campaigns to accept PAC support (i.e., the logic that unilateral PAC disarmament was a recipe for failure), the Sanders campaign was able to acquire a uniquely effective toehold in the news media coverage that it simultaneously criticized. The result was a remarkably robust interface between a democratic ethos performed as persuasive prefiguration in the transparent disclosure of self-organization of the campaign that responded to the media environment the campaign was operating in. The idea that the exchange between the campaign and its supporters was a type of authentic communication was central to this persuasive prefiguration of a democratic ethos.

News coverage of the campaign's fundraising strategy was extensive and continued even after it became clear that Clinton would be the Democratic Party nominee. One aspect of the fundraising—the status and use of the personal data of the individual donors—was of particular concern to pundits late in the campaign. The main question was whether the Sanders campaign would be giving its list of donors and their contact information to the Clinton campaign and the DNC. Attention to this decision was the result, in part, of how the controversy dramatized the question of whether Sanders and his campaign were actually going to follow through on promises to pursue party unity after Hillary Clinton had won the nomination.

The news coverage of the fate of the donor data reveals in even greater detail how the campaign was able to extend a discourse about politics, ethics, integrity, and authenticity into otherwise instrumentalist logics that dominate electoral campaigns at the national level. Because the tendency of most news outlets is to cover the competitive benchmarks, alliances, polls, and predictions of election cycles, these features of campaigns become integral to the way campaigns establish their internal goals.[59] In other words, it is difficult to separate the instrumentalism of campaign structures from the instrumentalism that dominates the news coverage of the campaigns; the campaigns seek instrumental success in order to cultivate positive news coverage. A close look at the news coverage of the Sanders campaign's fundraising and data management reveals how difficult it was for news coverage to maintain a "neutral" or purely instrumentalist approach when reporting on the controversy over the fate of the Sanders donor data.

The Anti-instrumental Defense of Donor Data

In the wake of Sanders's concession of the primary to Clinton and then her loss to Trump, the Sanders donor data—the personal data of those individuals who had donated to the Sanders campaign—took on a life of its own in news coverage of the Democratic Party and progressive politics.[60] The discussion of the data played out in national news media, the left press, and technology publications during several key moments. The data became a focal point in relation to Sanders's concession of the race to Clinton in 2016 as well as the election of a new chair of the DNC in February 2017. In both moments, the core question was about whether the Sanders campaign would be turning over its donor and volunteer data, most specifically its email list, as failed presidential primary campaigns had done in the past.

News coverage of this question—the fate of the Sanders donor data—reveals how the authenticity that the Sanders campaign attempted to cultivate in the mold of Occupy's democratic ethos modified the more typical instrumental ethos of a nationwide presidential nomination campaign. The centrality of the fundraising tactics to the campaign's message was at this point well established, making the donor data an even more compelling news story. The generosity and enthusiasm of these donors, according to commentators, had "reinvigorated American democracy,"[61] pointed "to a new reality for digital campaigning,"[62] and were "rewriting the rules of campaign finance and presidential politics."[63] The two million plus donors to the Sanders campaign had been the topic of intense, sustained celebration in the press for well over a year by the time the Sanders campaign came to a close.

In a surprising amount of the news coverage of the Sanders campaign, the fundraising tactics and technologies *themselves* were cast as the heroes, leaving human actors such as Sanders, his staffers, and his donors playing supporting roles. A *Slate* article argued that the groundbreaking innovations in political campaigning enabled by digital technologies were likely to have effects that were similar to the advent of direct-mail donation requests, the technology that had enabled the rise of conservatism in the United States[64] Some articles described the Sanders campaign's email list as the foundation or future of progressive politics, an assertion that was followed up with heated debates about how widely the "Sanders list" should be disseminated.[65] One commentator even went so far as to argue that the "major technological breakthrough" represented by the Sanders campaign "could revolutionize our campaign finance system," bypassing the need for Congress to act on campaign finance reform.[66]

The donor data began to garner attention as the Sanders campaign began using it to support other progressive candidates in the 2016 Democratic primary contests.[67] One of the first substantial articles about the fate of the Sanders donor data was published by *Politico* in April of 2016 as the outcome of the Democratic presidential nominating contest had become clearer.[68] *Politico,* a venue for professionalized and centrist political analysis, described the donor data's instrumental significance while sparely acknowledging the broader critique of ironic instrumentalism that the Sanders campaign demonstrated.[69] The article referred to the Sanders donor data in nearly fetishistic terms; much of the language of the article was reproduced in other publications.[70] A *Fortune* article, for instance, failed to link to the *Politico* article but nonetheless also referred to the donor data as the "crown jewel" of Democratic Party organizing.[71] A *Huffington Post* article similarly referred to it as "coveted."[72] In addition to this language, the *Politico* article called the data "the backbone of the Vermont senator's online fundraising juggernaut," "an electoral gold mine," "my precious," and quoted a Sanders supporter as describing it as "something greater there that needs to be used for generational change."[73] News coverage referred to the data's "vastness," its "massiveness," its "value," and its capacity to "fuel."[74] These metaphors solidified a sense of the data as an effective object or technology in itself, presenting an implied argument for the status of the technology as the hero of the campaign and the active agent in the production of democracy. Tech-savvy commentators contributed to this impression in other publication venues, describing the digital platforms used to assemble the data as the democratic actors. One political-tech blog figured a digital tool as itself being a pavement-pounding human canvasser, writing, "But just as email is the workhorse of digital brand marketing today, it is the intrepid ward heeler of digital political marketing, as well."[75] A major news network referred to the data as a "potent tool" and cited Democratic politics operatives making arguments about the power and utility of the data to continue the fight for Democratic victories.[76]

Sanders's supporters began objecting to the possibility that the DNC might obtain their data and that the Clinton campaign might begin marketing to them.[77] Many of their concerns were colored by frustration and disdain toward a DNC establishment they perceived as corrupt and utterly unworthy of support. Their concerns were also, however, shaped by long-standing concerns with privacy, surveillance, and data collection as important issues in themselves.[78] Some Sanders supporters, reacting to the possibility that their data might be shared with the DNC or Clinton campaign, expressed that they felt that the deep corruption of these organizations would make their data unsafe.[79] Early in 2016, the Electronic Frontier Foundation, a nonprofit organization dedicated to the development of the internet in a way that protects and empowers users, published a nonpartisan guide to protecting one's data while being involved in political campaigns.[80] The assumption and persuasive goal of this guide was that "data collection is an entrenched part of how modern political campaigns work, and that should concern you regardless of your political affiliation."[81]

This critical perspective on "privacy," however, is an extension (rather than critique) of the instrumentalism inherent in liberalism; opposition to government and large companies passively collecting user data is understood as in part guiding the internet toward a future that is more protective of individual rights as part of a neutral framework of government. Reliance on the language of privacy and individual rights was, in a sense, another way that more radically leftist commitments were performed in and through a more instrumental set of values. In other words, though some Sanders supporters may have been truly concerned about their privacy, the easily recognizable language of privacy and individual rights may have been a convenient discourse to funnel deeper critiques of how the Clinton campaign and the DNC were beholden to corporate interests. In the wake of WikiLeaks's publication of Hillary Clinton's emails (which showed the extent of the cooperation and collusion between the Clinton campaign and DNC leadership), Sanders's supporters were especially angry and convinced that the corruption in these organizations had led to an illegitimate primary contest result. Some vocal Sanders supporters made it clear that they already saw the DNC and Clinton as powerful interests on par with the NSA, big media, and big corporate data collectors who should never receive their personal information.

After some of the Sanders's staffers used the data to form the organization Our Revolution, there was less speculation in the press about the possibility that the data might go to the DNC or Clinton campaign. Instead, Sanders's staffers turned to the task of justifying the decision not to share the list. This involved generating metaphoric descriptions of the list that emphasized its static ineffectiveness in the absence of candidates with the proper abilities and democratic ethos: integrity, an antiestablishment message, and morality. Becky Bond, a senior advisor to the 2016 Sanders campaign, argued that access to the list wouldn't help most candidates. She compared such candidates' fantasies of success to someone buying a $12,000 bicycle and imagining that it would allow them to win the Tour de France.[82] Both Weaver and Tim Targaris, the campaign's digital fundraising director, described the irrationality of demands for the list using the metaphor of an ATM machine.[83] Targaris asserted: "They still need to figure out the PIN."

Other staffers, when speaking to the press, came up with even more imaginative metaphors for the data that emphasized Sanders's role as a mythical savior. The *Atlantic* reported that "a fundraiser [. . .] tweeted that the senator's list was like King Arthur's Excalibur: 'Lots of people might think they can use it, but it takes someone special for it to work.'"[84] In another interview, a fundraiser compared the data to Mjölnir, the hammer of Thor: "You can have it, but only a few people can wield it."[85] These analogies directed attention to the instrumental effectiveness of the list, but in the context of human (or superhuman) ethical agency essential to the effective operation of the technology.

Rather than accepting the framing of professionalized political publications such as *Politico,* in which the technology or the data was itself the savior and agent, these approaches pushed back to emphasize the ethos of the candidates as individuals and the way that the data had been constituted by a process of authentic democratic communication with supporters. Sanders himself used interviews with major news networks to insist that the list would only be used to support candidates who shared his campaign's commitment to policies that addressed economic inequality.[86] Other articles concretized and explained this perspective in more realistic and thorough ways by extensively interviewing staffers about how the campaign organized and communicated with volunteers; one such article argued that it was not "Big Data" but "Big Organizing" that built the Sanders campaign's successes.[87] Another staffer argued that the data, far from being an object, tool, or technology, was itself a powerful democratic "community of people."[88] This way of describing the data departed from figuring it as a technology in order to emphasize its status as a self-organizing human collective. A *Los Angeles Times* article took a similar approach, using ActBlue's records of small donors to locate and interview some of the individuals donating to Sanders and describing their motivations, goals, and values.[89] The *Los Angeles Times* article argued that detailed records kept by ActBlue—their way of compiling donor data—enabled greater understanding of the identity and values of everyday supporters of progressive democracy.

All these ways of recasting the data—as a tool that could only be effectively used by an on-message hero, as a small piece in a larger process of innovative community organizing, as *itself* a community, as a window into the values of citizens—moderated the instrumentalist media coverage of the data controversy with a commitment to the democratic ethos of Sanders himself and the campaign as a whole. Descriptions of the campaign's internal organizing techniques and the candidate's personal integrity were repeatedly deployed to counter the narrative that mere acquisition of the data was equivalent *in itself* to political success. In doing so, the Sanders campaign and its supporters described the management of the donor data as a dimension of the campaign's authentic internal democratic communication structure and performative consistency.

This authentic communication was not exclusively conducted by the candidate or the campaign. It was also the communication of the donation as an honest expression of the integrity and morality of the donors themselves as they responded to and participated in the campaign. The data was, and continues to be, described as a two-way conduit between the Sanders campaign and its supporters. This "dialogue" stands in contrast to instrumental forms of communication: the one-to-many communication technology of televised campaign ads and the logics of professionalized campaigning with their emphasis on efficiency and effectivity.

The news coverage of the fate of the data, however, demonstrates that the "small donor" fundraising strategy is not a simple refusal of instrumentalist campaigning logics in favor of a purely idealistic refusal. On the contrary, the small-donor fundraising strategy was also implemented as a means of accomplishing specific political objectives; it was a clear example of persuasive prefiguration. Small-donor cultivation was a very useful, effective, and efficient opportunity for the campaign to accomplish several things. These included building a contact list to help other like-minded candidates, demonstrating the ethos of the campaign to bolster anticorruption claims, and forcing moderate and left-leaning publications to cover the campaign's core message by attending to its internal communicative ethics of fundraising and data management. The result was the adaptation and animation of a deeply instrumental facet of election campaigning—fundraising—with the democratic ethos of authenticity.

Conclusion

The Sanders campaign claimed that the democratic qualities of its digital tools could be found in their capacity to foster more authentically democratic communication within the community of the campaign (a community that included Sanders, staff, volunteers, donors, and other supporters). The central logic that underwrites the projection of a democratic ethos through fundraising relies on long-standing left and progressive narratives of the conflict between the instrumentality of communicative forms such as television advertising and more dialogic, authentic forms of political speech. Because super PAC support has been so closely linked to television advertising, cultivating and managing small donors and their data helped the campaign persuasively prefigure a more authentically democratic mode of communication and ethos. This is not to say that the Sanders campaign's performance of a democratic ethos was without its instrumental value; it just found a foil in the media and super PACS that was more ironically instrumentalist than itself.

By engaging directly with the news media's "horse race" style of campaign coverage, the Sanders campaign was able to perform its version of the democratic ethos more widely and effectively. Much as Occupy strove for news media coverage by pushing out its own narrative of its activities via newer digital channels, the Sanders campaign performed a democratic ethos in a way that attended to and translated itself into instrumentalist categories. Rather than a merely ethical or prefigurative rationale for the refusal of super PAC support, the Sanders campaign persuasively performed that refusal for others to instrumentally bolster its own democratic credibility. When projected outward, its "authenticity" became instrumental in the sense that it was done not just for its own sake but to recruit and cultivate support and increase the probability of winning an election.

In the Sanders campaign, television advertising and the media in general nonetheless continued to be identified as relatively undemocratic forms of communication, but they will not necessarily remain so in the future. As digital campaigning becomes more professionalized, it is certainly poised to become more expensive than television advertising. In the controversy over the fate of the Sanders donor data we can see how the narrative frame of a conflict between authentic and instrumentalist communication is already being reproduced in ways that have nothing to do with television. The authentic/instrumental frame is the more permanent feature of the landscape of democratic political rhetoric.

The Sanders campaign has probably not permanently changed how progressive election campaigns are funded. There is no doubt, however, that its refusal of super PAC support has infiltrated subsequent campaigns—in part because campaigns that refuse super PAC support have in many cases received and relied on the Sanders donor data to make such a move work for them. Such effects demonstrate how cultivating small donors and refusing PAC support have deeply instrumental potentials even as they operate as performances of anti-instrumental radical values.

As it pursued a major party nomination, the Sanders campaign reckoned more directly with the instrumental logics of liberalism than the Occupy demonstrations did in 2011. The innovation in prefigurative politics that Occupy initiated, however, was the crucial mechanism that the Sanders campaign adopted. The Occupy demonstrations were intently focused on building a collective ethos based on internal organizing techniques that had previously been considered "merely" prefigurative in the sense that they happened behind closed doors and primarily impacted only those who participated in them. Just as the Occupy demonstrations projected these internal decision-making processes outward to demonstrate values and cultivate support and participation, the Sanders campaign projected its internal fundraising ethics outward to build a democratic ethos for the candidate and the campaign. Occupy's willingness to engage the instrumental rhetorical logics of ethos as a matter of persuasion (and not just mere ethical composition) provided a roadmap for other instrumental forms of left-leaning politics to do so, too.

In the case of the Sanders campaign, this meant the reinvention of a form of political action—the campaign donation. Various academic leftisms have critiqued the instrumental and neoliberal logics that support a model of politics in which donating would be a way to pursue political change. Nonetheless, when such instrumental actions are seen as having performative potential and are contrasted with more undemocratic, instrumentalist versions of themselves, they can still be projected as elements of authentic left democracy.

Although Bernie Sanders's personal ethos was an important element of the campaign, the ethos of the campaign was not reducible to his individual character and credibility. Describing the ethos of *the campaign* helps to explain several important elements of the way that leftist and horizontal values have permeated more moderate forms of political action. Conceptualizing and describing a collective (rather than individual) ethos highlights a variety of factors that are more salient to questions about leftist political action, including the rhetorical role of communication technologies, the balance between instrumentalism and authenticity in the leftist advocacy of democracy, and the significance of the internal processes of self-organization. As iconic as Bernie Sanders is, the persistent emphasis in the type of leftist political tradition he represents requires theoretical concepts that are flexible enough to provide insight into collective dimensions of his campaign ethos.

FOUR

Amending the US Constitution with Transparent Deliberation

Five middle-aged white people in professional attire sit at the front of the conference room. The room is full of many careful rows of padded, stackable chairs. The location is Suffolk Law School in Boston, Massachusetts. In front of them are five identical black microphones. Behind these composed, professional white people is a pull-down screen upon which a message is projected. The message on the screen thanks the audience for participating in a poll that measured their opinions about a constitutional amendment. Later in the event, the audience will be polled again to measure how the event has changed their perspective. The audience, primarily consisting of composed, middle-aged white people and a smattering of law school students, listens to thoughtful formal presentations and interjections from the moderator. After this structured conversation, audience members line up on either side of the room to take turns contributing their own comments and questions. The panelists appear to listen attentively and occasionally respond to the audience until the time allotted for the event runs out. Bold claims are made about continuing the conversation at a local pub.

Academic conference? No. This is the scene of the first "Interactive Town Hall" held by the organization American Promise as part of its Writing the 28th Amendment project.[1] The event was billed as an opportunity "to discuss what the next amendment should to do" and going through the process of "vetting [amendment] proposals to address political spending."[2] This vision of "town hall" democracy uncannily resembles a well-established ritual of expert knowledge building—with all of its exclusions, limitations, and blind spots—that is all too familiar. In addition, the audience members for the expert presentations are themselves treated as a source of polling data. Their opinions are measured and aggregated for some obscure organizational purpose, relegating them to the uneasy status of both persuasive targets and informants.

The imbrication of liberal democracy and scholarly expertise demonstrated by this "town hall" event illustrates a tension that has arisen within the contemporary movement to amend the US Constitution in the wake of Occupy and the election of Donald Trump. Most advocates of a constitutional amendment addressing corporate political influence recognize in the abstract that such an amendment will require broad public support and mass mobilization in order to be ratified. But not all amendment advocates seem to be equally skilled or focused in the pursuit of such public support. As legal experts debate the exact wording of the amendment, they reinforce their commitment to a scholarly ethos based on measurable results, constitutional history, and above all a technocratic, instrumentalist logic that privileges measurable political results over all other goals. Such an instrumentalism conceptualizes communication as the transparent transmission of data.

Other amendment advocates have more fully absorbed and reproduced a democratic ethos derived from the Occupy demonstrations and horizontal ideals. For these advocates, who often refer to themselves as "community organizers," communication is part of a process that strives for inclusivity, confrontation, critique, and organizational self-fashioning that is disclosed as part of the performance of democratic authenticity. Between lawyers and community organizers there are very different assumptions about what type of expertise is most relevant to amending the Constitution. These differing assumptions have led to different ways of self-organizing, cultivating grassroots support, and prioritizing inclusivity in democratic deliberation.

At first glance, the political goal of passing a constitutional amendment, any amendment, seems to directly contradict the anti-instrumental, anti-statist approach of Occupy. Striving toward a constitutional amendment, after all, demonstrates a sense of faith in not only constitutional power itself but also the liberal mechanisms established for transforming it. Occupy's refusal of such liberal and institutional forms of politics is at odds with the foundational assumptions driving amendment advocacy. Amendment advocates pursue the goal of constitutional reform without self-conscious irony. The most centrist of them strive for performative consistency by attempting to organize and persuade through deliberative democratic norms such as transparency, reason, expertise, inclusiveness, and neutrality.

In the wake of Occupy, however, some leftist amendment advocates have absorbed the values and culture of horizontalism enough to demonstrate key components of its democratic ethos. These amendment advocates have put increasing emphasis on authenticity and horizontal values in their own organizational practices and have leaned left. Others, such as American Promise, continue to support a more moderate and right-leaning version of a constitutional amendment. Organizations such as American Promise are narrowly focused on tweaking donation disclosure laws and increasing states' abilities to regulate campaign finance. More radical leftist groups, on the other hand, seek to amend the US Constitution to deny corporations *all* constitutional rights, including free speech, due process, equal protection, and others. Interactions between the leftist and centrist branches of the "amendment community" demonstrate how the democratic ethos of Occupy has disseminated unevenly and can foster conflict and change in the strategies of movement organizations even as they try to work together. Moreover, the conflict between the left and moderate advocates of an amendment also demonstrates how persuasive prefiguration demands the disclosure of self-organization processes. Such disclosures can be uncomfortable or even impossible for collective actors who have not fully embraced the values of democratic authenticity consolidated by Occupy.

American Promise, sponsor of the "town hall" meeting at Suffolk Law School, was founded in 2016 and is directed by Jeffrey Clements, lawyer and author of *Corporations Are Not People.*[3] As a newer organization, American Promise was built in part with the goal of bringing amendment advocates of multiple political orientations together to pursue a constitutional amendment that all could agree on, including leftists and conservative Republicans. American Promise argues that corporate involvement in political affairs runs counter to democratic ideals. They argue that the influence of wealth compromises the potential of the US government to enact democratic principles. They agree with leftist amendment advocates that broad popular action is the route to achieving constitutional reform; relying on a president or the courts will not work.

As American Promise pursues performative consistency in its demonstration of democracy, it places a great deal of emphasis on the ideals of transparency and deliberation. On the surface, commitments to deliberation and transparency have some similarities to the persuasive prefiguration central to the democratic ethos of Occupy. After all, liberal organizations such as American Promise attempt to model the deliberation and transparency they seek in their own forms of self-governance. Moreover, as we will see, American Promise has also attempted to publicize its internal organizational decision making to build its own ethos. If the democratic ethos consolidated by Occupy is a matter of revealing the internally constitutive democratic procedures, how is this performance of authenticity really any different from the long-standing liberal ideal of transparency? Is the performance of authenticity simply a matter of disclosing information about how a collective makes decisions, funds itself, and organizes relations between individuals?

The performance of authenticity and the liberal ideal of transparent deliberation have crucially different assumptions about the nature of communication. The ideal of deliberative transparency assumes that communicating "transparently" is simply a matter of unblocking the flow of "information" and making it available to all. The performance of authenticity, on the other hand, assumes that any and all ways of communicating what is internal to a collective reflects the values and commitments of that collective; the concept of "information," which would be a type of pure, unmediated factuality, has no role in that process. The result of these different assumptions about the nature of communication, especially deliberative communication, is that an ethos based on transparency comports much more seamlessly with a notion of expertise based in scientific rationality and instrumental reason; if transparent political communication is simply a matter of freely transmitting facts, data, or legal research, then expert knowledge in those areas is the central facet of political ethos. The performance of authenticity consolidated by Occupy, on the other hand, presumes that collective ethos is something that is continuously created in the process of adhering to horizontal deliberative values such as "step up, step back," anti-instrumental critique and protest, and affectively grounded mutual aid and care. Experience in and knowledge about the process of prioritizing those elements of collective self-formation is then a type of expertise that is central to the democratic ethos.

A liberal, instrumental commitment to "transparency" continues to presume the value-neutrality of communicative procedures and the information they transmit. This assumption, one that has been repeatedly called into question, opens liberal, instrumentalist organizations such as American Promise up to accusations of ironic performative contradiction from those further on the left. Rifts between leftists and centrists in the "amendment community" show how claims to transparent deliberation remain wide open to accusations of ironic contradiction from the perspective of horizontalism and the democratic ethos of authenticity. Even though centrist amendment advocates are not intentionally ironic about their commitment to transparency, the division they presuppose between means and ends creates opportunities for more radical advocates to critique the moments of self-contradiction that happen during the pursuit of transparency. Leftists highlight the failure to reveal how and why decisions have been made about what type of expertise is valued, who is included in deliberation, and how communicative procedures are arrived at.

The critique of the centrist approach made it impossible for American Promise to follow through on their commitment to the deliberative ideal of transparency, demonstrating how the performance of authenticity can undermine a simple instrumental commitment to "information" and transparency. The instrumental ethos might in theory be able to demonstrate a certain level of performative consistency. The ongoing adherence to the ideal of transparency and communication as information-transmission, however, means that the instrumental ethos can be made to appear performatively inconsistent when the authentic ethos is leveraged against it. Conversely, the authenticity of the democratic ethos depends on contrasting itself with a more ironic, instrumental alternative.

The tension between left and centrist advocates of the constitutional amendments is most clearly demonstrated through an analysis of direct conflict in attempts to come to terms with one another. In 2017, American Promise hosted a series of mass conference calls that included various leaders and supporters of different constitutional amendments. Recordings of the mass conference calls were initially made publicly available through the organization's website, ostensibly demonstrating a commitment to the deliberative ideals of transparency and inclusion. After a year or so, however, the recordings were inexplicably taken offline, contradicting the organization's initial commitment to transparency and open, "informational" deliberation. The retraction of the recordings seems to have been the result of concerns about how conflicts between the participants stymied the deliberations and undercut the ethos of American Promise.

The transparently available and then nervously retracted conference call recordings provide a unique window into how the liberal deliberative ideal of transparency differs from democratic authenticity but resembles it enough to generate the opportunity for critique of performative contradiction by more radical advocates. Pointing out performative inconsistencies in liberal politics bolsters the democratic ethos of the radical critic by providing a sense of other, more authentic, and internally consistent values. Beyond that, however, leftist efforts to intensify and amplify the performative contradictions of American Promise's advocacy prevented the organization from continuing to use the conference calls to bolster their ethos. As we have seen, the performance of a democratic ethos includes both a critique of corporate rights that is strident and uncompromising as well as an outward demonstration of commitment to inclusive, power-sensitive organizing techniques.

Before describing the way this dynamic between liberalism and radicalism was made apparent in the 2017 mass conference calls, a brief description of two of the most prominent versions of the Twenty-Eighth Amendment helps to illustrate the stakes of the breakdown in the conference call deliberations. At the time of the conference calls, the participants were already mostly on record as supporting one of two versions of an amendment addressing corporate political influence. The goal of the calls was greater unity, but the divisions were already well understood before the calls even began.

Two Amendments: Corporate Personhood and Campaign Finance

Many different versions of a "money in politics" constitutional amendment have been proposed every congressional session since the 2010 *Citizens United* decision. Supporters of these amendments see their work as a long-term battle; amending the Constitution is a difficult task that requires deep and widespread support in both houses of Congress and the state legislatures. Two general versions of the amendment have been repeatedly proposed in Congress.[4] The first of these amendments, which has been called the We the People Amendment, would forbid corporations from claiming all constitutional rights, including the rights to free speech, equal protection, due process, and other rights.[5] The Democracy for All amendment, on the other hand, has been more narrowly tailored to enable greater campaign finance regulation, including regulation of corporations.[6]

The We the People Amendment, as the more left-leaning and radical change in constitutional law governing corporations, would potentially require far-reaching changes in the ways that corporations operate as legal entities, including as donors to election campaigns. Its radicalism has garnered support from congresspeople such as Pramila Jayapal, Barbara Lee, Ayanna Pressley, and Alexandria Ocasio-Cortez. The amendment has been defiantly reintroduced in session after session despite its current poor prospects of being passed. There are two primary components of the proposed We the People Amendment. First, it declares that corporations should be stripped of *all* constitutional rights, and second, that federal, state, and local governments *must* pass laws to regulate campaign finance expenditures.[7]

The centrist Democracy for All Amendment, on the other hand, says that state and federal governments *may* regulate campaign finance and distinguish between natural and artificial persons while doing so.[8] This centrist approach has more congresspeople supporting it than the We the People Amendment and has been cosponsored by figures such as James McGovern, John Katko, and Jamie Raskin. The Democracy for All Amendment, despite being more centrist, has also been described as being unlikely to pass into law anytime soon.[9] The more moderate amendment creates room for state legislators to *voluntarily* regulate campaign finance, whereas the more leftist "We the People" approach would impose a strong *requirement* to do so. In addition, however, by stripping corporations of all constitutional rights, the leftist amendment would go beyond denying corporations the first amendment right to free speech. It would fundamentally change the way corporations relate to governmental institutions in the United States. For instance, supporters of the leftist amendment argue that corporations enjoy and regularly exercise their constitutional rights to protection against search and seizure, due process, equal protection, among others.[10] The leftist amendment would strip all of these rights from corporations, allowing such rights to be exercised only by individual employees and shareholders.

Fully dismantling corporate personhood has not garnered much support from Republican lawmakers.[11] Part of the impetus for the formation of American Promise as an organization was to craft and support a centrist version of the amendment acceptable to moderate Republicans and neoliberal Democrats. The "We the People" amendment has a radical thrust because it goes far beyond denying corporations participation in election campaigns and advocates changes in corporate constitutional rights that would produce far-reaching and uncertain effects. Supporters of the We the People Amendment often cite radio personality and author Thom Hartmann's position on the problems with corporate claims to multiple constitutional rights, articulated in his book *Unequal Protection.*[12] Even more frequently, they reference the work of the Program on Corporations, Law, and Democracy (POCLAD), a relatively academic group that began talking and writing about corporate personhood in the 1990s.[13] Even in that early work, leaders in POCLAD such as Richard Grossman argued that "it is not enough to get big money out of politics. Rather, We the People [. . .] must remove corporations entirely from our elections, our law-making, and public education."[14]

Supporters of the We the People Amendment acknowledge that denying corporations all personhood rights would be a broad change with potentially uncertain results. Citing the work of POCLAD, they argue that addressing only one or two of the ways corporations use the Constitution to gain power will not be effective.[15] For instance, they describe how claims to the Fourteenth Amendment protect corporations from being "discriminated against" as a class of persons the government is attempting to regulate.[16] Claims based on the Fourth Amendment allow corporations to avoid subpoenas and other forms of compliance with the law.[17] But beyond these and other specific analyses of "corporate rights" claims, leftist amendment advocates argue that corporate personhood is, as a legal doctrine, immoral and must be abolished in the name of justice and democracy.[18]

Some leftist amendment advocates identify strongly as community organizers and work for membership-based organizations such as Move to Amend. Move to Amend, as an organization, demonstrates many of the hallmarks of horizontalism and other types of leftist and antiracist organizing. For instance, at their 2018 annual national conference they opened proceedings with an explanation of how and why everyone should share their chosen personal pronouns as well as an Indigenous land acknowledgement.[19]

They have employed deliberative formats such as the People's Movement Assembly that draw on horizontal democratic principles.[20] They also prescribe extensive antioppression training for all movement chapters.[21] Not all these deliberative features evoke the democratic authenticity of the Occupy demonstrations, but the People's Assembly format and some other technics, when compared with the deliberative format of American Promise, provide a far stronger sense of a leftist approach, especially when combined with advocacy of a more radical amendment text that abolishes all corporate constitutional rights.

One of the key founders of American Promise, Jeffrey Clements, published a book in 2012 in which he also argued that corporate personhood is itself one of the fundamental problems of government and law in the United States.[22] The version of the amendment he advocated in that book was fairly close to the We the People Amendment in the sense that it would abolish all corporate personhood, not just corporate free-speech rights or election campaign expenditures. Since then, however, sympathetic skeptics of the movement against "corporate personhood" have argued that denying corporations all constitutional rights is too drastic and radical.[23] One of the strongest voices of this position has been Adam Winkler, a law professor at UCLA, who has argued that "corporate personhood has not led to expansive constitutional protections" and that abolishing all corporate constitutional rights is a risky proposition.[24] Another skeptic of critiques of corporate personhood is Justice Strine, the former Chief Justice of the Delaware Supreme Court and an authority on corporate law.[25] Figures such as Winkler and Strine have urged caution in amending the constitution to address problems related to corporate personhood.[26] Clements, in spite of his early support for abolishing all corporate rights, seems to have turned in a more moderate direction. Both Strine and Winkler were given ample opportunity to present their positions during the mass conference calls hosted by American Promise.[27]

Seemingly as a result of these voices and others, Clements and American Promise have adopted a more cautious posture as they move forward with their efforts to draft and support a constitutional amendment related to corporate involvement in politics. At the time of the mass conference calls, however, American Promise was still positioning itself as a sort of neutral arbiter of various amendment "factions."[28] One of the purposes of American Promise's 2017 mass conference calls was to see if supporters of the different amendments could be brought together as a first step in "building a national consensus about the specific language of the Amendment."[29] American Promise has subsequently come to endorse the centrist Democracy for All Amendment while maintaining that all advocacy for an amendment is a good thing. By dealing exclusively with campaign finance issues, the amendment attempts to preserve a sense of the fundamental correctness of the balance of power in the US federal government. The concept of "corruption" is central to this approach, wherein representative government in the United States is understood as having been weakened by the influence of money on elections but still strong in its essential constitutional structure.[30] This approach tends to lay a lot of blame on *Citizens United* while also identifying some of the Supreme Court campaign finance cases that preceded it as laying part of the groundwork for the flood of dark money funding election campaigns.

American Promise and other advocates of the centrist Democracy for All Amendment support it in part because they imagine that limiting campaign expenditures from wealthy individuals and corporations will have a set of effects that are predictable, positive, and far-reaching. The more unruly, uncertain results of abolishing *all* corporate constitutional rights are set aside for a narrower path that such advocates imagine will lead straight to political equality for all citizens and a cascading wave of democratic reforms that will restore elections and representative government to some imagined previous state of high functioning.

The Democracy for All Amendment has clarified the extent to which the We the People Amendment attempts to address a set of issues that go far beyond campaign finance and protections of corporate speech. The result is that supporters of the We the People Amendment are now seen as radically rejecting the status quo and "mere" reformist solutions. It is difficult to predict the precise effects of the We the People Amendment, but that uncertainty and imprecision contributes to the sense that the amendment divides itself from the complacency and instrumentalism represented by the Democracy for All Amendment. Much like the Declaration of the Occupation of New York City, the We the People Amendment prefigures a vision of law and government that is aspirational in its level of opposition to existing constitutional law. Support for the We the People Amendment articulates a radical approach to law and the Constitution that would excise corporate power and result in a large transformation in the relationship between wealth and government.

A central dimension of the mobilization that American Promise has sought from its inception is "cross-partisan" inclusion of Republicans. This "centrist" stance (though largely in name only, with very few Republican politicians actively involved) was part of the justification for "reasonableness," open-mindedness, and exposure to "information" provided by legal experts. This vision of an amendment movement free of "partisanship" is not unique to American Promise. Other amendment organizations, such as Wolf PAC, have made strong pushes to include Republicans as they articulate an amendment platform. Harvard Law School faculty member Lawrence Lessig, a one-time presidential candidate, Democracy Voucher advocate, and persistent supporter of cross-party cooperation to "fix corruption," spoke vehemently at a 2018 Wolf PAC event about the urgent need to cooperate across party lines. He argued that if the framers of the US Constitution could bracket their disagreements about slavery, "we should be able to bracket our arguments about health care, or the minimum wage."[31] This startlingly strident commitment to cross-partisan cooperation *modeled on cooperation with slaveholders* (an historic moment of cooperation which Lessig freely admitted probably extended the institution of slavery by over fifty years) demonstrates the intensity of instrumentalist commitment to the goal of passing an amendment even if the means of doing so abandon basic human rights and the pursuit of racial justice.[32] Couching the goals of deliberation about a constitutional amendment in these terms was part of the effort to avoid the "hyper-partisan rancor" that could potentially be voiced by more left-leaning and radical amendment advocates.[33] The neutrality sought by American Promise in its deliberative procedures and tone was part of an effort to be more inclusive of somewhat hypothetical conservative or Republican supporters of a constitutional amendment.

The work of the mass conference calls was initially framed as public outreach, information gathering for elected officials, and recording deliberations for historical purposes.[34] The assumption made by the organization from the outset was that the calls would model precisely the type of reasonable, rational, cross-partisan, and expert deliberation that should be similarly informing policy deliberation. To these ends, posting the calls online was an important part of the performance of "transparency"; the deliberations were intended to model a level of openness that strongly contrasted with backroom deals and dark money donations.

From the perspective of leftist advocates of the We the People Amendment, however, criticizing elements of the calls was a necessary component of the deliberation. As the conference calls went on, the supposed transparency and inclusivity of the mass conference calls was repeatedly called into question by leftists who described themselves as community organizers. They did this by pointing out the performative contradictions of the instrumentalism in the procedural design of the conference calls, implying that the calls were actually designed to convince grassroots organizers to moderate *their* version of the amendment rather than seek a truly inclusive consensus among all participants. This unstated goal of the conference calls became increasingly apparent over the months as the community organizers failed to see their justifications for the We the People Amendment represented in the "information" that was "transparently" gathered and transmitted by American Promise. In the end, the conflict that happened during the calls led

American Promise to perform the ultimate performative contradiction: abdication of transparency through the withdrawal of the recordings of the mass conference calls. The persuasive potential of making the idealized, rational deliberations available to "the public" or "the historical record" foundered on its failure to take prefigurative political priorities seriously.

Undermining Deliberative Transparency with Authenticity

Among advocates of a constitutional amendment, centrist actors tend to put a strong emphasis on counteracting the Supreme Court's *Citizens United* decision and reforming campaign finance law. These advocates see a "campaign finance" constitutional amendment as a sort of silver bullet that will enable a cascading wave of democratic and economic reforms "by the people" and "for the people." This assumption—that campaign finance reform is the key to better political representation and hence reduced economic inequality—participates in an instrumentalist approach similar to reform efforts such as the Seattle Democracy Voucher program. There is a crucial difference, however: where many advocates of the Seattle Democracy Vouchers embraced and acknowledged the irony of their approach, most advocates of a constitutional amendment seem to strive for a performative *consistency* between their means and ends; they do not openly embrace the ironies of their instrumentalism. Their instrumentalist ethos opened up the possibility that democratic elements of their collective ethos could be undermined by critiques from leftists determined to perform prefigurative authenticity.

In spite of working with the business community to pass an amendment, American Promise has neither embraced nor reproduced the market logics that are so characteristic of neoliberalism.[35] Its more straightforward liberal instrumentalism remains, relative to the Seattle Democracy Vouchers campaign, unselfconsciously ironic. Instrumental liberalism that is conducted without self-conscious irony differs in important ways from market logics and other clever neoliberal technics. In both instances, the techniques of politics are valued and deployed primarily (or significantly) according to criteria such as efficiency and effectiveness—and the ethos of the instrumentalist politics reflects and affirms these values alongside the ultimate goals of politics.

Instrumentalism without self-conscious irony offers opportunities for leftism to leverage a critique of performative contradiction (and, in essence, a critique of irony that is not preempted by the self-conscious embrace of irony) that is essential to the performance of the democratic ethos. This is because unironic instrumentalism does not explicitly value technics that are opposed to political equality. The contradiction between the means and ends might still be there, but they are not openly acknowledged. This provides rhetorical purchase for a leftist critique of performative contradiction.

Nonetheless, liberalism continues to require expertise in the machinery of government. This expertise is not the same as expertise in neoliberal market-based mechanisms. Instead, liberal instrumentalism is political action that pursues a goal clearly defined by legal, technological, or scientific experts as the solution to a problem. In this case of a constitutional amendment, the political victory represented by the enactment of laws reducing corporate political influence is the goal. Experimenting with different solutions (such as campaign finance vouchers or specific kinds of amendment language) may be part of a process of fine-tuning technical solutions to the problem. Even that experimentation, however, is part of a larger process in which the ends of political action are seen as distinct from and more important than the means employed to accomplish those ends.

The emphasis that liberalism puts on technical knowledge reminds us that ethos is also a matter of credibility—the extent to which a speaker might be believed as an authoritative source of knowledge. Credibility is closely tied to epistemology in the sense that it is a matter of whether the content of what is said is to be taken as a reliable representation of the world. If ethos is a rhetorical proof exclusively tied to the persuasive speech or writing of an individual human, it is relatively easy to describe the distinct but related qualities of credibility and character in rhetorical acts, as Johanna Hartelius does in her description of the rhetoric of expertise.[36] If an individual possesses (or plausibly presents themselves as having) the character trait of honesty, for instance, their description of the world is more credible. In the context of collective ethos, however, the relationship between knowledge and ethos is somewhat trickier.

Theorizing collective ethos provides a way of describing how "reasoned deliberation" is a knowledge-production process that contributes to the credibility of an organization such as American Promise. Technical expertise and knowledge play an important role in predicting, measuring, and achieving liberal political goals. As we saw in the case of the Seattle Democracy Voucher program, the expertise of political consultants, fundraisers, public relations professionals, and the translation of market logics to processes of political participation were prized forms of expertise. In the context of attempts to pass the Twenty-Eighth Amendment to the US Constitution, most of the technical expertise that has contributed to the enactment of American Promise's instrumentalist ethos lies in the area of legal history and jurisprudence. The organization has made important efforts to showcase and integrate citizen participation and experience when it can. Most of its efforts to do so, however, seem to be attempts to counterbalance its dedication to guiding the organization's work based on legal history, training, experience, and forms of argument.

As the organization strives to re-establish the liberal communicative values of transparency and deliberation in government and public discourse, it has sought to model communicative alternatives to dominant modes of political discourse. A series of regional "town hall" meetings, hosted mostly in law schools, were just one example of this type of effort; the mass conference calls were another.[37] These communication forums ostensibly provided opportunities to participate in self-directed political action that supported the cause of constitutional reform. The creation of deliberative and transparent communication forums within American Promise's own activities is an important component of how the organization conceptualizes democracy and strives for performative consistency. Somewhat idealistically, it has followed broad trends in political science and attempted a regeneration of "deliberative democracy" and transparent, "information-based" communication as a solution to corporate rule, stymied congressional debate, and grandstanding, biased news media.[38] Because so many forms of political deliberation (in the US Senate, House of Representatives, or national news media) are so completely corrupted, nonconsequential, and disconnected from the will of the people, amendment advocates must make an effort to create deliberative events that are transparent, consequential and demonstrate what democracy could be in the absence of corporate power. American Promise's commitment to deliberative ideals closely hews to broad trends in political theory and practice that have emerged out of the "deliberative democratic" synthesis of Jürgen Habermas and John Rawls.[39]

In spite of the fact that all amendment advocates seem to embrace working within systems of representative government, amendment advocates to the left of American Promise strive to produce an ethos that demonstrates the type of authenticity that the Occupy demonstrations cultivated and projected. This more radical, less liberal approach embraces performative consistency, or a balance between American Promise's internal and outward-facing communication and its critique of the absence of performative consistency in the communicative technics of centrist advocates. The leftist critique of performative contradiction was central to how American Promise's ethos buckled under pressure during a series of mass "amendment community" conference calls in 2017–18, leading to the retraction of the conference call recordings.

The leftist response to the mass conference call forum created by American Promise illustrates the complex way that irony contributes to the performance of an authentic democratic ethos. In the case of the conflict between leftist and moderate amendment advocates, leftists accused American Promise of contradicting its own values. This accusation of ironic contradiction had excellent rhetorical traction in part because transparency and deliberative procedures can never simply be a matter of mere information transmission and neutral inclusion.[40] The performance of authenticity needs only point at the ways that communicative transparency and deliberation are also rhetorical performances to demonstrate the difference between the democratic ethos and an instrumental ethos.

The leftist critique of American Promise echoed some of the most long-standing activist critiques of deliberative democratic forums. Iris Marion Young argues that deliberative forums may promote a certain type of reason, but they can fail to be transparent about their own self-constitution and expert power by controlling the deliberative setting.[41] Ostensibly transparent deliberative forums generate decisions about goals and questions that are predetermined by expert designers behind closed doors. For instance, because deliberative democratic forums generally set instrumental goals well ahead of involving deliberative participants, critics such as Young argue that they are not genuinely transparent about their methods.[42]

Critics of deliberative democracy such as Young and Chantal Mouffe have frequently identified the valorization of "reason" as a problem with the idealized models of deliberation derived from the works of John Rawls and Jürgen Habermas.[43] As Simone Chambers has argued, one of the many consequences of the overarching idealization of reason is the condemnation (especially among political scientists) of the irrationality of actually existing public deliberation.[44] Frustration with the state of public discourse has led to the creation of hothouse deliberative forums in which the use of reason and evidence can be carefully prescribed and tightly monitored by social scientists.[45] Gerard A. Hauser has pointed out some of the problems that have arisen as a result of "transferring deliberation on public problems from citizen forums to [Walter] Lippmann-like enclaves of technically educated elites."[46] Simone Chambers has even more specifically identified the construction of "mini-publics" by James Fishkin and others as increasing the risk that we might turn "our backs on the broader democratic public sphere as a place to pursue reasonable politics."[47] In fact, this tension between hothouse deliberation involving experts and irrational public deliberation is very similar to that between American Promise and more leftist community organizers.

The concept of "reason," however, should not be taken as a simple reference to the absence of emotion. In fact, if we take seriously the unavoidable imbrication of emotion in cognitive processes, as many contemporary researchers and theorists do, we are left with the task of describing what precisely is at fault with norms of reasonability, which have never convincingly pretended to describe actually existing practices of communication. Critiques of mini-publics often cite Young's concerns about how putting too much emphasis on "reason" excludes important rhetorical features of deliberation such as rhetoric, emotion, trope, passion, storytelling, refusal, and the body.[48] Scholars of public culture and movement rhetoric agree wholeheartedly with these concerns and point out that deliberation almost never happens without such "irrational" elements.[49] Mouffe argues that the affective dimensions of deliberation are essential and that an emphasis on reason in deliberation fails completely to provide an account of the democratic potentials of politics.[50] American Promise's persistent focus on rationality, effectiveness, and expert knowledge reflected a deep and unexamined commitment to deliberative democracy's liberal and technocratic assumptions.

One of the most significant elements of Fishkin's version of deliberative democracy, for instance, is that it requires that participants in a deliberative process be able to choose between *realistically* available options. Fishkin glosses over the question of where such choices in policy come from in genuinely deliberative situations, arguing only that they must be able to be actually enacted to be realistic.[51] There are obvious and difficult problems for this formulation of genuine deliberative choice and its relationship to the filtering effect of the deliberative forum designers. The question of what kind of reforms are "realistically" attainable is obviously open to debate and depends on circumstances and the extent to which political actors strive for various goals. Young, Lynn Sanders, and Nancy Fraser (among others) have argued convincingly that one of the main problems with deliberative democracy's faith in reason is that such faith fails to grasp how social difference and inequality affect various senses of what reason is and how it operates.[52]

For critics such as Wendy Brown and others following the work of Michel Foucault, Herbert Marcuse, and Louis Althusser, the deeper problem is that "reasoned" deliberation is actually shorthand for a complex set of values closely tied to the instrumental qualities of efficiency and effectivity; these are some of the features of the way of reasoning we have called "neoliberal."[53] The value placed on instrumentalist logics may have very little to do with "reason" conceived of as logic, cognition, or other elements that have been described as dispassionate, anticorporeal or antiaffective.

In hothouse deliberations that are tightly controlled by social-scientific designers or legal experts, instrumental values such as effectivity and efficiency may account for and even attempt to instrumentalize rhetorical elements related to the body, affect, passion, and other factors. For instance, the physical comfort, transportation needs, hunger, passions, identities, and abilities of the deliberating bodies might be taken into account within a framework that ultimately sees those elements as impediments to or aids in producing effective, efficient, clear, deliberative outcomes. The result is to continue to integrate such elements of deliberation into a larger instrumental framework rather than seeing them as reasons to ask more fundamental questions about the purposes and possibilities of deliberation (as practitioners of participatory democracy and direct democracy with prefigurative priorities do).

Young also argues that one way around the problems that arise when hothouse deliberations fail to account for structural inequalities is to give participants input on the *topics* and *general approach* of a deliberative forum and not simply the opportunity to weigh in on issues that are selected and described by the designers of the forum.[54] Opening the deliberative structure *itself* to input from participants was, of course, one of the primary goals of the assemblies found in the Occupy demonstrations, which allowed anyone to join the assembly and raise issues for consideration, including issues about the procedures of the forum itself. The ways that issues are selected and framed, in this way of thinking, is an important element that has powerful effects on the outcome of deliberation and who is able to participate.[55] Additionally, the structure of the forum itself may need to be up for deliberation before a specific topic can even be addressed; this self-reflexive gesture ideally can foster continuous improvement in the capacity of deliberation to respond to inadvertent exclusions and blind spots produced by systemic inequalities that precede it.

Careful attention to the parameters of deliberation within a defined assembly structure has had specific implications for the prefigurative reflexivity of Occupy in the performance of the democratic ethos of authenticity. As we have seen, the authenticity that is central to the democratic ethos consolidated by the Occupy demonstrations requires performative consistency between the critical message and the democratic values that shape the organization of political action. Without opening up the structure of deliberation to input from participants—or at least acknowledging such opening as a possibility that has been bypassed—any claim to be "transparent" with "information flow" misses the larger context of how deliberative forums are conceptualized and structured. Centrist amendment advocates committed to "transparency" in both government and political advocacy have thus been critiqued by leftist amendment advocates who accuse them of failing to meet the standards of democratic authenticity because they have not created space to open their own values and organizational choices up to contestation.

Advocates of reflexivity and performative consistency in deliberative structures seem to assume that the authentically democratic character of deliberation is grounded in the extent to which its technical apparatus is responsive to the possibility of being continuously revised by its participants. In the case of the Occupy assemblies, this commitment to reflexivity was prioritized over instrumental dimensions of the deliberative format such as efficiency, effectiveness, reason, or integration of evidence. The assemblies famously went on for hours without accomplishing anything concrete, a process that was valued by many participants nonetheless for how it helped to cultivate attachments, values, and sensibilities. It was also frustrating enough to discourage participation for many others and alienate strong supporters.[56] Prioritizing an open and reflexive structure that encouraged participants to set the agenda, however, allowed the assemblies to persuasively claim to be authentically democratic rather than merely instrumentalist.

If we follow Young's logic, self-reflexive values and their relationship to systemic inequality must be built into deliberative forum design in order to be meaningful.[57] Baking in such democratic values, however, requires jettisoning mere "transparency" as well as replacing expertise in the tasks of producing efficient and effective deliberative results with different types of expertise. This does not mean totally abandoning the role of expertise in deliberation, but it does mean going beyond subject-area expertise (such as legal expertise) and acknowledging the importance of expertise in other types of political activity that are constituted by different kinds of communication: movement building, movement history, community organizing, and the experience of structural inequality.

This was the type of expertise leveraged by "community organizers" and left-leaning amendment advocates on American Promise's mass conference calls. These organizers participated in the long tradition of community organizing that Occupy also expressed, asserting ownership of what they sometimes call an "anti-oppression" approach to political action.[58] The antioppression approach to amending the constitution includes training membership chapters in coalition building across social differences, forming partnerships with antiracist leaders and groups, and contextualizing their work with reference to other movements, both historical and contemporary.[59] They also built their ethos by attempting to privilege the experiences of those who are most affected by corporate rule—especially Black people, Indigenous people, poor people, and immigrants. The result of all these elements was an ethos that attempted to integrate prefiguratively-inflected democratic principles into communicative priorities. The critique performed by the community organizers on the conference call, however, would have fallen flat without the unironic commitment to consistency between expert liberal means and expert liberal ends that was performed by American Promise.

Performing Deliberation in Mass Conference Calls

Over the course of about six months in the second half of 2017 and early 2018, American Promise hosted a series of mass conference calls to "gather information" and foster "deliberation" about the wording and underlying principles of some version of the Twenty-Eighth Amendment that all amendment supporters might be able to agree on.[60] On the first call, the project was heralded by its own organizers as an "unprecedented" collection of Congresspeople and their staffers, legal scholars, and advocacy professionals.[61] A list of invited participants and supplementary materials for the call was provided online, including an overview of the Writing the 28th Amendment project that described the role of American Promise as bringing "constitutional expertise to deliberative citizen processes."[62] The overview document of the young organization argued that the plurality of amendment bills (including both the Democracy for All and the We the People Amendments) was a good problem but a problem nonetheless and that the purpose of the calls was to build consensus about amendment language while avoiding factionalism and "movement politics."[63] The overview document claims that the process of bringing constitutional experts, politicians, and advocacy professionals together with committed citizens from both parties will "counter hyper-partisan rancor with a model of effective deliberative democracy."[64] This commitment to deliberation as the mode of engagement is reiterated across multiple documents and mentioned frequently throughout the seven conference calls. Further, the deliberative processes hosted by the organization (and instantiated in the mass conference calls and other planned events) are described as modeling "deliberative self-government for a politically and demographically diverse people."[65] In this early document, when deliberative democracy is being juxtaposed with "hyper-partisan rancor," deliberation was described as being primarily a matter of transparency, creating consensus about the wording of the amendment, inclusivity, and comprehensive study.[66] In the absence of genuine deliberation in congressional bodies, the overview argued, part of the work of the organization was to exemplify such deliberation in its own work.[67]

Ahead of each of the mass conference calls, American Promise made available on its website a collection of background documents for the call participants to review and reference. These included transcripts of congressional testimony, think tank reports, law journal articles, Supreme Court case decisions and dissents, and other documents. The documents also included lists of "participants" on the calls, though it was unclear how many of those invited on the list were actually on the mass conference calls. Unlike a video conference call, the presence of participants was only revealed when they actually spoke.

The first call, held on May 30, 2017, was devoted to providing an overview of the process and assumptions of the mass conference calls. The calls were directed by Jeffrey Clements, the attorney who cofounded American

Promise and author of *Corporations are Not People: Reclaiming Democracy from Big Money and Global Corporations.*[68] Clements framed the general purpose of the calls as that of creating a forum that could be "a deliberative process about what we can do to ensure an effective amendment, not to decide whether we need one or not."[69] He said the first task was to make sure "we all have access to the information and thinking and writing needed to help us do a good job on this."[70] From the beginning, this sense of *effectiveness* as the primary criterion for an amendment and *information* dissemination as the purpose of the calls were front and center.

Clements introduced several Congresspeople on the call who spoke about their hope that the calls could lead to consensus about amendment language and greater unity among amendment advocates. This hope for consensus was immediately framed by multiple congressional staffers and legal scholars, however, as being possible only if it was about an amendment that focused only on campaign finance and not corporate rights. Legal experts determined that this was the proper type of amendment and that grassroots support should be directed toward it by leadership.

In this first call, a couple of community organizers spoke up, stating that they thought amendment language and goals should be decided on by the grassroots mobilization rather than leadership deciding on the best amendment. One of these organizers expressed some concern right away about how congressional staffers and legal experts were framing the "involvement" of the grassroots: "When I hear right off the bat sort of, uh, statements about, um, sort of *using* the mobilizations from below in order to get something that the grassroots have not been agitating for that raises the question for me of whether we'll actually be able to reach a consensus and maybe we should be prepared for there to be multiple amendments and for some sort of strategy that is at least cooperative."[71]

This comment identified a potential tension between the tasks of democratic mass mobilization and reaching an instrumentally motivated "consensus" on amendment language that would be "effective" in the sense that it could be approved of and passed by existing congressional bodies. Clements quickly acknowledged the importance of "the grassroots" and argued that the deliberative process of the mass conference calls could be valuable even if no consensus was reached.[72] Another community organizer jumped in to comment that it felt like the grassroots movement was already being shoved aside on the call, which Clements denied, asserting that the deliberative process of the calls was "inclusive" and that deliberation requires "lot of listening and a lot of learning."[73]

After this emergence of the core conflict between sitting politicians, legal experts and community organizers in the very first call, the goal of consensus about amendment language seemed to be shelved in the second call on June 27, 2017. Instead, Clements kicked off the session by declaring that the task of the calls was the production of white papers about constitutional principles that might inform deliberation about the Twenty-Eighth Amendment both in the public discussion and among the call participants. The white paper production process, he stated, was an opportunity to "focus our work [. . .] and to practice what we preach about deliberation and listening and collaboration and so forth in the development of these white papers."[74] This shift to framing the purpose of the calls in terms of the goal of producing legal knowledge muted the conflict between community organizers, politicians, and scholars that had begun to take shape in the first call. It did so, however, by solidly repositioning the purpose of the mass conference calls as being prior to traditional forms of community organizing by privileging the expertise of legal scholars.

After the white paper process had been outlined, one of the participants asked how American Promise planned to engage the public. Clements's reply to this query set the stage for subsequent calls as framed by the relationship between the "white paper" process of expert knowledge building and those outside of the calls (including grassroots supporters of an amendment or the general public) who were not legal experts:

> One thing we've already done is there is a live link on our website where anybody can follow along and see everything we're doing, essentially. So our first call, the recording is there, this one will be available to the public to listen to. All the readings we provide and our agendas and everything else is there. And that's just the sort of, transparency and the way for people to follow along. That is only the beginning. [. . .] So we anticipate, especially once we get the white papers going, to have a, uh, an interactive, a large process for both learning about what this group has done but also weighing in with views, so we anticipate using all of our various tools to do that. So we'll have a national call where people will have the draft of the white paper or a public, um, sort of, depending on how wonky the white paper gets [chuckle], an executive summary as well, but we'll get basically the thinking we're doing, the direction we're heading available, for deliberation, weighing in. People now can comment at any time, and electronically that'll still be available, but we'll also have a national call like this one where we'll have some of you, I hope, be our guests speakers to describe what we're doing and then take in input and deliberation from people around the country over this facilitated phone call. We'll do the same thing with webinars and other tools.

This extended comment reveals the extent to which transparency—the making visible of the information compiled by participants on the calls both verbally and in writing—was central to the way that democratic "public engagement" was conceptualized at this stage of the work of American Promise. Rather than respond to the claims made by community organizers that grassroots organizing supported a more radical amendment, American Promise responded that providing educational, informational resources produced by legal scholars—if those resources weren't too "wonky"—would satisfy the imperative to democratically engage "the public." Rather than push for the grassroots-supported version of the amendment, American Promise would "educate" the public about relevant legal cases and principles, presumably in order to convince them of the necessity of getting behind a more instrumentally feasible version of the amendment. Rather than prefigurative persuasion in which the democratic, egalitarian decision-making processes were broadcast, American promise offered "transparent" information flow.

American Promise's use of the nouns "the public" versus the community organizers' use of "the grassroots" suggests the disparate assumptions that these political actors made about the nature of democratic politics and its relationship to expertise. The sense of "the public" in Clements's formulation above seems to involve fairly Habermasian ideals in which an educated, literate group of privileged citizens deliberates about matters of concern.[75] In fact, Clements spoke of eventual public input on the white papers as a process of "peer review," suggesting the entire deliberative process as one akin to knowledge production.[76] Community organizers, on the other hand, spoke of "the grassroots" in a way that referred to the interests, concerns, and values of that group prior to any acquisition of legal knowledge. Organizers assumed that the "grassroots," unlike the public, had a type of agency and force of their own and were not in need of educating so much as they were in need of mobilizing and amplifying.

The difference between educating the public about constitutional principles and mobilizing the grassroots to express their opposition to capitalism informed the way that American Promise and others on the calls instrumentalized the grassroots. Community organizers expressed concern that existing grassroots support for a more radical amendment was only being considered by American Promise as a resource to efficiently and effectively get a more moderate amendment passed. Clements, the cofounder of American Promise, responded to this statement of concern about framing grassroots mobilization as a mere means to an end by vaguely confirming that he believed that grassroots mobilization was in fact essential to the project. He stated, "This doesn't get done without a grassroots effort. You don't get to 38 states ratifying an amendment without broad cross-partisan support at the local level. So that's our intention as well."[77] Although he went on to agree that multiple amendments might be necessary, he avoided the more fundamental question of how to think about the possibility that the opinions of *legal* experts on the precise wording of the amendments might be quite different in substance from what activists and grassroots supporters had been agitating for (i.e. an amendment that denies corporations all constitutional rights, not just the right to free speech). His comment, framed as an agreement with the community organizers, nonetheless revealed a reiteration of the instrumental approach: we can't get it done without grassroots support. Rather than expressing a commitment to respecting and adhering to existing grassroots perspectives, this response did little more than restate precisely the (arguably ironic) instrumental approach that the community organizers had initially expressed concern about.

One of the community organizers, Kaitlin Sopoci-Belknap of the organization Move to Amend, responded to Clements's vague affirmation of the need for grassroots support by verbally rehearsing the organizational histories and missions of different amendment-oriented groups. After describing how Clements and others had broken off from the more radical groups such as her own, she said, "[Y]ou all felt as though it was a more strategic agenda to address just the first amendment rights of corporations rather than all corporate constitutional rights. Not because you don't agree with us and we're on the same page about corporations are not entitled to constitutional rights and all the damage that that creates, but again the strategic question that's coming up."[78]

The "strategic" question that Sopoci-Belknap emphasized by this point in the mass conference call process, now the sixth call on November 28th of 2017, was precisely the question of the extent to which instrumental concerns should guide the decision made about what type of amendment to advocate for. By this point in the process, it had become clear that American Promise had consistently prioritized input from attorneys, judges, and legal scholars advocating a more moderate amendment that dealt exclusively with campaign finance and corporate free-speech rights rather than the broader range of rights that more radical advocates wanted to call into question.

The result of the conflict over the instrumentalization of "the grassroots" as part of an effort to push for a more moderate amendment than grassroots support actually indicated was a quick retreat into knowledge building in the name of educating "the public." In other words, American Promise presented the "deliberative" features of the conference calls as being about the transparent dissemination of information. This conceptualization of transparency and deliberation was part of an attempt to consistently perform liberal values in spite of a general instrumental framing for that performance.

American Promise's soft commitment to a more moderate amendment (in spite of Clements's book that explicitly advocated a more radical position against all corporate constitutional rights) suggested a firm distinction between the political means of *steering* "the public" and the ends of curtailing corporate power by ultimately *empowering* the public. As community organizers pointed out regarding the performative contradiction between those particular means and ends, American Promise pivoted to de-emphasize the goal of unifying to pass an amendment.

The result was what one community organizer called an "intellectual exercise" that seemed to focus on testimony from a parade of attorneys, congresspeople, judges, and scholars who supported a moderate amendment.[79] In an effort to maintain performative consistency, "deliberation" was framed as a process of education and information dissemination rather than something that would be about airing and really discussing disagreement. The community organizers, however, took issue with this conceptualization of deliberation, arguing that the process of the mass conference calls was performatively inconsistent because it failed to create an environment in which competing perspectives and forms of knowledge were genuinely included, that is, included on equal footing. After American Promise and other participants in the calls retreated from their suggestion that "the grassroots" should be persuaded to support a more moderate amendment, the tension between advocates boiled over again. This time, however, the deliberative contradictions within the calls themselves was the source of conflict.

Interrupting Transparent Deliberation

During the sixth conference call on November 28, the process shifted from listening to the input of "invited experts" to "internal deliberation" among the core call participants.[80] Clements acknowledged that American Promise had received criticism from the group members since the fifth call because of the way that the speakers all seemed to be slanted toward the more moderate campaign finance amendment. He claimed, however, that the apparent bias of the speakers "was not by our design" and that it had emerged because supporters of a more radical amendment had not been responsive to American Promise's invitations to present to the group.[81] This disavowal of responsibility for the results of the design and structure of the conference calls was not accepted by the more radical community organizers. The sixth and seventh calls, the last ones, consisted in large part of a wide-ranging discussion of how the structure, design, and content of the conference calls had failed to live up to their democratic aspirations, with American Promise representatives and others on the defensive about their claim to have performed neutrality and transparency.

As the community organizers made their case that the deliberative forum of the conference calls had excluded their perspectives, tactics, and values, they attempted to argue that the conference calls contradicted their organizers' own stated commitments to deliberation and transparency—that is, that their instrumentalism was ironic. This was done in two ways: by criticizing the design of the forum and by themselves performing a different type of deliberation and authenticity. The result of this dual combination —critique and performance of alternative, more radical values—produced enough of a sense of performative contradiction in the conference call structure to compel American Promise to renege completely on its commitment to transparency and take the recordings of the calls offline.

From the beginning, American Promise had committed to posting recordings of the conference calls on their website along with copious documents, academic law journal articles, amendment text, and lists of participants invited to the forum. By the time tensions had risen in the sixth and seventh conference calls, community organizers had begun to ask pointedly for American Promise to publish not just the list of who was invited but also who was actually on the calls and listening in on the discussion. The organizers insisted that if American Promise was claiming that the process was "deliberative" and that certain points of consensus had been achieved, the silence of such parties was not actually "consensus" and that the claims of such needed to be seriously qualified. In response to American Promise's claims that the conference calls had reached a type of deliberative consensus, one of the community organizers said that such a claim, "paints a picture of something much more deliberative and deep than has actually occurred. So I just want to, I guess, just register that because I think if a public person looks at this what they are always wanting is for us to really get into it and you know, hash through it and come out with consensus and this sort of implies that happened and don't feel as a participant that that's what we've done at all."[82]

Another community organizer echoed this point, saying "we don't know if you're . . . we don't know who's on the call and we don't know who's agreeing in any kind of affirmative way. So that also kind of bothers me."[83] These comments revealed that for the community organizers and supporters of a more radical constitutional amendment, claiming that any type of "consensus" had been achieved was very much dependent on both the type of deliberation that had occurred and the level of disclosure about who was participating and how they felt about the discussion that was happening. These community organizers resisted the use of the word "consensus" to describe a process that was not transparent or deliberative enough in the sense that it unevenly and arbitrarily included some voices and not others and did not even reveal who was listening to the conversation much less require contributions from them. As a result of this pointed criticism, American Promise quickly pledged to send out a list of all the participants on the calls.

The type of transparency and disclosure that the community organizers sought, however, would have needed to go beyond this conciliatory gesture. In addition to questioning the bias of the experts who were selected to participate on the calls, one of the community organizers insisted that a higher level of disclosure about the history of the various approaches to an amendment was both important and missing from the deliberations. Kaitlin Sopoci-Belknap of Move to Amend articulated the concern during the sixth call by describing a disagreement about bifurcation of amendment advocacy into instrumental and authentic approaches in the early stages of responding to the *Citizens United* decision 2010. She described how Clements and others had broken away from more radical approaches early on because of the "strategic question" of which amendment would be easier to pass (rather than which one would accomplish the most or address the problem most fully). The instrumental approach to drafting and advocating for an amendment created, according to Sopoci-Belknap, a rift in the amendment community. She said, "That's the message that we still see coming from American Promise as the agenda is that this next amendment, the 28th amendment, the most viable option is one that addresses only the first amendment rights of corporations, certainly not all of them because of the strategic question, not because I don't believe you that you are opposed to corporate constitutional rights."[84]

Sopoci-Belknap argues here that Clements and American Promise, among others, support a moderate amendment not because they don't agree that a more radical one would be better, but purely because they believe that pursuing the more moderate amendment is the feasible, efficient, and strategic course of action. In disclosing the history of this "strategic" (or instrumental) approach, she says that she "wanted to make it more explicit in the interest of trying to get to the bottom of this all and figure out where we all go from here. So rather than talking around things, I hope this comes across not as an accusation, but as to help understand, you understand where our skepticism is coming from."[85] In the name of transparency, she presents the history of the rift between amendment advocates as a type of important background that will flesh out and explain the skepticism that community organizers have brought to the deliberations. As she performs the values of authentic disclosure of internal organizing communication ("let's all acknowledge our history and where we are really coming from") she undercuts and critiques the efforts made by American Promise to claim that its own process, in which the organizational histories remain unacknowledged, is just about gathering neutral information about the law.

A similar dynamic between the community organizers' critique of American Promise and their own performance played out as the organizers called into question the fairness, inclusiveness, and depth of the deliberative format of the conference calls. In addition to pushing back on the claim that the calls had led to any kind of "consensus," community organizers on the calls also questioned whether a moderate amendment would do anything for most people in the United States. Keyan Bliss, another staffer from Move to Amend, asked some pointed questions about who would be served by an amendment that focused narrowly on campaign finance issues. After asking the question in an abstract way, Bliss focused more narrowly on how the limited scope of the moderate amendment seemed to be the expression of the relative homogeneity of its supporters. Reflecting the long-standing emphasis that prefigurative politics puts on self-examination and growth in the internal organizing process, Bliss asked participants to examine their privilege:

> I realize this is probably going to make some of you feel very uncomfortable, but the reality is that the majority of this, like, most of this conversation that we've been having has been largely between a small minority of white male voices. Most of whom seem unanimously opposed to addressing anything more substantive than campaign finance reform and feel somehow entitled to explain this amend . . . to dictate what language goes into amendment that should pass. Any amendment that comes out of this project is going to take a massive coalition of movement to actually get passed, I mean if anyone here is under the impression that all we need to do is appeal to a handful of political figures in a tiny class of middle to upper class white folks is, that's like we're already setting ourselves up for failure.[86]

This statement was followed by a critique of the limited and exclusionary scope of the conference call deliberations. Bliss's extended comments happened toward the end of the sixth conference call after a series of white male voices had indeed questioned whether anything more than campaign finance should be on the table for consideration at that moment. As Bliss warmed to his topic and began to explain why true political equality requires more than "getting money out of politics," the conference call moderator cut him off to end the entire call at the preplanned one-hour mark. The conference calls had all stuck to a rigid one-hour timeframe and this call was no different. Bliss, the only audibly Black participant on the calls, was cut off mid-sentence and without apology.

On the next call, Bliss and his coworker Sopoci-Belknap explicitly called the transparency and deliberative equality of the conference call process into question. Sopoci-Belknap, toward the end of the call, pointed out that Bliss had "raised his hand" to participate in the final conference call multiple times and had been ignored by the same moderator who had cut him off during the previous call. Sopoci-Belknap's comments performed a more radical, democratic ethos on two levels. First, she critiqued the American Promise staff for failing to include her coworker of color. In doing so, however, she also performed some elements of the democratic ethos in the sense that she modeled a "step up, step back" approach by trying to create space for her colleague of color to participate. Additionally, she demonstrated the value of precisely the type of more direct negotiation of differences that she had been claiming was missing from the conference calls all along; she directly described what she saw as an important "deliberative" failure of the democratic values of the conference call process.

Awkwardly acknowledging this, the moderator finally let Bliss speak. After affirming that he had tried to participate in the conversation multiple times and been shut out, Bliss commented, "I'm really disappointed in this process, I don't think it's been very deliberative at all. And it's frankly, just disappointing and insulting."[87] Immediately after this comment, several more moderate participants jumped in to castigate radical community organizers, including Bliss, for making "personal attacks" and "trying to submarine the process."[88] Clements tried to smooth over the widening rift with vague comments about working together to get past "bumps in the road." The seventh conference call, however, was ultimately the end of the road for this particular deliberative forum. It was also the end of striving for the calls to be "transparent"; eventually they were taken off of American Promise's website. Without the type of prefigurative authenticity sought by more radical participants, the deliberative failure meant that the persuasive capacity of the deliberations was undercut completely.

Conclusion

It would be all too easy to tell a story about the obstructionism of radicals based on the story of the breakdown and retraction of American Promise's mass conference calls. After all, didn't the radical values of community organizers stop the conference participants from coming together around a unified version of the amendment that could have garnered enough support in Congress to be passed into law? This was certainly the perspective of conference call participants who accused the community organizers of failing to uphold civil discourse simply because they pointed out that the dialogue had been structured in a way that did not give due consideration to their preferred amendment nor them as speakers and participants in the conference calls.

The failure of movement leaders and advocacy professionals to agree on one version of an amendment, however, is probably not what is standing in the way of actually passing an amendment to the Constitution that would decrease the influence of corporations on government. In the end, the greater barrier seems to be one of political mobilization. Hothouse deliberations between movement leaders, such as the conference calls hosted by American Promise in 2017, have little consequence without more involvement and momentum among average voters.

As of 2021, American Promise is still active, but it has significantly shifted its tactical emphasis to put much more energy into community organizing. Its annual 2021 National Citizens Leadership Conference promotional materials prominently feature multiple people of color, as does its list of paid staff.[89] It now employs people with titles such as Empowerment Coordinator. It has shifted to a chapter-based outreach model, claiming to have active chapters in 18 US states.[90] It regularly holds trainings in advocacy skills such as tabling and lobbying elected officials as well as outreach sessions to educate new members about the core issues and activities of the organization and how they can get involved.[91] In other words, American Promise now looks more like Move to Amend and other membership-based advocacy organizations than it ever has. Gone are the "town hall" meetings at law schools and the push to write policy briefs and white papers that were the focus of the mass conference calls in 2017.

"Citizen engagement" was part of the game plan for American Promise all along, but the methods by which this goal is now being pursued for the organization look different. This shift may not have occurred exclusively because of the pressure exerted by community organizers in 2017. There is no doubt, however, that American Promise's current methods and staff look a lot more like the tactics of community organizers than they did before.

This doesn't mean that the organization is publicly pursuing (and broadcasting) deliberative assemblies that are genuinely open to contestation and revision by the participants—their annual conference, for instance, is still staidly committed to a model of knowledge dissemination that resembles nothing more than an academic conference. But at least the subjects of knowledge have diversified, and less emphasis is being placed on the law and what types of amendments are "realistic" according to legal precedent. It appears that the emphasis of the organization is now less on "education" and more on mobilization.

The "transparency" promised by the hosts of the mass conference calls ended up being unrealizable in the face of the radical demand for authentic input on the very format of the deliberation. American Promise presumably did provide participants with a list of everyone who was on the conference calls, but the call recordings were taken offline, further demonstrating the community organizers' core suspicion that the process of the conference calls was not really oriented toward resolving disagreement, much less consensus, through a thorough airing of differences among amendment advocates.

Because American Promise conceptualized deliberative transparency as unimpeded "information" flow, it was unable to fully account for and defend elements of its deliberative process that were not about expert knowledge production. This narrow understanding of expertise is merely a matter of being able to convey information rather than knowledge about how to foster deliberation, build community, or mobilize for action. The tension between community organizers and American Promise that cropped up in the mass conference calls is not simply a question of how instrumental the more moderate approach is. The difference between these approaches reflects different ways of conceptualizing expertise and knowledge itself as elements of ethos. If ethos is the expression of the values, habits, and accreted sensibilities of a collective, community organizers and American Promise derive their ethos from two distinct, if overlapping, sets of democratic practices.

The instrumentalism of American Promise takes the concept of corruption as central to the problem that an amendment must seek to address. Much like Lawrence Lessig and other supporters of democracy vouchers, American Promise describes money in politics as an "influence" that has undermined an otherwise sound technical governmental structure designed by the so-called Founding Fathers. Given this underlying conceptualization of democracy as a quasi-mechanical structure that must be expertly maintained, the most compelling technics by which to repair it, according to the instrumentalist way of thinking, should arise from the legal community. These technics are ultimately judged according to how or whether they can garner support from already-elected congressional representatives and move further toward being enacted. Engagement with the public is therefore a relatively mechanical process by which support is drummed up for an approach to reform that has been predetermined by legal experts.

Because American Promise embraces expert legal technics as one element in a range of ways that ethos can be built, it doesn't suggest an ethos that embraces performative contradiction so completely. In fact, because American Promise was attempting its own version of a performatively consistent commitment to transparency and deliberation, it opened itself up to critique from radical organizers. Unlike the campaign to pass the democracy vouchers in Seattle, which was fairly open about its own ironic self-constitution, American Promise made a case for its approach based on an attempt to embody and perform liberal values. The points of intersection between these liberal values and the radical commitments of community organizers on the call served as an opportunity for those organizers to then point out the performative contradictions demonstrated on the conference calls, particularly when it came to their transparency and the deliberative structure. Radical community organizers, influenced by horizontalism and its sense of "consensus," efforts to privilege marginalized voices and acknowledge and cultivate relationships between participants, argued and demonstrated that the American Promise conference calls had failed to create a space in which political disagreements could be openly aired and negotiated. Not only that, but when conflict erupted because of the failure to appropriately include the participation of a person of color, community organizers made it clear that "transparency" based merely on information flow was a poor substitute for a more robustly implemented and self-reflexive deliberative process that included hedges against discrimination, such as a progressive stack or "step up, step back" guidelines for facilitators. Perhaps the most vivid illustration of the difference between "transparency" and the type of authenticity performed as the democratic ethos is in the way that American Promise ultimately chose to contradict itself by taking the mass conference call recordings offline. Without American Promise's stated commitment to transparency and deliberation, however, community organizers would have lacked the opportunity and rhetorical foothold to demonstrate a more radically democratic approach to the work of deliberating about amending the Constitution.

FIVE

Rural Community Democracy and the Radicalism of Instrumental Reason

The Community Environmental Legal Defense Fund (CELDF) is a legal-aid nonprofit that represents municipalities attempting to legislate against corporate incursions in their communities. CELDF helps communities pass local laws in a way that simultaneously supports both effective environmental protections and a radical rejection of property-based liberal citizenship.[1] As a legal-aid organization, CELDF began its life in the mid-1990s by providing straightforward legal support for attempts to enforce federal environmental regulations such as the Clean Water Act of 1972. CELDF has subsequently moved on to more radical approaches that operate entirely outside of and against the federal regulatory system. CELDF leadership argues that community rights ordinances preface a turn in liberal and left politics toward state and local government action on issues such as marijuana legalization, sanctuary cities, and fracking.[2] They also argue for the importance of the rights of nature, not only in local communities but also on a global scale as a response to climate change.[3]

CELDF openly supports the rights of nature, Indigenous rights, and local community rights as part of a broader commitment to antistatist democratic action that would, in the long term, displace the current US Constitution entirely and require a radical, revolutionary shift in political culture and government structures. Many of the communities they work with, however, are primarily interested in how the ordinances have a narrowly instrumental value in the process of solving specific local problems.[4] In some cases, the ordinances have succeeded in accomplishing tasks such as preventing toxic sludge disposal and hydraulic fracturing within the municipal boundaries. In cases where they have not succeeded, however, things become more complicated. CELDF describes the failure to effectively legislate at the local level as an important opportunity to radicalize communities and educate them about the absence of genuine democracy in state and federal institutions. In publicizing failure and instances of corporate and federal (or state) supremacy, CELDF performs authenticity in a way that is not dissimilar from how radical protest performs authenticity by rhetorically capitalizing on police violence. Because of this general strategy, CELDF has tended to actively claim instrumental motivations (rather than radical ones) even as it describes its radicalism as the necessary expression of a thwarted instrumentalism. The result is that the claim to instrumentally meet the physical needs of a community proves the authenticity in the collective democratic ethos of CELDF.

CELDF strives assiduously to help communities prevent harm to themselves. On the surface CELDF is a liberal nonprofit organization that is not far from the type of instrumentalism that helped fund the campaign to pass Seattle's Honest Elections initiative. CELDF's team of legal experts designs legislation to solve a specific problem and then helps key allies in the community push it through local government. Local allies are invested because they think the expert legislation will directly solve a concrete problem, and they trust the legal experts from outside the community.

There are important differences between the ironic instrumentalism of the Honest Elections Seattle campaign and CELDF's approach. CELDF does conceive of the ordinances as mere means to the end of stopping specific harms wrought by corporate incursions. But they also recognize that the ordinances may fail (or are even likely to fail) and that they are part of a larger, more radical and long-term process. CELDF accepts this instrumental failure in its efforts to prevent physical harm in order to pursue instrumental success in persuading and radicalizing an audience. In some cases, the ordinances have been overturned or small towns have been sued by corporations or state government.[5] CELDF strives to radicalize community members when these negative outcomes reveal the force of corporate influence in politics. The result is the production of a democratic ethos that is persuasively prefigurative in the sense that it is both instrumental *and* radical while being rooted in communicative technics that simultaneously evoke "town hall" community deliberation and rebellious, dispersed direct action. Unlike some anarchist antistatism, however, CELDF's version of a democratic ethos actively justifies its radical refusal of federal and state government by describing how corporate influence currently makes effective local self-governance impossible. In CELDF's politics, the specific, active, immediate failure of pragmatic, live, and face-to-face communication is framed as *the reason why* existing laws should be radically refused and long-term planning for cultural and mindset change is needed. CELDF's ethos has continuously integrated these two approaches—the immediate, practical legal work and the radicalization of communities—as elements of its self-presentation as authentically democratic.

In the wake of Occupy, CELDF has also begun to perform its ethos with a stronger emphasis on strategic civil disobedience. This change has been a process of layering rather than a full-scale transformation. It has involved a shift in communicative technics from local organizing (through face-to-face meetings, local gatherings, and publications emphasizing practical issues) to publicizing the successes of local organizing through what John Durham Peters has called one-to-many or "broadcast" communicative technics that are asynchronous: books, film, and blog posts.[6] In these persuasive, outward-facing broadcast media, however, CELDF continues to describe the live, face-to-face communication of municipalities as the core feature of its own democratic ethos. The performative contradiction between how CELDF broadcasts and the importance of live, face-to-face communication within those broadcasts might seem to undercut the organization's ethos. To avoid this, CELDF carefully articulates a departure from strictly live, face-to-face democratic dialogue as a move that is justified by the failure of that dialogue to work effectively in all instances. The result of this careful, continued centering of a democratic dialogue somewhat prefigurative in its idealism but with a focus on instrumental problem-solving (albeit primarily on the failure of that instrumentalism) is the core technic of radical democratic strategic disobedience.

The Evolving Strategies of CELDF

CELDF is not *itself* a small town; it is a legal-aid nonprofit. An important component of its ethos has always been foregrounding the active self-rule of the municipalities that pass its community rights ordinances. Community rights ordinances have been pursued by local governments as responses to specific urgent problems such as fracking, factory farming, toxic waste disposal, oil drilling, hard-rock mining, and water extraction. In some US states (such as Pennsylvania, Alaska, Minnesota, Massachusetts, and Ohio), state constitutions grant local municipalities the ability, within limits, to pass binding legislation governing their own territory.[7] CELDF attempts to draw on this "home rule charter" legal tradition to claim the force of sovereign authority for community rights ordinances. The ordinances are different from petitions or resolutions, both of which are nonbinding forms of opinion expression through local government. The ordinances, in contrast, are binding local laws that confrontationally assert their right to override federal and state law.

Local municipal civil disobedience has taken on a new valence in the COVID-19 pandemic. State and federal government at some points left it up to local municipalities whether to impose mask mandates on the local population. At other points, however, state-level mask mandates have been imposed and actively resisted—either by passive refusal or activism—by local residents.[8] The question of whether to mandate mask usage in schools has prompted comparisons to 1950s local resistance to desegregation mandated by *Brown vs. Board of Education.*[9] All these issues—school desegregation, pandemic masking mandates, and community rights ordinances—draw on a long-standing libertarian current in US politics that sees civil disobedience to federal (and sometimes state) law as ethically and politically necessary for the protection of freedom and democracy. CELDF's work, though drawing on this conceptualization of democracy to a certain extent, promotes a right to local self-rule in the name of environmental protection—traditionally a left-progressive political issue. CELDF is aware of this overlap and has been careful to craft its community rights ordinances in such a way as to make a clear distinction between human rights and equality issues and corporate rights, arguing that local governments should still be obligated to follow federal law on issues such as gun control and racial equity.[10] Nonetheless, the resonance of the "community rights" tactics of CELDF with other issues prompts important questions about the overlap between far-right and far-left antistatism.

CELDF works primarily in the US but has also helped to establish new rights in other countries. For instance, the organization participated in drafting Ecuador's 2008 Constitution, which codifies the rights of nature, the right to food, the right to "free, intercultural, inclusive, diverse and participatory communication in all spheres of social interaction," and the right of access to airwaves and information technologies, among other rights.[11] In the United States, CELDF has facilitated the passage of local ordinances asserting communities' rights since 1998.[12] Since its pivot away from working within the regulatory system at the end of the 1990s, it has pursued the enactment and codification of new rights in local and state law.[13] The articulation of these rights— community rights, the rights of nature, the right to survive, and others—has expanded and become more detailed. The core approach to rights and the law, however, has remained consistent. Although strongly antistatist, it is also an approach that is consistent with a Deweyan account of a community or public as a group of people mutually affected by consequences.[14] The practical emphasis on community and environmental harms and problem-solving are the root its instrumentalism.

Because of the failures of state and national regulatory systems, CELDF argues, communities need to reassert their right to self-govern and legislate against corporate actions on the local level. The organization's move to begin assisting communities to draft legally binding laws came after years of fruitlessly attempting to enforce inadequate state and federal environmental regulations that were too permissive to corporations. One of the central problems with existing environmental regulations, they argue, is that their democratic appearance generates a shield whereby corporations cannot be held liable for the damages they inflict on local communities as long as their actions adhere to the letter of the regulatory laws. Additionally, CELDF argues, long-standing corporate constitutional rights guarantee Commerce Clause protections as well as protections based on the First, Fourth, Fifth, Sixth, and Fourteenth Amendments. Because of these legal protections, they aver, any successful efforts to more effectively regulate the actions of corporations should bypass state and federal regulatory frameworks and directly confront corporate rights claims to with the sovereignty of local governance. In other words, critiquing existing liberal articulations of corporate rights and the US Constitution itself is central to CELDF's strategies for preventing and abating damage to humans and ecosystems.

In the United States, hundreds of CELDF's community rights ordinances have been passed, primarily in rural areas. A few larger municipalities and counties have also passed them, the largest being the city of Pittsburgh.[15] Many of these ordinances have been effective at preventing destructive corporate activities. Other community rights ordinances have yet to be tested in actual legal battles and some have been overturned in litigation. Others simply fail to pass in popular votes. One of CELDF's opponents in the energy industry calls the ordinances "misleading, legally meaningless language," while a similarly inclined blog calls CELDF and its allies, "old-time pool hall hustlers, operating without consciences and taking in naive local officials who are led to believe they have previously unimagined powers to overrule every law standing in their way."[16] These critiques attempt to drive a wedge between the common sense of rural residents and CELDF's rhetoric by painting it as an organization of overeducated, excessively idealistic interlopers.

CELDF's organizational ethos has been built in part to express solidarity with rural communities and against the federal government. In its efforts to empower local communities, it turns away from national-level politics almost completely. It broadly assumes that amending the US Constitution to improve democratic representation by denying corporations rights, no matter how many rights, could not plausibly result in a meaningfully more democratic state. CELDF has declared that it does not endorse activism that focuses narrowly on "overturning" *Citizens United.*[17] The organization argues, much like Occupy demonstrators, that corporate influence on politics was a deep and persistent problem prior to *Citizens United.* In sum, CELDF takes the general position that processes of national representative governance are not and can never be truly democratic. So, says CELDF, "*we must become revolutionaries, not reformers.*"[18] Instead of attempting to restore a democratic system that never existed, they argue, we should be trying to build one from the ground up by creating a "new community civil rights movement" that does not involve "asking for permission" from authorities.[19] Building such a movement, of course, is precisely what CELDF claims to do through persuasively prefiguring change as it encourages "grassroots organizing that will grow community by community, lawsuit by lawsuit, local law by local law; pressing outwards to eventually change state law and then federal law."[20] CELDF argues that communities should assert their sovereign right to directly create the laws that govern places, activities, and natural environment. In other words, it is no stretch to say that CELDF strives for an idealized, nearly prefigurative form of community politics that is broadcast as ideal and part of an effort to persuade the broader public of the values and critique that the prefigurative community demonstrates. Much like Occupy, the organization has tended to distance itself from centrist critiques of corporate rights that focus on electing sympathetic politicians to state and federal office or amending the federal Constitution.[21]

At the same time, however, CELDF's core mission is about helping communities solve tangible, practical problems. Historically, CELDF has organized in hyperlocal face-to-face meetings—some of them in actual town halls. A cornerstone of this organizing has been hosting "Democracy Schools" in towns that were interested in the possibility of passing a community rights ordinance.[22] These two-day workshops encourage participants to engage directly with a variety of historical texts, including Edward Bernays on propaganda, W. E. B. Du Bois on colonialism and Reconstruction, and a variety of others. This approach familiarizes participants with critiques of the aristocratic and pro-corporate tendencies of the political leaders of the early US republic.[23] Alongside the critique of the founding assumptions of the US Constitution, CELDF has identified and amplified a historical democratic counter-discourse that includes the Levellers, Thomas Paine, Abolitionism, and women's suffrage as it has encouraged rural municipalities to stand up to corporate incursions.[24] The result is a form of education in Anglo-American jurisprudence that carefully constructs a counter-narrative of democracy as a local, practical effort to govern together only as much as is needed to solve common problems and resist illegitimate power from above.

This narrative of popular rule is essential to CELDF's work because the overarching mission of the organization is to conceptualize, popularize, and codify community rights and the rights of nature in local and state law. These rights are less individualistic, less anthropocentric, and overwhelmingly hostile to the corporate legal form, which is a mere tool. CELDF's ordinances themselves contain pointed descriptions of the difference between "natural" and "artificial" persons, a distinction that justifies communities' claims to legal rights. Corporations are artificial persons designed for exclusively instrumental purposes according to CELDF, and, as such cannot claim to be legitimate political actors. This distinction bolsters the sense that CELDF itself is authentically democratic.

Many of CELDF's ordinances aim to dismantle the legal basis for business corporations. CELDF's attacks on the legal basis for the corporation are not, therefor, purely instrumental tactics for stopping specific harms. They are performative devices for building the ethos of the actors passing the laws as the authentic source of democratic legitimacy.[25] The legal device by which the ordinances attempt to disassemble corporate law is language that specifically describes the protections of corporate limited liability as null and void within the boundaries of a town passing an ordinance.

An early example is the ordinance passed by the Tamaqua Borough in Pennsylvania in response to problems caused by the disposal of toxic sewage sludge within the town limits. The "Findings and Purpose" section of the ordinance explicitly states that part of the problem it seeks to address is that "it is also recognized that limited liability shields prevent financial recovery (and accountability) for damages caused by business entities because limited liability insulates the persons managing the corporation from harms caused by their decisions."[26] In addition to defining "the corporation" as nearly all the ordinances do, the Tamaqua Borough ordinance contains the following passage in its "Civil Rights Enforcement" section:

> *Any person* acting under the authority of a permit issued by the Department of Environmental Protection, any corporation operating under a State charter, or any director, officer, owner, or manager of a corporation operating under a State charter, who deprives any Borough resident, natural community, or ecosystem of any rights, privileges, or immunities secured by this Ordinance, the Pennsylvania Constitution, the United States Constitution, or other laws, *shall be liable to the party injured and shall be responsible for payment of compensatory and punitive damages and all costs of litigation, including, without limitation, expert and attorney's fees.* Compensatory and punitive damages paid to remedy the violation of the rights of natural communities and ecosystems shall be paid to Tamaqua Borough for restoration of those natural communities and ecosystems.[27]

This section effectively states, like many of the other CELDF ordinances, that permits and charters granted from state authorities (such as US state and federal governments) that are not the Tamaqua Borough have no legal standing if the persons using those legal tools violate the rights of the Tamaqua community. It goes on, as emphasized in italics above, to declare unequivocally that the implication of invalidating those permits and charters is that persons typically protected by the grant of limited liability that comes with the corporate legal form will instead be personally liable for those damages. The implications of this position are striking; the ordinances fundamentally attempt to supersede state and local law governing the corporate form. Much like the ways that anarchist direct action attempts to prefigure freedom from the state by breaking the law during protests, the ordinances enact a new basis for sovereignty and prefigure the law that would result from it. In neither case is the law actually changed, but in both the performance is then available to be mobilized as authentic ethos in the pursuit of persuasive tasks.

The radical goal of undermining the legal basis of for-profit corporations is rhetorically and practically subservient, however, to the larger goal of solving the community's problems. In other words, in some cases the community rights ordinances do actually stay on books and prevent harm. The practical, instrumental function of the ordinances is the primary reason why most towns have enacted them.[28] Pre-Occupy editions of CELDF's quarterly newsletter emphasized the tangible problems facing rural communities. These newsletters, mailed out to supporters and archived on the organization's website, were one of the key ways that the organization publicized its work prior to 2011. They also published a book with Gibbs-Smith, a Salt Lake City press, in 2009 titled *Be the Change: How to Get What You Want in Your Community.*[29] In both the early newsletters and *Be the Change,* the organization actively made direct connections between specific environmental harms and the failures of state and federal government. They also argued that the resistance they encountered from corporate actors was proof of the value of their approach, as this newsletter article asserted: "If you thought our prior work raised the hackles of the corporate establishment, just wait. When communities begin writing new constitutional frameworks that place the rights of people, communities, and nature above the rights of property and commerce, you'll see the corporate hacks come running, as if we'd broken the last seal prior to Armageddon."[30]

This passage draws an equivalence between CELDF, communities, people and nature while contrasting them with the corporate establishment and corporate hacks. This idea of corporate hacks as those who engage in routine, instrumental communication, and who lack in the expression of authentic values, is central to how CELDF's rhetoric performs the division between authenticity and instrumentality. While seemingly "spoiling for a fight," the newsletters did not yet take the step of attempting to describe community rights ordinances as forms of strategic civil disobedience. What they did do was outline the practical, instrumental importance of the environmental issues to the communities attempting to pass laws banning fracking, preventing water extraction, stopping toxic sludge disposal, among other issues. The general importance of these environmental issues is encapsulated by a local Pennsylvania organizer in the March 2010 newsletter: "No good citizen invites trouble with the state. However, when the state is seen as failing to protect the health, safety and welfare of its residents, law abiding people are forced to challenge existing state law in order to save themselves and their families from unwanted harm and possible health risks."[31]

So, while CELDF's newsletters accuse corporate actors of treating communities as mere means to an end, they also emphasize the practical goals (rather than radical antistatist ideals) of their own organizing efforts. The result is that a comparatively instrumental form of activism is framed as authentically democratic in part by comparing itself to a *more* instrumentalist form of corporate power. A variety of different "unwanted harms" and "possible health risks" resulting from corporate incursions are scattered throughout issues of the newsletters as justifications and warrants for the concern and involvement of communities in rebellion against state and federal law. The upshot is clear: the community rights ordinances are not being enacted by municipalities with state oppression as the first or even primary problem that they seek to address. Instead, the long-term and more abstract and radical "democracy problem" is secondary to the immediate health and environmental effects of gas drilling, waste dumping, resource extraction, and various forms of pollution. This is not to say that CELDF itself sees the broader democracy problem (in which communities don't have the right to legislate about what happens in their own municipalities and state and federal government have been captured by corporate interests) as secondary; on the contrary, convincing others that it is central is a large part of what their outward-facing publications seek to accomplish. But the newsletters, designed to cultivate financial and practical support from allies and recruit additional towns to their methods, carefully present accounts of the specific, practical problems that the ordinances will hopefully alleviate in the short term. This aspect of CELDF's self-presentation has not changed over time—the enumeration of specific environmental and human harms is still central to how they describe their work.

CELDF's own instrumentalism has a populist, alarmist tone and is often urgent and emotional in its denunciation of corporate political influence and state and federal authority. Nonetheless, the communicative technics by which the towns come to embrace the "community rights" approach are of substantial value to the ethos performed by the ordinances as well as CELDF itself. Ordinances are passed through ballot initiative or votes in town councils after deliberation. Therefore, they are framed as examples of a democratic process of local community problem-solving through democratic talk,[32] a framing that carries a certain rhetorical weight regardless of the content and process of the talk itself. The democratic technic that is most central to CELDF's ethos is that of face-to-face conversation and collective deliberation between community members who reside in the same place together and come together to discuss and solve problems that impact them all. The sense of practical, instrumental problem-solving is actually central to CELDF's version of persuasive prefiguration. The techniques of "local democratic talk" and their associated instrumentalism are important to CELDF's ethos despite that it is itself a nonprofit organization with national and international activities rather than being rooted in a particular location. CELDF elevates the stories of local action by communities and citizens in small towns as the central dimension of its work, downplaying the role of its own legal team and elevating the organizing work of townspeople.

Face-to-face democratic communication does not demonstrate CELDF's ethos on its own, however. It is figured as "authentic" because of the ways it is distinct from the more instrumental communication technics of corporate actors and state and federal government. In the early stages of its work, the abstruse legal language of "corporate rights" was the central target of CELDF's critique of corporate and state communication.[33] In contrast to the manipulations of lawyers and the "misuse" of rights discourse to support corporate actions, CELDF juxtaposed the authentic, face-to-face, town-hall democracy of rural communities.[34] Both of these types of democratic communication are instrumental in some sense, but the "ends" of corporate incursions and community politics are, of course, quite different. Emphasizing the difference in the *means* of communication, however, is the way of producing a sense of which type of persuasion is more authentically democratic.

A 2009 book coauthored by a CELDF founder and a community leader, titled *Be the Change: Get What You Want in Your Community*, focuses carefully on the role of democratic talk and practical problem-solving in four municipalities.[35] Each chapter details the problems that led residents to organize. The book also, however, lingers on the details of what happened in town meetings and organizing meetings as the different municipalities worked toward addressing the problems with a community rights ordinance. For instance, this passage describes a dynamic Tamaqua meeting in which a consensus emerged even when a supervisor had initially seemed unsupportive: "Because of the overwhelming support, he too voted to pass the ordinance. After the unanimous vote, the entire room gave the supervisors a standing ovation."[36] Another passage described the process of debate in terms of the positions and investments of the participants: "At the meeting for public comment, most people judged the new ordinance a good thing. [. . .] Only two people spoke against the ordinance—a representative from the coal company and an attorney, who threatened the supervisor with lawsuits."[37] Some of the descriptions emphasize the rough-hewn quality of town meeting deliberation and suggest their place in a longer and more abstract tradition of direct democracy that is less "prefigurative" than it is nostalgic—but no less idealized. For instance, this passage describes local democracy in New England: "These small towns are also places where democracy is still practiced at the local level, in the form of town meetings. In the state of New Hampshire, the annual town meeting is a forum for the community decision making in which elected representatives, called selectmen, answer directly to those they represent. Any registered resident may attend the town meeting and vote on every article brought up for discussion. [. . .] Some town meetings can get rowdy, and some even stretch into the following day."[38] This vision of democracy positions the meetings about the CELDF ordinances in a long tradition of "town hall" imagery.[39] In this case, the "rowdiness" of the meeting suggests communication that is the authentic exchange of ideas between community members known to one another and comfortable disagreeing with one another.

The ethos of local town-hall democracy and its communication practices also appears in CELDF's early newsletters, which regularly contain a column written by a community organizer. The newsletters frequently provide details about exactly how deliberation and organizing have happened by regularly featuring writing by community leaders and organizers. Articles before 2012 describe how "residents may go to their selectmen or board of supervisors," or what happens "when we talk to our friends and neighbors about what the obstacles are to getting what we want in our communities."[40] Other articles even more directly reference the role of deliberative gatherings, describing what happened "after several public meetings at the Lancaster Town Hall"[41] or describing how the deliberative structure of the meetings created advantages for different participants: "Many residents, who faced three-minute limits on their public comments, were frustrated that Ms. Smith was allowed to speak without a time limit."[42] Attention to details such as these reflect the important place of democratic technics—the procedures of democracy—in the democratic ethos of CELDF.

It is this sense of authentic communication that CELDF strives to cultivate by describing not only town meetings but also the interpersonal conversations of local volunteer organizers working in and for their own communities. The book describes how one organizer "had a good reputation, so she went door to door, talking to every neighbor, and then she traveled further into outlying areas. She talked people into attending public meetings. She told them about the situation."[43] The organizer is then quoted directly: “The most important part of organizing is the day-to-day conversations with neighbors around kitchen tables. That’s what builds a strong movement, sharing information and expertise and opinions. The great thing is that people begin to talk, not only about what they are against, but more importantly, what they want their community to look like and what rights they believe they possess.”[44]

Democracy as grounded in neighborly talk and the everyday processes of conversation between people known to one another suggests a Deweyian vision of authentic community as the basis for political ethos. It is this sense of authentic democratic communication that CELDF strives to both publicize and cultivate—not just in its own ethos but also in current and potential organizers and community members. Each book chapter begins with didactic, bullet-pointed “Lessons Learned,” such as “Change begins at the grassroots level. Talk with neighbors and community members, encouraging communication and debate”[45] and “Learn to solve differences of opinion through conversation and by developing relationships.”[46] These “lessons” suggest the very specific technics that not only get things done but also define the elements of authentically democratic communicative technics.

In a speech given in 2005, cofounder and executive director of CELDF Thomas Linzey described their work as occurring in venues that were not even as dignified or formal as a city council chamber. Speaking in a Methodist church in Seattle, he told his audience: “From 1998 to 2002, we rarely set foot in a city councilman’s office. Or some other formal venue such as a college campus that folks generally travel around and speak to. Our meetings instead took place in a much different kind of place. Salt sheds, where our municipal officials keep salt to clear the roads in the winter. The basements of the smallest churches in the smallest of places in central Pennsylvania. One room school houses that are still used for municipal buildings in south and north-central Pennsylvania. Churches were always a common place for us to speak.”[47]

This account of the type of communication engaged in by CELDF staff emphasizes the connection between the everydayness of political talk and democratic authenticity. Linzey’s description of the physical structures of the municipality—the salt, the repurposed building, the smallness of the church buildings—paints a picture of democracy as intertwined with the everyday work of the community as people go about their business in a sort of timeless, cyclical process bound to the rhythms of necessity. This sense of democracy taps into the idea that democracy is part of everyday life. It also refers to democracy as a matter of solving community problems: salting the roads, providing needed education, and offering spiritual comfort and guidance.

In sum, during the period leading up to the Occupy demonstrations, CELDF's political ethos reflected a radical antistatism, pragmatic instrumentalism, and a commitment to the communicative authenticity of everyday talk and town-hall technics. Since CELDF stopped working within the environmental regulatory framework in 1998, it has firmly and frequently proclaimed its radical and whole-hearted opposition to state and federal environmental laws as they are currently configured. Unlike the Occupy demonstrations, however, CELDF combined this antistatist radicalism with a relentlessly instrumental approach to specific actions that attempt to concretely and materially improve the conditions of life in the communities they assist. The "town hall" communication described in their early publications suggests that CELDF's ethos is closely tied to the rural communities and their (somewhat idealized) practices of problem-solving, self-representation, and solidarity with one another. CELDF's books, newsletters, and other rhetorics seemed to be primarily oriented around two tasks: defending communities in legal forums against specific harms propagated by corporations and federal agencies and spreading the word to other communities that might be interested in trying their tactics. After Occupy, this orientation shifted as CELDF's ethos also came to be constituted by its practices of alliance building and persuasively publicizing its work to a broader audience.

Persuasive Prefiguration in CELDF

Since the Occupy demonstrations in 2011, CELDF has continued to help pass the same types of environmentally focused community rights laws, but the leadership of the organization expanded into additional types of work.[48] They still demonstrate a strong commitment to the antistatism, instrumentalism, and face-to-face technics described in the previous section. What has changed is that CELDF and other community rights advocates are increasingly attempting to publicize their approach and the philosophy of democracy that underlies it. Their new audiences seem to be leftists not necessarily directly involved (or about to become involved) in passing community rights ordinances.

CELDF has signaled its affinity with the Occupy demonstrations in a variety of ways. Two CELDF leaders gave a speech at the Bioneers conference in 2016 titled "Occupy the Law," in which they spoke about the work of the community rights movement as "legalizing civil disobedience" and described how communities are prohibiting their police from arresting community members "who seek to enforce their laws through direct action."[49] A 2017 documentary film about the community rights movement facilitated by CELDF features footage from the Occupy demonstrations with a CELDF leader arguing: "Whenever you pick those fights in the right way and people understand what the fights are about, that begins to uncolonize, to take the veil away from millions of people that are living out there, because those fights are about showing that we don't live in a democracy. And if you live in a corporate state, there's only one option left to you, which is to dismantle it and build something new."[50] This call to overhaul and decolonize the structure of government itself has resonance with prefigurative politics, especially as it has come into dialogue with contemporary antiracist activism. The film also creates a visual connection between community rights organizing and the act of marching in protest that was a central feature of Occupy's direct action tactics. CELDF's recent books are no longer with the lifestyle press that published *Be the Change* in 2009 and have either been self-published or published by PM Press, an anarchist press in Oakland, California. All these moves signal solidarity with Occupy and the traditions of anarchism, horizontalism, and prefigurative politics.

CELDF's forays into broadcasting its approach to community rights have facilitated greater collaboration on new issues. One of these was Denver's 2019 Right to Survive ballot initiative, which would have made urban camping legal in Denver.[51] The Right to Survive initiative was developed by Denver Homeless Out Loud, an organization that describes itself as "a horizontal and consensus-based group" that developed the specifics of the initiative based in part by surveying people experiencing homelessness.[52] The ballot initiative, which CELDF helped to draft, was supported by dozens of organizations in Denver. The measure was designed to overturn a ban on urban camping passed in 2012 and make houselessness more tolerable for many people living outdoors.[53] The Right to Survive initiative failed to pass in 2019 after it was challenged by a well-organized opposition campaign funded by local developers and real estate organizations.[54]

The failure of the Right to Survive initiative was framed by CELDF organizer Ben Price in this way: "This idea of a real human right to survive in the 21st century did not die in Denver. It was born—through the determination and commitment of the people who live here. Those who anted up $2.5+ million to defeat the measure have not ended the struggle for basic rights sparked by Denver residents advancing this remarkable initiative."[55] This framing of the failure of the 2019 initiative as a beginning rather than an ending is an extension of the way that CELDF has fundamentally adopted the strategy of persuasive prefiguration. The collaboration with an urban, horizontally inflected organization fighting for the rights of people experiencing homelessness illustrates how CELDF has adapted its instrumental emphasis on face-to-face and "town hall" democratic technics in dialogue with horizontalism. Part of this adaptation is leaning into *publicizing failure* in order to sharpen critiques of plutocracy. Instrumental failures are persuasively described by emphasizing how those failures demonstrate state and corporate repression and then using that demonstration as a recruiting and education tool. Failure to accomplish specific ends is touted as evidence of the necessity of the ongoing prefigurative performance of radical authenticity.

Failure is not the primary goal, of course. CELDF has continued to help rural communities enact their own laws as part of attempts to forestall immediate environmental harms. As they attempt to account for the specific failures of some local organizing efforts, however, they draw on horizontally inflected ways of framing political struggle to build an ethos that moves beyond claiming that local laws are effective instruments for immediately stopping environmental harm and stopping corporate incursions. Part of this transition is moving from the goal of effectively halting environmental destruction to the more long-term and abstract goal of changing the way people think about and believe in democratic values.

CELDF has increasingly framed the community rights ordinances as a form of *strategic civil disobedience* in which federal and state law is broken by passing local law.[56] Civil disobedience has a long history in leftist politics, of course, but CELDF's version of it is particularly anarchist in its orientation. This is because the stated goal of CELDF's civil disobedience is not only the immediate amelioration of harms with an appropriate reform but also the performance of a conflict that reveals the violent illegitimacy of the state itself. The aforementioned quotations from the Bioneers speech and the film *We the People 2.0* are simplified condensations of a much more in-depth and long-term orientation toward rebellion. Earlier publications contained elements of this framing, but the framing has subsequently been expanded and enhanced as some ordinances have failed and the organization has reckoned with those defeats.

The deepening of CELDF's commitment to conceptualizing their work as strategic civil disobedience has resulted in a more complicated ethos for CELDF as an organization. CELDF has taken on the tasks of broadcasting the successes and core philosophy of the community rights and rights of nature approach through conferences, books, blog posts, and films. They still provide direct legal aid to municipalities contacting them for assistance and circulate newsletters and press releases to communities they have organized with or might organize with in the future. They also, however, are increasingly forming collaborations with movement organizations, publishers, international NGOs, and media companies. This has meant supplementing the face-to-face deliberations of the Democracy Schools, town halls, and interpersonal conversations of local organizing with communication technologies such as film, more books, interviews, conference presentations, and digital periodicals.

These communication technologies are, of course, not exclusive to anarchist and horizontal democracy; they are most certainly also elements of liberal and even neoliberal democratic persuasion. In fact, they seem to have the potential to cut against the way that CELDF has claimed an authentic democratic ethos based on its radical antistatism, pragmatic instrumentalism, and face-to-face, local communication. Books, films, digital periodicals, and conferences are communicative technics that suggest more urban and distributed forms of communication than local, face-to-face meetings. Their longer-term influence and dispersed forms of production and circulation also mitigate their capacity to help with immediate instrumental problem-solving. One-to-many "broadcast" technologies such as books and films have a long-standing association with forms of elite expertise and persuasion, especially when contrasted with the types of face-to-face interpersonal communication that are required to organize a small community to pass a new law. Peters argues that historically, "By virtue of its reciprocity and interaction, dialogue is taken as superior to the one-way communiqués of mass media and mass culture."[57] Although this association is neither necessary nor inherent in broadcast media, CELDF has cultivated an ethos that is deeply reliant on the technics of democratic action conducted through comparatively idealized, dialogic means. The active, willing, and passionate self-rule of "the people" in the communities they work with are an absolutely central component of CELDF's presentation of their own work as democratic in the face of instrumental corporate and state incursions.

It would seem as though CELDF's increase in broadcast communication might run the risk of tainting the rebellious democratic ethos they have so carefully cultivated. As CELDF's long-term democratic ethos is performed through this expanded array of more instrumental, persuasive communication technics, how is its sense of authenticity holding up? As it has increasingly branched out through these communication technologies, CELDF has balanced its move into broadcast media by describing its activities as strategic civil disobedience with a quasi-prefigurative texture. The militant qualities of their own self-description present their broadcasting efforts as being part of a direct action in which attention to strategic law-breaking is part of raising consciousness, education, and planning for long-term change. Radical antistatism is a continuing feature of this ethos. But persuasive instrumentalism and conversational and deliberative communication in local forums continue to be no less essential. This is because CELDF actively justifies its radicalized civil disobedience based on the failure of the pragmatic, face-to-face communicative technics to succeed in every instance.

In this new range of broadcast media, CELDF continues to claim an authentic democratic ethos based on disclosing and narrativizing the instrumentalist and face-to-face core of its community rights ordinances. It is this orientation and its failure that justifies the democratic necessity of more abstract, long-term, and impractical forms of democratic communication. For instance, the film *We the People 2.0* (2017) begins with a series of stories about communities in which harmful corporate activities threatened the lives, employment, water, and health or other conditions of people living in US municipalities.[58] It describes in detail how and why some efforts to ameliorate these harms have failed to be effective and then describes how community rights ordinances have sometimes been able to protect communities that pass them. But before this hopeful story and the opening credits begin, the film opens with a series of aerial shots of landscapes, some pristine and some polluted, interspersed with footage from protests and maps of the United States marked with various environmental hazards. The background audio blends tense music and protest chants layered with narration: "A revolt is emerging in towns across America, and it started with a frustration. Why is it, that by almost every environmental statistic, things are worse now than they were 50 years ago? Why are communities still facing toxins, dumps, abuse and sickness? Even though we have tried, why can't we protect our health and welfare? A small nonprofit law firm found the answer to these questions when they tried in vain to stop the destruction. And the answer took them far beyond local problems. It took them to the very foundation of our country and to the question of democracy."[59] Before describing the details of community rights ordinances and the problems they have been passed to address, this cinematic introduction frames CELDF's work as part of a process of failure and persistence. CELDF "tried in vain" to work through regulatory agencies and then learned from its mistakes, demonstrating the authentic evolution of its radicalism based on the impossibility of working through established channels to solve problems.

The books CELDF has published about its own work go even further to explain the process by which the organization abandoned conventional legal challenges and began codifying community rights at the local level. In 2016, PM Press published a book titled *We the People: Stories from the Community Rights Movement in the United States* by Thomas Linzey and Anneke Campbell, the two authors of *Be the Change* (2009). Over half the material in *We the People* is the exact text of *Be the Change.* Each chapter is supplemented with updates about the outcomes of community rights organizing since the 2009 publication of *Be the Change.* This unusual publication format allows the authors to carefully map the trajectory of their activism in several instances. In addition to describing the details of lawsuits, corporate activities, municipal elections, and changes in leadership, *We the People* also describes changes in strategy: "CELDF has evolved the rights-based ordinances over the years to invite specific confrontations with the corporations, the state, and the courts. Mainly the ordinances are now designed to force the courts to pick a side and answer the question: Whose rights are greater within the community? The corporation's "rights" or the community's rights?"[60] This tactic of performatively *inviting* confrontations with corporate and state actors is the core feature of all strategic civil disobedience. Not only a principled, prefigurative refusal of bad law, this strategy is part of a larger persuasive effort to draw attention to bad law by performing the event of refusal.

Civil disobedience plays several different roles in demonstrating CELDF's ethos and authentic commitment to democracy. First, it is educative in the sense that it encourages conventional, self-protecting communities to see the bigger picture of the system of corporate power and state capture. In other words, it reveals a truth to them: that the state is not democratic. Second, civil disobedience of CELDF's type grounds and justifies a radical antistatism that is projected outward to a broader audience not directly involved in the specific local conflicts.

CELDF's broadcast communication clearly argues that the failure of local laws can awaken and radicalize community members by revealing a truth below the surface that they previously could not see. This position has been refined and more clearly stated as CELDF's tactics have played out and as they have collaborated with horizontally inflected groups. *We the People* argues that the moment when a local law is brushed aside by the judiciary is "a powerful teaching moment the first time a state directly intervenes, which clarifies for many that the enemy is not just the corporation but the state as its enforcer."[61] Some of CELDF's broadcast materials describe how this process works in very specific detail. For instance, *We the People* recounts the legal machinations of a gas company in Pennsylvania: "The [Pacific Gas and Electric Company] lawyers' strategy was to throw enough stuff to scare the supervisors, lots of depositions and subpoenas, including a motion for injunctive relief, as if they were being previously harmed by not being able to dump their fracking waste water in that one well in Grant Township."[62] These are types of events in which the disjunct between commonsense awareness of the needs of corporate actors and their legal strategies is heightened and enhanced to produce a descriptive sense of the vast power and domineering influence of corporations and government agencies.

CELDF has done extensive work to locate its civil disobedience and its educative capacities as part of the legacy of important historical movements in the United States. They argue in a PM Press pamphlet titled *On Community Civil Disobedience* that the movements for abolition and women's suffrage paved the way for their approach: "They failed time and time again. In the face of a strong and angry opposition, however, the Abolitionists were able to slowly build their movement by using the actions and words of slavery's defenders to bring more people into their fold."[63] Much like anarchist street protestors drawing violence from police, recording such interactions, and disseminating the recordings, the civil disobedience of CELDF relies on overenforcement of corporate rights in the courts to perform a demonstration of precisely that which is being resisted. They argue that they are following in the footsteps of historical movements because "by being forced to leverage corporate rescues and publicly illustrating (in real time) how the existing structure nullifies community lawmaking, more and more people arrive at the realization that the structure is inherently unjust and undemocratic."[64] In addition to raising awareness and revealing the truth about oppressive systems of government, "disobedience to existing laws was the hallmark of [abolitionist and women's suffrage] movements, and breaking existing laws served to both reveal the unjust nature of those laws and to portray what a new system of law would look like."[65] Not only does civil disobedience reveal the truth of the corruption of the state apparatus, it also demonstrates the vision of the future of democratic politics that is being fought for. Although CELDF does not use the term "prefiguration" to describe this aspect of civil disobedience, the resonance with the concept is clear. The "vision of the future of democratic politics" that CELDF helps to enact and defend is the authentic version, whereas the legal perfidy of corporations and the state is composed of purely instrumental, profit-driven motivations.

The authenticity of CELDF's ethos and the democracy it enacts is not merely a product of contrasting itself with instrumental corporate political tactics. The sense of authenticity is also produced through CELDF's ongoing commitment to the role of democracy in solving the practical, urgent problems of people harmed by corporate rights and their enforcement by the state. As we have seen, one of the long-standing critiques of radical and horizontal politics that strive primarily to raise awareness of state-based oppression is that they fail to really address the needs of the people on the ground in a way that leads to institutional change. CELDF itself critiques a related version of this approach as mere "advocacy" and argues that it generates a sense of an event without leading to lasting change. They closely associate such tactics with social media communication technologies and argue: "Advocacy—and organizations that fund advocacy—are tailored to generate the immediate headlines and create the online storm of e-mails, blogs, and web postings that suggest that *something is happening.* But a listserv does not a movement make."[66] The pragmatics and instrumental qualities of local, face-to-face and town-hall communication technics, on the other hand, make sure that political action revolves around solving real problems in people's lives rather than simply generating a sense that action is occurring.

In early 2015, cofounder Thomas Linzey began writing a regular column about CELDF's work and philosophy for *In These Times,* a leftist periodical about labor, climate, race, and economic issues. Under the section title "Rural America in These Times," Linzey argues that self-governance is a myth in the United States and that mere critique is an empty way to address it. In one column, he argues vehemently that radical politics must first attempt to address the practical problems of folks on the ground or else radical critique is worthless: "Those wishing to change that system must come to grips with the fact that people do not embrace wholesale change immediately. First, a corporate hog farm sites next door to them, or pesticide spraying threatens their organic garden. Logically, their focus is on stopping those activities that are threatening to harm them. When they learn that the current system of law forces them to endure those harms, they begin to understand that what is happening in their community is not an isolated example. Instead, their problem is structural, and not easily fixed. Without the community's firsthand experience, and the guidance of those who have seen it before, a critique of the system at the outset simply finds no purchase."[67]

On face, this analysis supports a general argument about the difficulty of educating people in the problems of structural power without concrete problems to attribute to that power. In addition, however, this passage demonstrates the authenticity of CELDF's ethos in the sense that it grounds its radicalism in an attention to the needs of specific people aware of and deliberating what is best for their communities according to instrumental logics. CELDF's pamphlet *On Community Civil Disobedience* figures this authentic ground of democracy as one that appears through the communicative trope of conversation, which implies a local, face-to-face process of talking about what needs to be done with others who are similarly affected. The pamphlet argues: "Movements start not only small but local—and they begin with people who are personally impacted by a harm legalized by the existing constitutional structure. They begin with conversations among people with shared belief systems and then broaden to an ever-widening group."[68] This way of describing the origins of authentic democracy as grounded in the talk of people who share a certain common sense is the core of CELDF's ethos even as the organization branches out into new political projects and technics. This way of claiming democratic authenticity is not only about face-to-face communication; it is also about how political action must have an instrumental character if it is to claim to be genuinely democratic. By continuing to stake this claim to ground their politics in the real, material, needs of specific people, CELDF is able to continuously produce a democratic ethos. The explicit priority placed on the principles that ground their strategic choices is put front and center even as their communicative technics diversify into work that embraces other types of action.

CELDF's ordinances and community legal assistance are instrumental in that they begin with specific goals (such as reducing pollution, sickness, waste, etc.) and then work toward accomplishing them through whatever means are effective. Considering these efforts against the backdrop of the more long-term, abstract, and revolutionary goals articulated by the organization's leadership, however, a different sense of "means" and "ends" emerges. This is the sense that the practical problem-solving "means" of the ordinances and the type of communication strive toward the long-term "goal" of constitutional change. On that "goal-level" the means of local politics are a demonstration of an instrumentalism as itself the means to a long-term goal, demonstrating that long term revolutionary or radical change is accomplished through the performatively consistent means of local democratic politics.

Conclusion

CELDF frames their practical decisions about how to forestall direct environmental and human harms as the basis for their antistatist, anarcho-libertarian philosophy. Their earlier instrumental posture (community rights ordinances and the rights of nature as a means to the end of saving human lives) has not been abandoned so much as it now serves as a justification (in that instrumentally effective action is not always or currently possible) for a far less practical effort to shift thinking about the relationship between democracy, corporate power, nature, and human life over the long-term and through communication technologies that suggest a more cosmopolitan (if not urban) horizontal ethos. Instrumental failure fosters prefigurative persuasion.

When instrumentalism is deployed as the guiding logic for pursuing concrete life-saving political goals, the performance of authenticity centers the instrumental logic itself. This centering, however, depends on the concrete goals being of a certain type. In the case of CELDF and its communities, the instrumentalism of corporate actors that the communities are in conflict with is the foil that makes it clear how something like "democratic instrumentalism" or "community instrumentalism" differs from doing what needs to be done in the name of profit-making.

Moreover, the communicative media of CELDF's work in small towns—the face-to-face conversation and town-hall meetings—operate as more than simply the means by which the anticorporate community goals are pursued. They are the means, but they are also the performance of a certain idealized nostalgic/prefigurative sensibility about the nature of democracy as itself an instrumental, problem-solving endeavor. This generates a performative consistency between the instrumentalism of the small-town work and CELDF's larger and more long-term radical goals as it builds bridges—albeit with a tension that emerges from the way that the more radical and long-term goals are ultimately pursued by descriptively and persuasively broadcasting the community rights movement rather than actually *engaging in* the more conversational and town-hall forms of communication that are touted.

CELDF's work shows us how persuasive prefiguration is not simply a matter of instrumentally broadcasting prefigurative internal organization. Instrumental logics have a certain idealized democratic shape of their own as they are linked to processes of cooperation, local problem-solving, or mutual aid. While the camp activities of the Occupy demonstrations (related to food, medical care, sleeping, and hygiene, etc.) were quite practical in certain respects, the performance of these activities as a form of public protest in semipublic space reduced or eliminated their instrumental character. In the case of the community rights ordinances and the "town hall" democratic processes that necessitated and facilitated them, however, we can see how instrumentalism is in fact at the core of a certain type of prefiguration. For strategic civil disobedience like CELDF's, the instrumentalism of "persuasive prefiguration" not only obtains in the outward-facing persuasion; it is also the central justification for the existence of the organization.

Conclusion

There are various explanations for why it has been so difficult for left politics to find purchase in popular politics. These explanations range from the psychoanalytic to the infrastructural.[1] Stuart Hall, for instance, argued that leftism's distance from popular politics was because of the absence of a moral-political vision appropriate to the character of the times rather than being the result of internal divisions within the Left.[2] Hall acknowledged that the failure of the Left to summon broad support was the result of its suspicion of "cultural politics," that is, its suspicion of deploying rhetoric embedded in the language of liberal democracy and its historical institutions. This suspicion has not vanished, but it also seems as though contemporary leftism is tying itself more closely to liberalism than it has for some time.

A larger historical question remains regarding whether radical refusal to engage with liberal institutions is responsible for the rise of neoliberal "third way" compromises, the evisceration of social safety nets, and ultimately the rise of right-nationalism in the United States. This question serves as the backdrop against which some left intellectuals have attempted to shift the definition of "radical" politics to include more institutionally engaged forms of politics. For instance, Cornel West, a public intellectual well known for his antiracist advocacy as well as his Marxist influences and commitment to democratic ideals, continues to espouse hope for the possibility of radical democratic politics engaged with governmental institutions. Post-Marxist intellectuals Chantal Mouffe and Ernesto Laclau have pointedly criticized autonomous Marxist intellectuals such as Michael Hardt and Antonio Negri for advocating a politics of "exodus" from the battle for hegemony in liberal political institutions.[3] Leftist political theorists such as Wendy Brown have pointed out that there are different kinds of state institutions and that while liberal states are not ideal, the neoliberal and subsequent plutocratic right-nationalist capture of previously liberal states is clearly much worse.[4] Lawrence Grossberg argued that we should continue to ask how antistatist politics can be combined with more hegemonic political tactics.[5] West, Mouffe, Laclau, Brown, Grossberg, and others have advocated for diverse and complex forms of political engagement that produce imaginative, radical, and even utopian alternatives while continuing to do the persuasive work of changing institutions in the here and now.

Occupy demonstrated, to a certain extent, how radical, anti-institutional "other worlds" might appear in full view of legacy media, unions, and liberal reformers. Occupy preserved the memory of the 1999 Seattle WTO protests, was heavily influenced by critical theories of politics, committed itself to embodied performance, refused engagement with a hierarchical state apparatus, and embraced communist values. In defiance of critics, the Occupy demonstrations put certain types of radical, neovitalist academic leftisms on display for a broad audience.

Many of the commendations of Occupy demonstrate a faith in the broadly "disruptive" capacity of embodied, live occupation, even though such capacities have been called into question.[6] A more modest claim seems easier to support: Occupy may have initially been a kind of startling disruption to politics as usual, but its long-term importance rests in how many of its performative techniques have been folded back into more common, less "interruptive" forms of politics. As a form of democracy, the Occupy demonstrations were certainly niche in the sense that they refused to acknowledge many traditional liberal institutions as democratic. But because the concept of democracy was so central to how the demonstrations took shape and were subsequently described, the demonstrations built and reinforced an important and influential set of performative tactics that have intersected with and re-invigorated progressive and even liberal notions of democracy—while also appearing in some kinds of antiracist activism. The resulting changes in the democratic ethos of advocacy and activism ensure the enduring legacy of the Occupy demonstrations.

I recall arguing over dinner with friends in 2011 about the importance of Occupy as the demonstrations were unfolding. It is with great discomfort that I remember now how I dismissed the demonstrations by vaguely parroting the language of a news article I'd read and actually thought little about: "What do they want? They don't have any demands!" My dear friends, their patience boosted by the fact that we had fed them dinner, explained carefully that Occupy was important because it was "changing the discourse" about inequalities in wealth and turning attention to the injustice of collusions between government and capital. This argument has always seemed difficult to dismiss. In fact, it might be the most widely claimed "success" of the demonstrations. I hesitate to include this brief anecdote because it makes me cringe. I do so to demonstrate the position of privilege, relative ignorance, and implicit white-liberal bias that I began from as I started to research anticorporate political rhetorics in the early twenty-first century.

Occupy certainly "brought attention" to some problems and in that sense was a "disruption" of the commonsense discourse about the relative fairness of economic opportunity in the United States. A decade later, it also may very well be that part of Occupy's lasting legacy has been to simply draw attention to a loose, overlapping series of concerns around campaign finance, deregulation of banking, predatory lending, rising education costs, low wages, contingent labor, employment precarity, housing insecurity, and related issues. When journalists revisit the meaning and impact of Occupy, they sometimes point to certain reforms related to these issues that have been pursued and enacted.[7]

This perspective on Occupy, however, seems far too simple. Occupy's rhetoric, its ways of presenting itself, its message, its radicalism, and its tactics have had far more complex effects on movement politics. The 2011 demonstrations have changed what "counts" as credibly democratic and how democracy is performed among progressives and liberals. These changes in ethos were increasingly apparent in the resistance to the Trump administration—but they were growing even before Trump was elected. Occupy may have "changed the discourse" by drawing attention to specific institutional problems that could be fixed with relatively straightforward reforms, but most of those reforms have yet to materialize. In spite of the overwhelming attention that economic inequalities and political corruption now receive from the Left *and* on the Right, a common assumption about the Occupy demonstrations is still that they *failed* to meet instrumental goals.

If specific policy outcomes directly connected to the actions of encampments are the measure, it is difficult to reach any other conclusion. In fact, the narrative of Occupy's failure (much like the narrative of its overwhelming importance from radical-left academics with preexisting commitments to its foundational philosophies) is overdetermined by the larger instrumental narrative that frames it. If the *only* measure of success is electoral, legislative, and judicial impact, Occupy was stillborn.

But the 2011 demonstrations did not generally attempt to extract concessions from state institutions. Instead, many of them aimed to enact a performative intervention in political language, values, and embodied practices of democracy. If the measure of radical democratic value is whether it performatively "disrupts" dominant instrumentalist liberal norms, did Occupy succeed simply by existing?[8] One way to avoid the recursive analytical problem of narrowly viewing Occupy in terms of whether it "succeeded" is to take the demonstrations as attempts to protest plutocracy while altering the way people speak, act, and organize democratically in non-governmental political groupings. Many nongovernmental organizations exist under this banner of reformist progressive and liberal democracy. Unevenly, but distinctly, we can see results from radical efforts to change how democracy is both practiced and pursued by such groups.

The emergence of the radical democratic ethos in the work of contemporary reformist organizations signals a new instrumental role for prefiguration in left politics, which in turn should prompt scholars of movement rhetoric to push toward more robust conceptualizations of *collective* ethos. As we saw in the Sanders campaign, the outward projection of the internal composition of an election campaign, for instance, is an important source of democratic credibility. The demands of community organizers in the fight for a constitutional amendment shows us how battles over the procedures for internally organizing can result in a shift in priorities away from technocratic expertise and toward the performance of authentically integrating the voices of those with no training in the law. Much like CELDF's radical framing of instrumentality (and its failure) as the core of its mission, the Sanders campaign and amendment advocacy have not abandoned instrumental, state-oriented reform efforts as they carefully craft their collective ethos. Instead, they find ways to adopt internal organizing and communication tactics that are more authentically democratic and can be projected outward as such to build their credibility and strengthen their collective voices as they instrumentally engage with various types of mass media, including social media. Moving beyond individualistic concepts of movement leadership and rhetorical production means adapting concepts such as ethos to collective political action.

One resulting implication of the emergence of the democratic ethos in progressive politics is a new way of conceptualizing "prefiguration" and its long tradition in radicalism. Rather than being a primarily internal phenomenon that erects a barrier to entry for newcomers unfamiliar with the rituals and procedures of radical democratic organizing, *persuasive prefiguration* attempts to educate, inform, and persuade a broader audience about the democratic values that guide the self-composition of an advocacy collective. This means that the horizon of success for such organizations is not just reforms enacted in and through state institutions. The horizon is also the awareness of democratic values enhanced and made visible in the conduct of the organization itself. This persuasive task is no less instrumental than working to reform state institutions, but it is less likely to be open to accusations of irony.

The Irony of Ethos

The only conceptualization of "ethos" adequate to capturing the emergence of prefigurative authenticity in less radical or more reformist democratic politics is one that foregrounds collective rhetorical production and does not shy away from the instrumental qualities of the concept. In fact, it is precisely because prefiguration is now being used persuasively that the link between "ethos" and prefiguration makes sense. Conceptualizing ethos as a ground, dwelling, or collective ethical spirit gives little to the study of movement rhetoric—except to the extent that such things are mobilized by a *specific* collective in the process of intentional political action that is persuasive and that has an instrumental component.

Most scholars who work with the concept have, of course, thought carefully about the relationship between cultural values and practices and the way they are mobilized by individual speakers. Investigating the ethos of *collective* political agents (campaigns, organizations, demonstrations, etc.) creates a whole new set of exciting possibilities for upending this somewhat stale "individual/social" theoretical frame. Collective political agents aware of themselves as actors with goals and internal cultures have the potential to project an ethos in all kinds of ways that are analogous to individuals but really quite distinct.

The most powerful dimension of the ancient Greek concept is how it demands emphasis on the relationship between what is said by a rhetor and what they have done, a feature of the concept which captures part of the dynamic of critique in left politics. This is precisely what is most central to the emergence of persuasive prefiguration. Internal prefiguration emphasizes performative consistency, but the emphasis has been on whether an individual conducts themselves according to the broader organizational values rather than using the organizational structure to support the outward-facing mission of the organization. One of the most notable aspects of the emergence of the democratic ethos (a type of persuasive prefiguration rather than internal prefiguration) in more reformist political organizations is the way that it reveals a long-standing critical dynamic between authenticity and irony in left rhetoric. Arguably there is no political rhetoric of any type completely free from instrumentalism, but accusations of instrumental rationality nonetheless ground accusations of irony in left critique. A robust and complex conceptualization of collective ethos that includes its instrumental dimension helps to explain the roles of irony and authenticity in left politics and scholarship.

The idea of an "authentic" culture, self, creativity, voice, or political representation has been repeatedly called into question by rhetorical, posthumanist, and Marxist critics.[9] Even Charles Taylor acknowledges some of the problems that arise when authenticity is assumed to be the expression of a true interior self.[10] Media critics such as David Shumway and Sarah Banet-Weiser have insightfully pointed out that modern striving for authenticity exists in dialectical tension with a fear of the inauthenticity, commercialism, and misrepresentations of mass media.[11] All the forms of left-progressive politics described in this book have borne this out; the performance of democratic authenticity was inseparable from their critique of performative contradictions in existing forms of democracy accused of "merely claiming" to be democratic.

A number of tricky questions that have been avoided up until this point, however, are these: Is any given action or text inherently ironic? Is democracy itself ironic? Or is irony something that must be pointed out by a critical observer from a certain vantage point that assumes access to the truth? The stakes of these questions are nothing less than the irony of the democratic ethos itself. Further, is any claim to "authentically" embody and enact democracy fated to be accused of ironic instrumentalism?

From Giambattista Vico onward, irony has been closely identified with a posture of detachment and observation.[12] In Hayden White's reading of *The New Science,* he argues that an immersion in "Christian truth" encouraged Vico to view the tropological trajectory of history into an ironic age as part of a larger dialectic.[13] Consequently, White argues, Vico's observation of irony was simultaneously implicated in the very dialectic it presumed to witness. Kenneth Burke agrees that true irony relies on the observation of a whole composed of multiple contradictory perspectives, but that "true irony, humble irony" recognizes that it needs the other that is ironically observed in order to define itself.[14]

If identifying irony requires the performance of an observational, supposedly noncontradictory perspective (such as that of a distant scholar), then the ethos of that observer relies on the identification of ironic performative contradiction somewhere else in order to perform its *own* supposedly contrasting internal consistency. In the performance of the democratic ethos, this means that the demonstration of internal consistency between political means and ends (what we have also been calling authenticity) happens in and through the critical observation of the ironic performative contradictions of a different and self-contradictory claim to enact democracy. The authenticity of the democratic ethos is no less a performance—and *potentially* also ironic—than a more contradictory version that it observes and critiques, but the clarity and force of the most recent performance of authenticity relies on the identification of some previous, more contradictory and hence ironic performance.

Because instrumentalism overtly embraces a distinction between means and ends, it creates an opening for the critic to perform the identification of ironic performative contradiction. The destructive force of this critique—which is basically the identification of performative contradiction and a direct attack on an ethos—is part of what has led Richard Rorty, for instance, to argue that ironic observations must be kept private.[15] Political instrumentalism, which is virtually required by liberalism, perpetually creates the risk of being accused of irony, especially when it happens in the context of the rhetoric of democracy.[16] All this is just to lay the analytical groundwork for a relatively simple claim: authenticity is always a performance that can also be accused of ironic self-contradiction. This means that the democratic ethos, as a performance of authenticity, can certainly be subject to the same accusation of irony. For such an accusation to do very much, however, it would have to be voiced by a collective agent performing the democratic ethos more effectively.

The absence of a firm set of activities or actions deemed essentially, finally, and permanently the most authentically democratic is a challenge for the theorization and analytical usage of the concept of the democratic ethos. It is also, however, its analytical strength—the concept names a dynamic, ongoing political process rather than a set of static criteria. This process of posing collective action as being more performatively consistent than the ironically instrumental efforts that have come before is one that has no end in sight and is beginning to be felt in aspects of left politics less directly concerned with elections, voting, economic inequality, and corporate power.

The Potential of Authenticity

Occupy's tactics have also, however, had a new life in the democratic practices of movement organizations associated with antiracist and pro-immigrant organizing and progressive election campaigns. These types of democratic practices are not exclusive to Occupy; many of them preceded the Occupy demonstrations and others have been important aspects of movement culture and rhetoric in the United States for some time. For instance, the ideas of "participatory democracy" and "civil disobedience" have obviously been closely tied to left politics in the United States since at least the student movements and Black freedom politics of the 1960s; they are also related to the radical-leftist intellectual formation expressed by Occupy.[17] Occupy did not invent most of its tactics out of nothing; it invented them out of previously existing movement rhetorics that were consolidated, tweaked, and then disseminated by the demonstrations.

The Occupy demonstrations in 2011 included a basic sort of consideration of the racial privilege of the majority of the participants (we can recall the "step up, step back" deliberative principle and the progressive stack) but it nonetheless remained an instantiation of North American horizontalism that was overwhelmingly white.[18] The extensive resurgence of the movement for Black lives in the wake of the murders of George Floyd and Breonna

Taylor has impacted the way movement groups self-organize in ways that are still unfolding. It seems to be leading to a greater emphasis on hiring and retaining BIPOC staff in nonprofit, campaign, and movement organizations that are not specifically focused on issues of racial justice, including some of the collectives described in this book. American Promise, for instance, seems to be working much harder than ever before to seek input from BIPOC leaders and staff on its general direction, membership recruiting, and messaging. Among activists focused on anticorporate democracy issues, the intersection of racial justice and voting rights has risen in priority. Bernie Sanders's second run for the presidential nomination, cut short by the COVID-19 pandemic, included a much stronger emphasis on involving staff and communities of color as well as registering and turning out young voters of color. The cofounders of the Community Environmental Legal Defense Fund have left the organization they founded to pursue work that is more informed by Indigenous and decolonial perspectives on the rights of nature. In all these cases, decolonialism and antiracism and their demands for greater accountability from white-liberal democracy advocates have shifted the way that organizations perform their own practices of self-composition. We can hope that these trends toward greater awareness of the racialized and colonial elements of democracy continue to prompt liberal political organizations to reevaluate their work.

Additionally, however, resurgent Black radicalism has been performing a relationship between authenticity and instrumentalism that bears a strong resemblance to the tactics of CELDF. The core demands of Black radical activism, including greater safety for Black bodies, less death, and more financial security, are much like CELDF's demands that communities be free of deadly toxins, fracking, and other problems. Although these types of threat to health and safety have very different histories, the failure of any state agency to meaningfully address such core demands is precisely the leverage that enables, justifies, and validates the expression of a radical refusal of conventional political channels in both instances. A practical, conventionally intelligible goal, because it is continuously refused, justifies radical means of pursuing it. The result is a politics that is ostensibly instrumental (trying to solve a practical problem) and one that uses a state-based refusal to justify a turn to radicalism.

As the influence of antiracist and decolonial perspectives continues to unfold, it will be important to carefully consider the ways that such values inform the performance of collective ethos in campaigns, nonprofits, and movement organizations: What does it mean to be authentically antiracist? How is performing collective antiracism similar and different to persuasively prefiguring democratic values? Is it appropriate to ask such questions? Are there forms of communication (e.g., face-to-face, deliberative, broadcasted) that connote antiracist authenticity? For instance, what does it mean to figure social media activity as collective "conversations" about race? These question and others will continue to be informed by emerging political action.

Whether or not there is enough overlap between emergent antiracist activism to warrant comparison with the types of political action described in these chapters, it is apparent that such activism does call majority white organizations to task for their failures to effectively commit to antiracist principles in deed rather than just in word; the whole concept of "performative activism" has emerged to pinpoint precisely this problem.[19] It is one thing to release a statement condemning racism and police brutality. It is another to recruit, retain, and prioritize BIPOC staff and leadership and make antiracist programming a priority or embrace Black radical perspectives on the need to reject white supremacist institutions. The performative consistency between what is said and what is done is important in antiracist advocacy, whether or not it should be referred to as "authenticity." The ironic instrumentalism of claiming antiracism in order to boost sales or avoid political pressure is wide open to the same type of critique levied against nominally democratic campaigns like those of Seattle's Democracy Voucher program.

As the radical values, communication tactics, and performative features of the Occupy demonstrations seep into the culture and tactics of liberal advocacy, it is important to consider that lamenting the integration between radical and conventional politics too quickly—as Thomas Frank did when discussing Occupy—is to fundamentally misunderstand the role of radicalism. Radical political tactics, values, theories, and forms of political action must be embraced on their own terms, as they shift the ways that advocates think, feel, and guide the evolution of collective actors. The consolidation of persuasive prefiguration and its relationship to internal prefiguration is a development that took time to happen and become recognizable. Rushing to critique the instrumental failures of radicalism—be they anticapitalist, antiracist, queer, or any other type of radicalism—is an effort to derail this process and suck the vitality out of political action. Likewise, of course, radical purity tests mute the force and potential of radical values and tactics as they spread and inspire.

The tension between authenticity and instrumentalism has been posed in stark terms by progressives, liberals, and leftists. If we recall Thomas Frank's scathing early critique of the Occupy demonstrations, we have a clear illustration of the vitriol and frustration that can accompany differing commitments to instrumentalism and authenticity. These differences have driven wedges between activists, politicians, organizers, and communities that might otherwise consider themselves allies, especially when it comes to reining in the worst implications of corporate power and capitalist logic.

The events of the Trump presidency created uneasy allies of liberals, progressives, radical leftists, and even some principled conservatives. The fragile coalitions wrought by opposition to right-wing extremism, however, are difficult to sustain when such extremism loses some of its institutional foothold. This means that differences between sympathetic political actors still play out in terms of their competing assumptions about the value of instrumentalism and authenticity. The Occupy demonstrations were a form of radicalism that engaged quite directly with instrumental logics, especially around questions of publicity, messaging, and outreach to news media. This shift from internal prefiguration to persuasive prefiguration for an audience—as a deliberate effort to persuade—marks the integration of a lightly instrumentalist approach with the type of horizontalist left radicalism that has often eschewed instrumentalism of any kind. Occupy's social and deliberative practices were not simply the enactment of more radically democratic and egalitarian modes of social life and decision making as part of an autonomous collective. They were done, quite deliberately, in public space and while being broadcast for an audience in order to persuade that audience of their value and long-term democratic vision.

Recognizing the radical, instrumental approach to media and audience helps to put to rest the excesses of the liberal condemnation of Occupy as well as the self-righteous radical refusal to see horizontal self-organization as anything more than an end in itself. In other words, the consolidation of the left-democratic ethos exhibited in the Occupy demonstrations confirms that left radicalism has engaged with instrumentalism all along. It also confirms that Occupy's effort to perform core precepts of that radicalism as part of an outward-facing persuasive demonstration has opened up new ways of conceptualizing how the balance between instrumentalism and authenticity is being negotiated by activists, politicians, advocates, and organizations in the wake of the demonstrations.

Recognizing the instrumental qualities of radical rhetoric like Occupy's should perhaps prompt a reconsideration of the status of instrumental conceptualizations of rhetoric. For several decades, scholarly emphasis on rhetoric as constitutive, on "intention" as unknowable, on context and trope as primary sites of explanation, and on affect, the body, space, and objects in general have all directed attention away from traditional conceptualizations of "persuasion" as a process of humans striving to generate intentional, specific effects. Rhetorical scholars no longer tend to ask what specific, intended effects of persuasive speech might have been or whether they were accomplished. The rejection of persuasion as a meaningful rhetorical concept happened alongside broader rejection in humanistic scholarship of individualistic human subjects such as authors or historical leaders as loci of explanation for the structure of texts, artworks, or historical events. Instead, explanation has turned to social forces, forms, material objects, technology, and other types of "actors." To center *ethos,* in the classical sense of the concept as the intentionally produced impression of goodwill, knowledge, good judgment, or other factors that assist in the accomplishment of a persuasive goal, is to return (to a certain extent) to acknowledging the instrumental character of political rhetorical and communication. When ethos is an expression of collective action, however, it is difficult to maintain the centrality of individual human subjects. With a figure such as Bernie Sanders, the role of an individual carries a certain importance within the collective of a campaign. But the actions and relationships of other individuals as well as the communication technologies that help form the collective are also important factors that contribute to the performance of the ethos of a collective subject. Acknowledging the instrumental elements of the rhetoric of collective subjects does not mean that such rhetoric is reducible to intentional, conscious human action. It does, however, allow for consideration of how instrumentalism nonetheless factors into how collectives are not just formed but attempt to perform political actions.

Instrumentalism, the acknowledgement and embrace of the difference between the means and ends of action, has been critiqued by twentieth- and twenty-first-century scholars particularly concerned with its manifestation in capitalism. These critiques, however, leave room for us to consider the range of political potentials in different ways that means and ends are put in relation to one another as collective actors attempt to accomplish specific goals while performing their self-constitution as part of a democratic ethos. More attention needs to be paid to how critical attention to means and various ends in any given political situation suggests different performances of collective ethos and different targets of criticism. There are multiple levels on which an observer or critic can identify means and ends and their relationship to one another. One level may contain a performative contradiction while another may not. Awareness of these levels and the distinctions between means and ends allows more precise pinpointing of the role of the act of identifying instrumentalism and irony and how it plays into the performance of ethos. Collective actors influenced by radical ideas such as horizontal democracy strive for performative consistency between their political goals and their methods of internal self-constitution. To ignore the instrumentalism of such political performances as *persuasive* efforts is to not only ignore a crucial dimension of them but also to refuse to allow them to, in a sense, speak for themselves.

The long association of the concept of authenticity with originality, creativity, and fidelity to cultural or individual genesis has made it difficult to see how performative consistency is also a form of authenticity especially relevant to the concept of ethos. Without a sense of the distinction between means and ends of political action—i.e., instrumentality—it is difficult to grasp the rhetorical stakes of attempts to bring means and ends into alignment or agreement as performative authenticity. In the context of political performance according to democratic values, authenticity is not just the matching of the means and ends of political action that strives to enhance and strengthen democracy. It is also the ideal of the absence of performative contradiction. Authentic, noncontradictory democratic action animates critiques of existing, problematic performative contradictions that wallow in their own ironic instrumentalism.

NOTES

Introduction

1. Frank, "To the Precinct Station"; Meredith Hoffmann, "Protestors Debate What Demands, If Any, To Make," *New York Times,* Oct. 16, 2011, http://www.nytimes.com/2011/10/17/nyregion/occupy-wall-street-trying-to-settle-on-demands.html; Miranda Leitsinger, "To Demand or Not to Demand? That Is the 'Occupy' Question," NBC News, November 17, 2011, http://www.nbcnews.com/id/45260610/ns/us_news-life/t/demand-or-not-demand-occupy-question/#.WU1S3DOZNE4; Taylor et al., *Occupy!*
2. Frank, "To the Precinct Station."
3. Ibid.
4. Burke, *Grammar of Motives*; Cintron, *Democracy as Fetish.*
5. Wanzer-Serrano, *Young Lords.*
6. Bray, *Translating Anarchy;* Clough and Blumberg, "Toward Anarchist and Autonomist Marxist Geographies"; Graeber, *The Democracy Project;* Hammond, "The Anarchism of Occupy Wall Street"; van de Sande, "Fight with Tools."
7. Grossberg, *We All Want to Change the World.*
8. Grossberg, *Under the Cover of Chaos.*
9. Acosta, "Occupy Wall Street: The Tea Part of the Left?," CNN, October 6, 2011, http://www.cnn.com/2011/POLITICS/10/06/tea.party.left/index.html; Michael Bauwens, "Gideon Rosenblatt and Lawrence Lessig: What To Think of the Framing of the #OccupyWallStreet Movement as a 'Tea Party of the Left,'" P2P Foundation blog, October 16, 2011, https://blog.p2pfoundation.net/gideon-rosenblatt-what-to-think-of-the-framing-of-the-occupywallstreet-movement-as-a-tea-party-of-the-left/2011/10/16; Sidney Tarrow, "Why Occupy Wall Street Is Not the Tea Party of the Left," *Foreign Affairs,* October 10, 2011, https://www.foreignaffairs.com/articles/north-america/2011-10-10/why-occupy-wall-street-not-tea-party-left; Chris Weigant, "Notes From the Occupation: Occupy Wall Street Is Not the Tea Party of the Left," *HuffPost,* December 6, 2017, https://www.huffpost.com/entry/guest-column-occupy-wall-_b_1084788.
10. Brown, *In the Ruins of Neoliberalism.*
11. Freeman, "The Tyranny of Structurelessness"; L. A. Kauffman, "The Theology of Consensus," *Jacobin,* May 27, 2015, https://www.jacobinmag.com/2015/05/consensus-occupy-wall-street-general-assembly/; Ober, *Demopolis*; Osborne, *Athens and Athenian Democracy;* Shein, "Whose Occupation?"; Smith and Glidden, "Occupy Pittsburgh"; Taylor et al., *Occupy!*, 46–49, 65.
12. Juris et al., "Negotiating Power and Difference"; Maharawal, "Radical Politics of Inclusion."
13. Frank, "To the Precinct Station."
14. Polletta, *Freedom Is an Endless Meeting.*

15. Boggs, "Workers' Control," 98.
16. Ibid, 106.
17. Ibid, 121.
18. Hardt and Negri, *Multitude.*
19. Azzellini and Sitrin, *They Can't Represent Us!*; Graeber, *The Democracy Project;* Holloway, "Power and Democracy."
20. Garsten, *Saving Persuasion.*
21. Foss and Griffin, "Beyond Persuasion."
22. Gross and Keith, *Rhetorical Hermeneutics;* Lundberg and Gunn, "Ouija Board."
23. Polletta, *Freedom Is an Endless Meeting.*
24. Polletta, *Freedom Is an Endless Meeting.*
25. Polletta, *Freedom Is an Endless Meeting.*
26. Chávez, "Counter-Public Enclaves."
27. Connolly, *Ethos of Pluralization.*
28. Hyde, *Ethos of Rhetoric.*
29. Gaonkar, "The Idea of Rhetoric."
30. Amossy, "Ethics at the Crossroads of Disciplines"; Doxtader, "Characters in the Middle of Public Life"; Halloran, "Aristotle's Concept of Ethos"; Sattler, "Conceptions of *Ethos.*"
31. Ryan, Myers, and Jones, eds. *Rethinking Ethos.* Conceptualizing ethos as a function of how individual rhetors appropriate and express various values is consonant with the general move to denaturalize culture in rhetorical studies after the introduction of feminism and critical theory. This has meant a transition from a universal and singular model of ethos (based on masculinist Aristotelian notions of good sense, good will, and good judgment) to an acknowledgement of how differences in cultures and discourse communities produce *ethē* (or multiple and overlapping ways of projecting one's character as part of persuasion that makes sense within a cultural framework for a specific audience). Ruth Amossy, for instance, frames ethos in the context of the relationship between the individual rhetor and the culture in which they participate. *Culture* affirms and exceeds, or even determines, individuals and their deployment of those values for persuasive ends. *Cultures,* however, are also plural, diverse, and in frequent conflict with one another. Ryan et al. is another example of this general trend.
32. Carey, "The Mass Media and Democracy"; Jasanoff, "Future Imperfect."
33. Thimsen, "The Lessons of Community Rights Ordinances."
34. Stiegler, *Technics and Time.*
35. Connolly, *Ethos of Pluralization,* xiv.
36. Connolly, *Ethos of Pluralization*, 180; Jasanoff, "Future Imperfect."
37. Jasanoff, "Future Imperfect," 4.
38. Taylor, *The Archive and the Repertoire.*
39. Derrida, *Dissemination.*
40. Halkin, "Outside the Indigenous Lens," 160; Martinez-Torres, "Civil Society"; Wolfson, "From the Zapatistas to Indymedia."
41. Carey, "Commentary"; Peters, "Satan and Savior."
42. Community Environmental Legal Defense Fund, "CELDF Celebrates 20 Years!," CELDF (website), published December 2, 2015, https://celdf.org/2015/12/celdf-celebrates-20-years/.
43. Dixon, *Another Politics Is Possible.*

CHAPTER ONE

The Democratic Ethos of Authenticity in the Occupy Wall Street Demonstrations

1. Castells, *Networks of Outrage and Hope;* Cram et al., "Civic Sights"; DeLuca et al., "Occupy Wall Street on the Public Screens of Social Media"; Deseriis, "The People's Mic"; Ewalt et al., "Activism, Deliberation, and Networked Public Screens"; Happe, "Parrhesia, Biopolitics, and Occupy"; Jones, "Compensatory Division in the Occupy Movement"; Kavada, "Creating the Collective"; Kelp-Stebbins and Schifani, "The Medium Is the Masses"; May and Synk, "Contradiction and Overdetermination in Occupy Wall Street"; Maharawal, "Radical Politics of Inclusion"; Min, "Occupy Wall Street and Deliberative Decision-Making"; Protevi, "Semantic, Pragmatic, and Affective Enactment at OWS"; Radovac, "Mic Check"; Winslow, "'Not Exactly a Model of Good Hygiene.'"
2. Taussig, "I'm So Angry I Made a Sign."
3. Ibid.
4. Gitlin, *Occupy Nation.*
5. Butler, *Notes toward a Performative Theory.*
6. DeLuca et al., "Occupy Wall Street on the Public Screens of Social Media"; Kavada, "Creating the Collective."
7. Castells, *Networks of Outrage and Hope.*
8. Karpf, "Digital Politics After Trump."
9. Castells, *Networks of Outrage and Hope;* DeLuca et al., "Occupy Wall Street on the Public Screens of Social Media."
10. Todd Gitlin, "Where Are the Occupy Protestors Now?" *Guardian* (US edition), June 17, 2014, https://www.theguardian.com/cities/2014/jun/17/where-occupy-protesters-now-social-media; Josh Harkinson, "Occupy Wall Street—Where Are They Now?" *Mother Jones,* September 17, 2012, http://www.motherjones.com/politics/2012/09/occupy-wall-street-anniversary-where-are-they-now/; Michael Levitin, "The Triumph of Occupy Wall Street," *Atlantic,* June 10, 2015, https://www.theatlantic.com/politics/archive/2015/06/the-triumph-of-occupy-wall-street/395408/; Accra Shepp, "Occupy Wall Street: Where Are They Now?," *New York Times,* September 17, 2016, https://www.nytimes.com/interactive/2016/09/17/opinion/Occupy-Wall-Street.html?mcubz=0&_r=0.
11. Kate Linthicum, "Occupy Movement Protesters Fight On—Now in Support of Bernie Sanders," *Los Angeles Times,* February 1, 2016, http://www.latimes.com/nation/politics/la-na-0201-sanders-occupy-20160201-story.html; Eric Westervelt, "Message to Resistors from Occupy Co-Creator: Stop Protesting. Run for Office," NPR, March 28, 2017, http://www.npr.org/2017/03/28/520971836/message-to-resistors-from-occupy-co-creator-stop-protesting-run-for-office; White, *The End of Protest.*
12. Reich, "The Organizational Trace of an Insurgent Moment."
13. Adam Gabbatt, "Former Occupy Wall Street Protestors Rally around Bernie Sanders Campaign," *Guardian* (US edition), September 17, 2015, https://www.theguardian.com/us-news/2015/sep/17/occupy-wall-street-protesters-bernie-sanders; Gregory Krieg, "Occupy Wall Street Rises Up for Sanders," CNN, April 13, 2016, https://www.cnn.com/2016/04/13/politics/occupy-wall-street-bernie-sanders

-new-york-primary/index.html; Tessa Stuart, "In Battle for New York, Occupy Wall Streeters Turn Out for Bernie," *Rolling Stone,* April 19, 2016, https://www.rollingstone.com/politics/politics-news/in-battle-for-new-york-occupy-wall-streeters-turn-out-for-bernie-178430/.

14. Move to Amend, "Endorsing Organizations" (website), accessed July 20, 2018, https://movetoamend.org/organizations.
15. Greene and Kuswa, "'From the Arab Spring to Athens"; Pason, "Phenomenon or Meaning?"; Varga, "Occupying the Picket Line"; Zemlicka and Hazeltine, "The Reality of Contingency."
16. DeLuca et al., "Occupy Wall Street on the Public Screens of Social Media."
17. Bray, *Translating Anarchy.*
18. Bray, *Translating Democracy;* Schneider, *Thank You, Anarchy.*
19. Nathan Jurgenson, "Occupy Audio: The Soundscape of the Protests," *Atlantic,* November 28, 2011, https://www.theatlantic.com/technology/archive/2011/11/occupy-audio-the-soundscape-of-the-protests/249123/; Richard Kim, "We Are All Human Microphones Now," *Nation,* October 3, 2011, https://www.thenation.com/article/archive/we-are-all-human-microphones-now/; Una Spenser, "Witnessing #occupywallstreet: The Power . . . of the People . . . 's Mic," DailyKos, September 29, 2011, http://www.dailykos.com/story/2011/09/29/1021211/-Witnessing-occupywallstreet-the-power-of-the-people-s-mic.
20. Jeff Sharlet, "Inside Occupy Wall Street: How a Bunch of Anarchists and Radicals with Nothing but Sleeping Bags Launched a Nationwide Movement," *Rolling Stone,* November 24, 2011, http://www.rollingstone.com/politics/news/occupy-wall-street-welcome-to-the-occupation-20111110.
21. Carrie Kahn, "Battle Cry: Occupy's Messaging Tactics Catch On," NPR, December 6, 2011, http://www.npr.org/2011/12/06/142999617/battle-cry-occupys-messaging-tactics-catch-on.
22. Bray, *Translating Anarchy;* Schneider, *Thank You, Anarchy.*
23. Bray, *Translating Anarchy;* Gitlin, *Occupy Nation;* Schneider, *Thank You, Anarchy.*
24. Levitin, "The Triumph of Occupy Wall Street."
25. Buckley, "The Arc of Communism"; Reich, "Occupy Democracy"; Taylor et al., *Occupy!* 2, 4–6.
26. *Yes! Magazine,* "Declaration of the Occupation of New York City," Oct. 4, 2011, http://www.yesmagazine.org/people-power/declaration-of-the-occupation-of-new-york-city.
27. Gitlin, *Occupy Nation,* 110.
28. Bray, *Translating Anarchy*; Polletta, *Freedom Is an Endless Meeting.*
29. Markovits, *The Politics of Sincerity*; Shumway, "Authenticity"; Trilling, *Sincerity and Authenticity.*
30. Taylor, *The Ethics of Authenticity.*
31. Frank, "To the Precinct Station."
32. Taylor, *The Archive and the Repertoire.*
33. Vogel, *Stolen Time.*
34. Pleyers and Touraine, *Alter-globalization.*
35. Azzellini and Sitrin, *They Can't Represent Us.*
36. Azzellini and Sitrin, *They Can't Represent Us;* Castañeda, "The Indignados of Spain"; Nail, "Zapatismo and the Global Origins of Occupy."
37. Greene and Kuswa, "'From the Arab Spring to Athens."
38. Bray, *Translating Anarchy.*

39. Azzellini and Sitrin, *They Can't Represent Us;* Graeber, *Democracy Project;* Polletta, *Freedom Is an Endless Meeting.*
40. Polletta, *Freedom Is an Endless Meeting.*
41. Chávez, "Counter-Public Enclaves."
42. della Porta, *Social Movements in Times of Austerity.*
43. Polletta and Hoban, "Why Consensus?"
44. Alinsky, *Rules for Radicals.*
45. Polletta, *Freedom Is an Endless Meeting*; Sitrin, *Everyday Revolutions.*
46. Some strongly anarchist conceptualizations of "direct action" limit the term to political activities that break the law anonymously. Although this specific understanding of "direct action" is important, I am working here with a broader conceptualization of "direct action" that includes the type of civil disobedience conducted by individuals and groups who disclose their identities.
47. The role of democratic practices and ideals in these Latin American movements is described by many. They include della Porta, *Austerity;* and Sitrin, *Everyday Revolutions.*
48. Dixon, *Another Politics Is Possible.*
49. Polletta, *Freedom Is an Endless Meeting.*
50. Grossberg, *We All Want to Change the World,* 196.
51. Polletta and Hoban, "Why Consensus?"
52. Bray, *Translating Anarchy;* Schneider, *Thank You, Anarchy.*
53. Bray, *Translating Anarchy;* Gitlin, *Occupy Nation;* Schneider, *Thank You, Anarchy.*
54. Bray, *Translating Anarchy;* Gitlin, *Occupy Nation;* Schneider, *Thank You, Anarchy.*
55. New York City General Assembly, "QuickFind: Summaries, Minutes, and Livetweet Links," NYCGA Official Website, November 23, 2011, Internet Archive, https://wayback.archive-it.org/2950/20111227014512/http://www.nycga.net/2011/11/23/quick-find-minutes-livetweet-links/.
56. Bray, *Translating Anarchy;* Schneider, *Thank You Anarchy;* Taylor et al., *Occupy!*
57. Happe, "Parrhesia, Biopolitics, and Occupy"; Pason, "The Revolution Will Not Be (Food) Reviewed."
58. This episode of Occupy is described in several places, including Mark Bray's *Translating Anarchy* and in Taylor et al., *Occupy!*
59. The distinction between these two groups does not map easily onto the distinction that some commentators have made between the "occupiers," or those who lived in the camp, and the "organizers," or those who lived off-site but invested time, energy, and money into planning events, speaking with the press, coordinating resources, and trying to think about next steps. The distinction I have in mind concerns more a set of activities that both groups (campers and those living off-site) participated in at different moments. Many occupiers who were living in the camp, for instance, seemed to be the most active on protests and marches.
60. New York City General Assembly, "General Assembly Minutes 9/18/11," NYCGA Official Website, September 18, 2011, Internet Archive, https://wayback.archive-it.org/2950/20111227070255/https://www.nycga.net/2011/09/18/assembly-minutes-3pm-91811/.
61. New York City General Assembly, "NYCGA Minutes 10/20/2011," NYCGA Official Website, October 20, 2011, Internet Archive, https://wayback.archive-it.org/2950/20111227084803/http://www.nycga.net/2011/10/20/nycga-10202011/; New York City General Assembly, "NYCGA Minutes 10/28/2011," NYCGA Official Website, October 28, 2011, Internet Archive, https://wayback.archive-it.org

/2950/20111227070030/https://www.nycga.net/2011/10/28/nycga-minutes-1028 2011/.

62. Dixon, *Another Politics*; Polletta, *Freedom Is an Endless Meeting;* Sitrin, *Everyday Revolutions.*
63. Bray, *Translating Anarchy.*
64. Polletta and Hoban, "Why Consensus?"
65. Danisch, *Building a Social Democracy*; Min, "Occupy Wall Street and Deliberative Decision-Making."
66. New York City General Assembly, "NYCGA Minutes 10/4/2011," NYCGA Official Website, October 4, 2011, Internet Archive, https://wayback.archive-it.org/2950/20111227085031/http://www.nycga.net/2011/10/04/general-assembly-minutes-104-7pm/.
67. New York City General Assembly, "NYCGA Minutes 10/25/2011," NYCGA Official Website, October 25, 2011, Internet Archive, https://wayback.archive-it.org/2950/20111227070030/https://www.nycga.net/2011/10/28/nycga-minutes-1028 2011/.
68. Bray, *Translating Anarchy;* Gitlin, *Occupy Nation.*
69. Polletta and Hoban, "Why Consensus?"
70. New York City General Assembly, "General Assembly Minutes 9/29/2011, 7PM," NYCGA Official Website, September 29, 2011, Internet Archive, https://wayback.archive-it.org/2950/20111227064546/http://www.nycga.net/2011/09/29/general-assembly-minutes-929-7pm/; Maharajah, "Standing Up."
71. New York City General Assembly, "General Assembly Minutes 9/29 7PM"; Maharajah, "Standing Up."
72. Habiba Alcindor, "How People of Color Occupy Wall Street," *Nation,* November 4, 2011, https://www.thenation.com/article/archive/how-people-color-occupy-wall-street/; Meerkat Media Collective, "Consensus (Direct Democracy @ Occupy Wall Street)," filmed October 13, 2011, in New York City, YouTube video, 8:25, https://www.youtube.com/watch?v=6dtD8RnGaRQ&t=256s.
73. Polletta, *Freedom Is an Endless Meeting.*
74. Azzellini and Sitrin, *They Can't Represent Us;* Sitrin, *Everyday Revolutions.*
75. Sitrin, *Everyday Revolutions,* 3–4.
76. New York City General Assembly, "General Assembly Minutes 9/19 10 PM," NYCGA Official Website, September 19, 2011, Internet Archive, https://wayback.archive-it.org/2950/20111227070247/https://www.nycga.net/2011/09/19/general-assembly-minutes-919-10pm/; New York City General Assembly, "General Assembly Minutes 9/21/2011," NYCGA Official Website, September 21, 2011, Internet Archive, https://wayback.archive-it.org/2950/20111227070220/https://www.nycga.net/2011/09/21/nycga-minutes-9212011/.
77. New York City General Assembly, "NYCGA Minutes 10/19/2011," NYCGA Official Website, October 19, 2011, Internet Archive, https://wayback.archive-it.org/2950/20111227084817/http://www.nycga.net/2011/10/19/nycga-minutes-10192011/; New York City General Assembly, "Minutes 10/25/2011."
78. New York City General Assembly, "NYCGA Minutes 9/28/2011," NYCGA Official Website, September 28, 2011, Internet Archive, https://wayback.archive-it.org/2950/20111227070127/https://www.nycga.net/2011/09/28/general-assembly-minutes-928-2pm/; New York City General Assembly, "NYCGA Minutes 10/2/2011, 7:30pm," NYCGA Official Website, October 2, 2011, Internet Archive, https://wayback.archive-it.org/2950/20111227085056/http://www.nycga.net/2011

/10/02/308/; New York City General Assembly, "NYCGA Minutes 10/3/2011, 7:30pm," NYCGA Official Website, October 3, 2011, Internet Archive, https://wayback.archive-it.org/2950/20111227085044/http://www.nycga.net/2011/10/03/305/; New York City General Assembly, "Minutes 10/4/2011"; New York City General Assembly, "NYCGA Minutes 10/17/2011," NYCGA Official Website, October 17, 2011, Internet Archive, https://wayback.archive-it.org/2950/20111227084844/http://www.nycga.net/2011/10/17/nycga-minutes-101711/.

79. Happe, "Parrhesia, Biopolitics, and Occupy"; Pason, "Occupy Kitchen."

80. Bray, *Translating Anarchy;* DeLuca et al., "Occupy Wall Street on the Public Screens of Social Media."

81. New York City General Assembly, "Minutes 10/20/2011."

82. Castells, *Networks of Outrage and Hope;* Cram et al., "Civic Sights"; DeLuca et al., "Occupy Wall Street on the Public Screens of Social Media"; Ewalt et al., "Activism, Deliberation, and Networked Public Screens"; Jones, "Compensatory Division in the Occupy Movement."

83. Kerbel and Bowers, *Next Generation Netroots;* Lessig, *The USA Is Lesterland.*

84. Bray, *Translating Anarchy;* New York City General Assembly, "General Assembly Minutes 9/29 7PM."

85. New York City General Assembly, "Minutes 10/2/2011"; New York City General Assembly, "NYCGA Minutes 10/1/2011," NYCGA Official Website, October 1 2011, Internet Archive, https://wayback.archive-it.org/2950/20111227070109/https://www.nycga.net/2011/10/01/general-assembly-minutes-930-7pm/; New York City General Assembly, "NYCGA Minutes 10/16/2011," NYCGA Official Website, October 16, 2011, Internet Archive, https://wayback.archive-it.org/2950/20111227084858/http://www.nycga.net/2011/10/16/nycga-minutes-10162011/.

86. New York City General Assembly, "NYCGA Minutes 10/21/2011," NYCGA Official Website, October 21, 2011, Internet Archive, https://wayback.archive-it.org/2950/20111227084747/http://www.nycga.net/2011/10/21/nycga-minutes-10212011/.

87. New York City General Assembly, "Minutes 10/20/2011"; New York City General Assembly, "NYCGA Minutes 10/23/2011," NYCGA Official Website, October 23, 2011, Internet Archive, https://wayback.archive-it.org/2950/20111227084739/http://www.nycga.net/2011/10/23/nycga-minutes-10232011/.

88. New York City General Assembly, "Minutes 10/28/2011."

89. New York City General Assembly, "NYCGA Minutes 10/13/2011," NYCGA Official Website, October 13, 2011, Internet Archive, https://wayback.archive-it.org/2950/20111227084920/http://www.nycga.net/2011/10/13/nycga-transcript-10132011/.

90. Logan Burruss, "Occupy Wall Street Has Money to Burn," CNN, November 21, 2011, https://money.cnn.com/2011/11/21/news/occupy_wall_street_money/index.htm; John Carney, "Occupy Wall Street Flush with Cash, But Not from Soros," CNBC, October 13, 2011, https://www.cnbc.com/id/44892333; Jeff Gordinier, "Want to Get Fat on Wall Street? Try Protesting," *New York Times,* October 11, 2011, https://www.nytimes.com/2011/10/12/dining/protesters-at-occupy-wall-street-eat-well.html; Adrienne Jeffries, "More Money, More Problems: How Occupy Wall Street Is Really Funded [Updated]," *Observer,* October 14, 2011, https://observer.com/2011/10/more-money-more-problems-how-occupy-wall-street-is-really-funded/.

91. Ben Berowitz, "Occupy Wall Street Finds Money Brings Problems Too," Reuters,

November 2, 2011, https://www.reuters.com/article/us-usa-wallstreet-protests-money/occupy-wall-street-finds-money-brings-problems-too-idUSTRE7A12DY20111102; Arun Venugopal, "Newly Acquired Wealth Gives Occupy Wall Street Opportunities and Challenges," WNYC, November 3, 2011, https://www.wnyc.org/story/168280-blog-newly-acquired-wealth-gives-occupy-wall-street-opportunities-and-challenges/.

92. New York City General Assembly, "Minutes 9/21/2011."
93. Radovac, "Mic Check"; Vogelaar, "Staging Revolution."
94. Graeber, *Democracy Project,* 240–58.
95. Bray, *Translating Anarchy;* Graeber, *Democracy Project,* 234.
96. Bray, *Translating Anarchy*, 135.
97. Graeber, *Democracy Project*.
98. John Holloway, *Change the Word Without Taking Power.*
99. Rehmann, "Occupy Wall Street and the Question of Hegemony"; Rowe and Carroll, "Reform or Radicalism."
100. Bray, *Translating Anarchy.*
101. Bray, *Translating Anarchy;* Gitlin, *Occupy Nation;* Polletta, *Freedom Is an Endless Meeting.*
102. Graeber, *Democracy Project;* Polletta, *Freedom is an Endless Meeting.*
103. Graeber, *Democracy Project;* Joosse, "Elves, Environmentalism, and 'Eco-Terror.'"
104. Bakunin, *Bakunin on Anarchism.*
105. Bray, *Translating Anarchy.*
106. Rasza, "Beyond 'Riot Porn.'"
107. Audrey et al., *99%: The Occupy Wall Street Collaborative Film.*
108. Craig Calhoun, "Societas: Evicting the Public Sphere at Zuccotti Park," filmed November 17, 2011, in New York City, YouTube video, 4:05, https://www.youtube.com/watch?v=G7hLrlLItPk; Vogelaar, "Staging Revolution."
109. Rasza, "Beyond 'Riot Porn.'"
110. Graeber, *Democracy Project.*
111. Bray, *Translating Anarchy.*
112. New York City General Assembly, "NYCGA Minutes 9/30/2011, 7PM," NYCGA Official Website, September 30, 2011, Internet Archive, https://wayback.archive-it.org/2950/20111227070104/https://www.nycga.net/2011/09/30/317/.
113. Al Baker et al., "Police Arrest More Than 700 Protestors on Brooklyn Bridge," *New York Times,* October 1, 2011, https://cityroom.blogs.nytimes.com/2011/10/01/police-arresting-protesters-on-brooklyn-bridge/.
114. Baker et al., "Police Arrest More Than 700"; NPR Staff and Wires, "Hundreds Arrested after Protest on Brooklyn Bridge," NPR, October 1, 2011, https://www.npr.org/2011/10/01/140983353/about-500-arrested-after-protest-on-brooklyn-bridge; Matt Wells, "Occupy Wall Street—The Story of the Brooklyn Bridge 'Trap,'" *Guardian* (US edition), October 3, 2011, https://www.theguardian.com/world/blog/2011/oct/03/occupy-wall-street-brooklyn-bridge-arrests.
115. Frank, "To the Precinct Station."
116. Frank, "To the Precinct Station"; Rick Perlstein, "Why Occupy Needs to Start Making Demands," *Rolling Stone,* March 22, 2012, https://www.rollingstone.com/politics/news/why-occupy-needs-to-start-making-demands-20120321.
117. Holloway, *Change the World,* Graeber, *Democracy Project;* Polletta, *Freedom Is an Endless Meeting;* Sitrin, *Everyday Revolutions.*
118. Pason, "Occupy Kitchen"; Winslow, "'Not Exactly a Model of Good Hygiene.'"

119. Levitin, "The Triumph of Occupy Wall Street."
120. Murray, "The Sphere, the Screen, and the Square"; Pietrucci, "YES WE CAMP!"

CHAPTER TWO

The Seattle Democracy Voucher Campaign and Ironic Instrumentalism

1. Brennan Center for Justice, "The Case for Small Donor Financing in New York"; Alan Greenblatt, "The New Strategy for Limiting Money's Role in Elections," *Governing,* August 31, 2017, https://www.governing.com/topics/politics/gov-public-finance-campaigns-elections.html.
2. Bruce Ackerman and Ian Ayres, "Democracy Dollars' Can Give Every Voter a Real Voice in American Politics" (opinion), *Washington Post,* November 5, 2015, https://www.washingtonpost.com/opinions/democracy-dollars-can-give-every-voter-a-real-voice-in-american-politics/2015/11/05/48100ae8-8345-11e5-a7ca-6ab6ec20f839_story.html?utm_term=.cadc37f7696e; Sarah Kliff, "Seattle's Radical Plan to Fight Big Money in Politics," *Vox,* November 5, 2018, https://www.vox.com/2018/11/5/17058970/seattle-democracy-vouchers; Lawrence Lessig, "More Money Can Beat Big Money" (opinion), *New York Times,* November 16, 2011, https://www.nytimes.com/2011/11/17/opinion/in-campaign-financing-more-money-can-beat-big-money.html; Mark Schmitt, "Seattle's New Political Vouchers Are an Experiment. How Will We Know If They're Working?" *Vox,* November 16, 2015, https://www.vox.com/polyarchy/2015/11/16/9743144/seattle-political-vouchers.
3. Josh Cohen, "'Democracy Vouchers' Aim to Amplify Low-Income Voices, to Conservative Ire," *Guardian* (US edition), July 7, 2017, https://www.theguardian.com/us-news/2017/jul/07/democracy-vouchers-seattle-politics-low-income-homeless; Lee Drutman, "Maine Passes Ranked-Choice Voting, South Dakota Approved Campaign Vouchers," *Vox,* November 9, 2016, https://www.vox.com/polyarchy/2016/11/9/13574478/maine-ranked-choice-voting-south-dakota-campaign-vouchers; Greenblatt, "Limiting Money's Role"; Mark Lisheron, "Seattle 'Democracy Dollars' Case That Could Influence Austin Goes to State High Court," *Texas Monitor,* January 9, 2019, https://texasmonitor.org/seattle-democracy-dollars-case-that-could-influence-austin-goes-to-state-high-court/; Tanvi Misra, "More Cities Want to Embrace 'Democracy Vouchers,'" *CityLab,* August 8, 2018, https://www.citylab.com/equity/2018/08/more-cities-want-to-embrace-democracy-dollars/566801/.
4. These include Every Voice, Represent.Us, Public Citizen, and Common Cause.
5. Brown, *Undoing the Demos.*
6. Alan Durning, "Who Funds Seattle's Political Candidates?" Sightline Institute, July 2015, https://www.sightline.org/research_item/who-funds-seattles-political-candidates/.
7. Durning, "Seattle's Political Candidates."
8. Mumford, "Authoritarian and Democratic Technics."
9. Jasanoff, "Future Imperfect."
10. Frank, "To the Precinct Station."
11. Damon Eris, "Occupy Wall Street Politics and Electoral Reform Group Seeking Input," *Independent Political Report,* October 11, 2011, https://independentpoliticalreport.com/2011/10/occupy-wall-street-politics-and-electoral-reform-seeking-input/; "Occupy NYC Working Group on Electoral Reform," We the People

Reform Coalition, accessed April 17, 2019, https://bigbatusa.org/electoral-reform/documents/b-occupy-nyc-working-group-on-electoral-reform/.

12. Bray, *Translating Anarchy.*
13. Lawrence Lessig, "Lawrence Lessig Occupy Wall Street Could Bridge Left and Right," filmed October 2011, in New York, New York, YouTube video, 1:37, https://www.youtube.com/watch?v=G1B5hn3Tnog; Reich, "Occupy Democracy."
14. Fraser, "The End of Progressive Neoliberalism."
15. Rich Smith, "Kshama Sawant Says She Won't Use Democracy Vouchers. Why Not?" *Stranger,* January 24, 2019, https://www.thestranger.com/slog/2019/01/24/38277781/kshama-sawant-says-she-wont-use-democracy-vouchers-why-not.
16. Biesecker, "Guest Editor's Introduction"; Biesecker and Trapani, "Escaping the Voice of the Mass/ter"; Brown, *Undoing the Demos;* Chaput, "Rhetorical Circulation in Late Capitalism"; Cherniavsky, *Neocitizenship;* Rose, *Inventing Ourselves;* Vivian "Neoliberal Epideictic."
17. Miller, "Technology as a Form of Consciousness."
18. Marcuse, "Some Social Implications of Modern Technology," 147.
19. Rorty, *Contingency, Irony, and Solidarity.*
20. Markovits, *The Politics of Sincerity;* Vlastos, "Socratic Irony."
21. Austin, *How to Do Things with Words.*
22. Rorty, *Contingency, Irony, and Solidarity.*
23. Burke, "Four Master Tropes."
24. Hariman, "Allegory and Democratic Public Culture in the Postmodern Era."
25. Ibid.
26. Lessig, *Republic Lost;* Teachout, "The Anti-corruption Principle."
27. Lessig, *America, Compromised;* Lessig, *Republic, Lost;* Lessig, *The USA Is Lesterland.*
28. Also see Zephyr Teachout, *Corruption in America.*
29. Paul Blumenthal, "Seattle Could Create an Entirely New Way to Fund Elections," *Huffington Post,* October 1, 2015, https://www.huffpost.com/entry/honest-elections-seattle_n_560d4018e4b0af3706dfaf02; Kliff, "Seattle's Radical Plan"; Lessig, "More Money."
30. Lessig, *Republic Lost.*
31. Lessig, *Republic Lost;* Lessig, *The USA Is Lesterland.*
32. In perhaps another ironic twist, the Mayday PAC failed to result in the election of any of the candidates it supported and is now defunct; see Schmitt, "Philanthropy, Politics, and Democracy."
33. Lessig, *The USA Is Lesterland.*
34. Lessig, *The USA Is Lesterland,* 72.
35. Brown, "American Nightmare"; Brown, *Undoing the Demos*; Green, "Rhetorical Capital."
36. Brown, "Neo-liberalism and the End of Liberal Democracy."
37. Chaput, "Rhetorical Circulation in Late Capitalism."
38. Vivian, "Neoliberal Epideictic."
39. Ibid.
40. Brown, "Neo-liberalism and the End."
41. Lessig, *Republic Lost;* Reich, *Saving Capitalism.*
42. "Seattle.gov | Ethics and Elections Commission | Campaigns | City Council District 3 | Sawant," City of Seattle, WA (website), accessed April 18, 2019, http://web6.seattle.gov/ethics/elections/campaigns.aspx?cycle=2015&type=campaign&IDNum=389&leftmenu=collapsed.

43. "Seattle.gov | Ethics and Elections Commission | Campaigns | All Campaigns," City of Seattle, WA (website), accessed April 18, 2019, http://web6.seattle.gov/ethics/elections/campaigns.aspx?cycle=2019&type=home&IDNum=0&leftmenu=collapsed.
44. *Seattle Times* Editorial Board, "The Times Recommends: Seattle Voters Should Reject Campaign-Finance Reform Measure, Initiative 122" (editorial), *Seattle Times,* September 27, 2015, https://www.seattletimes.com/opinion/editorials/seattle-voters-should-reject-campaign-finance-reform-measure-initiative-122/.
45. Daniel Beekman, "Seattle Initiative Puts Spotlight on Campaign Financing," *Seattle Times,* October 26, 2015, https://www.seattletimes.com/seattle-news/politics/seattle-initiative-puts-spotlight-on-campaign-financing/; Blumenthal, "Seattle Could Create"; Kliff, "Seattle's Radical Plan."
46. Kliff, "Seattle's Radical Plan."
47. Beekman, "Seattle Initiative Puts Spotlight"; Blumenthal, "Seattle Could Create"; Kliff, "Seattle's Radical Plan"; Gregory Krieg, "A New Way to Reform: 'Democracy Vouchers' vs. Citizens United," CNN Politics, November 10, 2015, https://www.cnn.com/2015/11/10/politics/democracy-vouchers-seattle-honest-elections-finance-reform/index.html.
48. Durning, "Seattle's Political Candidates."
49. Bruce Speight, "The Outsized Influence of Big Money in Seattle Elections: How Honest Elections Seattle Can Empower Regular Voters," WashPIRG, October 29, 2015, accessed April 17, 2019, https://washpirg.org/reports/wap/outsized-influence-big-money-seattles-elections.
50. Speight, "Big Money in Seattle Elections."
51. Durning, "Seattle's Political Candidates," 24.
52. Kliff, "Seattle's Radical Plan."
53. Beekman, "Seattle Initiative Puts Spotlight"; Amanda Clark, "Initiative 122 Would Bring Power Back to the People" (opinion), *Seattle Times,* September 30, 2015, https://www.seattletimes.com/opinion/initiative-122-would-bring-power-back-to-the-people/.
54. Laura Friedenbach, "Seattle's Democracy Vouchers Reduce the Power of Big Money and Expand Political Participation," Every Voice Center, November 15, 2017, https://everyvoice.org/wp-content/uploads/2018/08/2017-11-15-Seattle-Post-Election-Report-FINAL.pdf; Heerwig and McCabe, "Expanding Participation in Municipal Elections"; Mark Joseph Stern, "Janus Unleashed," *Slate,* December 26, 2018, https://slate.com/news-and-politics/2018/12/seattle-democracy-vouchers-elster-janus.html.
55. Friedenbach, "Seattle's Democracy Vouchers."
56. Friedenbach, "Seattle's Democracy Vouchers," 2.
57. Friedenbach, "Seattle's Democracy Vouchers," 3–4.
58. "Berk Consulting Final Report: Seattle Democracy Voucher Program Evaluation," City of Seattle Ethics and Elections Commission, April 2018, accessed April 17, 2019, http://www.seattle.gov/ethics/meetings/2018-05-02/item2.pdf.
59. Gene Balk, "Do Seattle's Democracy Vouchers Work? New Analysis Says Yes," *Seattle Times,* October 13, 2017, https://www.seattletimes.com/seattle-news/data/do-seattles-democracy-vouchers-work-new-analysis-says-yes/.
60. Clark, "Initiative 122"; Greenblatt, "Limiting Money's Role."
61. Dale Eisman, "Democracy Vouchers Leveling the Political Playing Field in Seattle," Common Cause, August 2, 2017, https://www.commoncause.org/democracy-wire/democracy-vouchers-leveling-political-field/.

62. Beekman, "Seattle Initiative Puts Spotlight."
63. Jimmy Tobias, "Imagine a Campaign-Finance System That's the Opposite of Today's Dark-Money Monster," *Nation*, July 26, 2017, https://www.thenation.com/article/imagine-a-campaign-finance-system-thats-the-opposite-of-todays-dark-money-nightmare/.
64. Durning, "Seattle's Political Candidates," 24.
65. Durning, "Seattle's Political Candidates," 24.
66. Speight, "Big Money in Seattle Elections," 7.
67. Kliff, "Seattle's Radical Plan."
68. Blumenthal, "Seattle Could Create"; Marcus Harrison Green, "Can Seattle Boot Big Money Out of Elections by Giving Everyone 'Democracy Vouchers'?," *Yes! Magazine*, October 30, 2015, https://www.yesmagazine.org/people-power/can-seattle-boot-big-money-out-of-elections-by-giving-everyone-democracy-vouchers-20151030; Krieg, "A New Way to Reform"; Tobias, "Imagine a Campaign-Finance System"; Teresa Mosqueda, "Seattle's Democracy Vouchers Helped Get Me Elected and Here's What I Want You to Know," *Bustle*, August 14, 2018, https://www.bustle.com/p/seattles-democracy-vouchers-helped-me-get-elected-heres-what-i-want-you-to-know-10052772; Schmitt, "Seattle's New Political Vouchers."
69. Blumenthal, "Seattle Could Create"; Krieg, "A New Way to Reform."
70. Kliff, "Seattle's Radical Plan"; Audrey McGlinchy, "Austin Voters Will Decide on 'Democracy Dollars: Here are 6 Things to Know about Prop H," NPR station KUT 90.5, April 21, 2021, https://www.kut.org/politics/2021-04-21/austin-voters-will-decide-on-democracy-dollars-here-are-six-things-to-know-about-proposition-h; Mosqueda, "Helped Me Get Elected."
71. Tobias, "Imagine a Campaign-Finance System."
72. Daniel Beekman, "I-122: Big Money Helping Wage Anti-big-money Campaign," *Seattle Times*, October 26, 2015, https://www.seattletimes.com/seattle-news/politics/i-122-big-money-helping-wage-anti-big-money-campaign/.
73. Durning, "Seattle's Political Candidates"; Speight, "Big Money in Seattle Elections."
74. Speight, "Big Money in Seattle Elections," 7.
75. "Honest Elections Seattle," Hamburger Gibson Creative (video), accessed April 18, 2019, http://hgcreative.com/work/project/honest-elections-seattle.
76. Russell Berman, "Seattle's Experiment with Campaign Funding," *Atlantic*, November 10, 2015, https://www.theatlantic.com/politics/archive/2015/11/seattle-experiments-with-campaign-funding/415026/; Green, "Can Seattle Boot Big Money."
77. Blumenthal, "Seattle Could Create."
78. Krieg, "A New Way to Reform."
79. Kliff, "Seattle's Radical Plan."
80. Schmitt, "Seattle's New Political Vouchers."
81. Ackerman and Ayres, "'Democracy Dollars' Can Give Every Voter"; Blumenthal, "Seattle Could Create."
82. Balk, "Do Seattle's Democracy Vouchers Work?"
83. "Seattle.gov | Democracy Voucher Program | Program Data | 2019 Allocated Funds," City of Seattle, WA (website), accessed April 18, 2019, http://www.seattle.gov/democracyvoucher/program-data.
84. Ibid.
85. "Berk Consulting Final Report"; Friedenbach, "Seattle's Democracy Vouchers."

86. "Seattle.gov | Democracy Voucher Program | External Reports," City of Seattle, WA (website), accessed April 18, 2019, http://www.seattle.gov/democracyvoucher/program-data/external-reports; "Seattle.gov | Democracy Voucher Program | Internal Reports," City of Seattle, WA (website), accessed April 18, 2019, http://www.seattle.gov/democracyvoucher/program-data/internal-program-reports.
87. *Seattle Times* Editorial Board, "Big Money Behind Initiative 122 Contradicts Its Purpose," (editorial), *Seattle Times,* October 15, 2015, https://www.seattletimes.com/opinion/editorials/big-money-behind-initiative-122-contradicts-its-purpose/; *Seattle Times* Editorial Board, "The Times Recommends: Seattle's Voters Should Reject."
88. *Seattle Times* Editorial Board, "Big Money Behind Initiative 122 Contradicts."
89. "Seattle.gov | Ethics and Elections Commission | Contributions to Honest Elections Seattle Initiative 2015 Election Cycle," City of Seattle, WA (website), accessed April 18, 2019, http://web6.seattle.gov/ethics/elections/poplist_v2.aspx?cid=441&listtype=contributors.
90. The closest campaign was that of Kshama Sawant, the Socialist Alternative candidate for city council, whose successful campaign raised $480,258 during the 2015 cycle—far less than half the HES campaign; see "Seattle.gov | Ethics and Elections Commission | Campaigns | City Council District 3 | Sawant."
91. Beekman, "I-122: Big Money"; Daniel Beekman, "Seattle's Richest, Whitest Areas Dominate Campaign Giving, Say Reform Backers," *Seattle Times,* July 21, 2015, https://www.seattletimes.com/seattle-news/politics/seattles-richest-whitest-sway-campaign-giving-say-reform-backers/; *Seattle Times* Editorial Board, "Big Money Behind Initiative 122 Contradicts"; Blumenthal, "Seattle Could Create"; Heidi Groover, "A New Plan for Public Campaign Financing Will Appear on Your Ballot this Fall," Slog, *Stranger,* July 13, 2015, https://www.thestranger.com/blogs/slog/2015/07/13/22537490/a-new-plan-for-public-campaign-financing-will-appear-on-your-ballot-this-fall; Reid Wilson, "Seattle's Bold Campaign Finance Experiment Could Cost a Lot of Money," Morning Consult, November 5, 2015, https://morningconsult.com/2015/11/05/seattles-bold-campaign-finance-experiment-could-cost-a-lot-of-money/.
92. Sarah Ellison, "The Complex Power Couple of Chris Hughes and Sean Eldridge," *Vanity Fair,* July 2015, https://www.vanityfair.com/news/2015/06/chris-hughes-sean-eldridge-new-republic-congress-run; Alex Pareene, "Sean Eldridge Earned His Politico Hit Piece," *Salon,* April 10, 2014, https://www.salon.com/2014/04/10/sean_eldridge_earned_his_politico_hit_piece/; Kevin Roose, "Political Donors Put Their Money Where the Memes Are," *New York Times,* August 6, 2017, https://www.nytimes.com/2017/08/06/business/media/political-donors-put-their-money-where-the-memes-are.html.
93. Beekman, "I-122: Big Money"; Beekman, "Seattle's Richest, Whitest Areas"; Shift Washington, "The Best WA Campaign Finance Reform—That Out-of-State Donors Can Buy," October 3, 2016, https://shiftwa.org/best-wa-campaign-finance-reform-state-donors-can-buy/; *Seattle Times* Editorial Board, "Big Money Behind Initiative 122 Contradicts"; Joel Connelly, "Only in Seattle: $1.3 million Campaign Warns of 'Unfettered Influence' of $43,966 Opposition," *Seattle Post-Intelligencer,* October 26, 2015, https://blog.seattlepi.com/seattlepolitics/2015/10/26/only-in-seattle-1-3-million-campaign-warns-of-unfettered-influence-of-43966-opposition/; Groover, "A New Plan"; Casey Jaywork, "Once Again, Big Political Money Is Backing an Effort to Get Money Out of Politics," *Seattle Weekly,* October 12, 2016,

https://www.seattleweekly.com/news/once-again-big-political-money-is-backing-an-effort-to-get-money-out-of-politics/; Wilson, "Seattle's Bold Campaign."

94. Shift Washington, "The Best WA Campaign Finance Reform"; *Seattle Times* Editorial Board, "Big Money Behind Initiative 122 Contradicts"; Connelly, "Only in Seattle"; David Kroman, "It's Taking a Lot of Cash to Get Big Money Out of Local Politics," *Crosscut,* October 5, 2015, https://crosscut.com/2015/10/local-campaign-finance-measure-attracts-east-coast-cash.
95. "Our Portfolio | Recommended Organizations," Democracy Alliance (website), accessed April 19, 2019, https://democracyalliance.org/investments/.
96. "Seattle.gov | Ethics and Elections Commission | Expenditures by Honest Elections Seattle Initiative 2015 Election Cycle," City of Seattle, WA (website), accessed April 19, 2019, http://web6.seattle.gov/ethics/elections/poplist.aspx?cid=441&list type=vendors; Kerbel and Bowers, *Next Generation Netroots.*
97. "Seattle.gov | Ethics and Elections Commission | Expenditures by Honest Elections Seattle Initiative 2015 Election Cycle."
98. Krieg, "A New Way to Reform."
99. Speight, "Big Money in Seattle Elections."
100. *Seattle Times* Editorial Board, "Big Money Behind Initiative 122 Contradicts."
101. Beekman, "I-122: Big Money."
102. Brown, *Undoing the Demos.*

CHAPTER THREE

Bernie Sanders and Authentically Democratic Donations

1. Selfa and Smith, "The Sanders Campaign and the Left."
2. Leonard, *Illiberal Reformers.*"
3. See, for instance, Herman and Chomsky, *Manufacturing Consent.*
4. Baudrillard, *Simulacra and Simulation;* Debord, *Society of the Spectacle;* Habermas, *The Structural Transformation of the Public Sphere.*
5. Capella and Jamieson, *Spiral of Cynicism.*
6. Lessig, *The USA Is Lesterland.*
7. Lessig, *Republic, Lost.*
8. Anna Massoglia and Karl Evers-Hillstrom, "2020 Presidential Candidates Top $100M in Digital Ad Spending as Twitter Goes Dark," *Opensecrets News,* November 14, 2019, https://www.opensecrets.org/news/2019/11/digital-ad-spending-2020-presidential-candidates-top-100m/.
9. Bowers and Kerbel, *Next Generation Netroots.*
10. Although this narrative of authentic digital communication and artificial broadcast communication has appeared recently in conversation with the concept of the "net roots," the work of John Durham Peters describes how it is an ancient distinction that dates to the Socratic critique of the sophists; see Peters, *Speaking into the Air.*
11. Connolly, *The Ethos of Pluralization*; Hyde, "Introduction," in *Ethos of Rhetoric,* ed. Michael J. Hyde.
12. Hyde, *Ethos of Rhetoric.*
13. Castells, *Networks of Outrage and Hope.*
14. Bray, *Translating Anarchy;* Kevin et al., "Occupy Wall Street on the Public Screens of Social Media."
15. Judis, *The Populist Explosion*; Michael Kazin, "How Can Donald Trump and Bernie

Sanders Both Be 'Populist?'" *New York Times Magazine,* March 22, 2016, https://essayzilla.org/wp-content/uploads/2020/12/20190526200933how_can_donald_trump_and_bernie_sanders_both_be____populist___.pdf; Mouffe, *For a Left Populism.*

16. Laclau, *On Populist Reason.*
17. Judis, *The Populist Explosion;* Kazin, "How Can Donald Trump and Bernie Sanders"; Laclau, *On Populist Reason.*
18. This narrative about the democratic potential of digital media is developed at length by Bowers and Kerbel in *Next Generation Netroots.*
19. Hardt and Negri, *Multitude.*
20. Parson, "Breaking Bread, Sharing Soup, and Smashing the State."
21. Greene, "Rhetorical Capital."
22. Dean, *Democracy and Other Neoliberal Fantasies.*
23. Mouffe, *The Democratic Paradox.*
24. Brown, *Undoing the Demos.*
25. Hauser, *Vernacular Voices;* Andrejevic, *iSpy.*
26. Pezzullo, *Toxic Tourism;* DeLuca, *Image Politics.*
27. Dewey, *The Public and Its Problems.*
28. Asen and Brouwer, "Introduction"; Jackson and Clark, *Trained Capacities.*
29. Carey, "Commentary."
30. Carney, "Occupy Wall Street Flush with Cash."
31. Weaver, *How Bernie Won.*
32. Stuckey, "Rethinking the Rhetorical Presidency and Presidential Rhetoric."
33. Bernard "Bernie" Sanders, "Bernie Sanders Announces Bid for Democratic Presidential Nomination," filmed May 26, 2015, in Burlington, VT, YouTube video, https://www.youtube.com/watch?v=fL12Gb_ixtU&t=65s; Sanders, *Our Revolution;* Bernard "Bernie" Sanders, "Senator Bernie Sanders Presidential Campaign Announcement," filmed May 26, 2015, in Burlington, VT, C-SPAN, YouTube video, 36:54, https://www.youtube.com/watch?v=fL12Gb_ixtU.
34. Sanders, "Announces Bid"; Bernard "Bernie" Sanders, "Bernie Sanders Dallas Rally," filmed July 19, 2015, in Dallas, TX, YouTube video, 1:00:02, https://www.youtube.com/watch?v=iquADz8Yve4; Sanders, *Our Revolution*; Sanders, "Campaign Announcement."
35. Bond and Exley, *Rules for Revolutionaries.*
36. Baldwin-Philippi, *Using Technology, Building Democracy;* Chávez, "Counter-Public Enclaves."
37. For instance, see Gitlin, *Occupy Nation;* and Taussig, "I'm So Angry I Made a Sign."
38. Bond and Exley, *Rules for Revolutionaries.*
39. Judis, *The Populist Explosion;* Laclau, *On Populist Reason.*
40. Bernard "Bernie" Sanders, "We Are Doing Something Very Radical in American Politics," Phoenix, AZ, March 15, 2016, YouTube video, 59:06, https://www.youtube.com/watch?v=_wwHxmEdyeU.
41. Weaver, *How Bernie Won;* Sanders, *Our Revolution.*
42. Sanders, *Our Revolution,* 90.
43. Ibid, 91.
44. Bernard "Bernie" Sanders, "Senator Bernie Sanders Primary Night Speech," Phoenix, AZ, March 15, 2016, https://www.c-span.org/video/?406669-1/bernie-sanders-primary-night-speech.

45. Sanders, *Our Revolution,* 31.
46. Sanders, "Announces Bid"; Sanders, "Campaign Announcement."
47. Cappella and Jamieson, "News Frames, Political Cynicism, and Media Cynicism."
48. John Cassidy, "What Bernie Sanders Has Achieved," *New Yorker,* March 17, 2016, https://www.newyorker.com/news/john-cassidy/what-bernie-sanders-has-achieved.
49. Clare Foran, "Bernie Sanders's Big Money," *Atlantic,* March 1, 2016, https://www.theatlantic.com/politics/archive/2016/03/bernie-sanders-fundraising/471648/.
50. Ibid.
51. Brent Budowsky, "Sanders' Small Donors Are the Rockstars of 2016," *Observer,* April 4, 2016, http://observer.com/2016/04/sanders-small-donors-are-the-rockstars-of-2016/.
52. Paul Blumenthal, "Bernie Sander's Small Donor Fundraising Continues to Set Records," *Huffington Post,* January 31, 2016, https://www.huffpost.com/entry/bernie-sanders-fundraising_n_56ae4f7ee4b0010e80ea7bdb; Brian Hanley, "Bernie Sanders Received More Individual Campaign Contributions Than Obama's Entire 2008 Campaign," *Huffington Post,* December 6, 2017, https://www.huffpost.com/entry/bernie-sanders-has-alread_b_9671406.
53. Jamelle Bouie, "Bernie's Change," *Slate,* July 13, 2016, http://www.slate.com/articles/news_and_politics/politics/2016/07/how_bernie_s_small_donor_revolution_could_change_politics_on_the_left.html.
54. Cassidy, "More Fighting Words from Bernie Sanders"; Sam Stein and Jason Cherkis, "The Inside Story of How Bernie Sanders Became the Greatest Online Fundraiser in Political History," *Huffington Post,* June 28, 2017, https://www.huffpost.com/entry/bernie-sanders-fundraising_n_59527587e4b02734df2d92c1; Jonathan Swan, "Clinton Campaign Adds $27 Donate Option to Woo Sanders Supporters," *The Hill,* July 12, 2016, https://thehill.com/blogs/ballot-box/presidential-races/287383-clinton-campaign-adds-27-donate-option-to-woo-sanders.
55. Seema Mehta et al., "Who Gives Money to Bernie Sanders?" *Los Angeles Times,* June 3, 2016, http://www.latimes.com/projects/la-na-pol-sanders-donors/.
56. Nick Corasaniti, "Bernie Sanders Campaign Showed How to Turn Viral Moments into Money," *New York Times,* June 24, 2016, https://www.nytimes.com/2016/06/25/us/politics/bernie-sanders-digital-strategy.html.
57. Robert Yoon, "$182 Million: Bernie Sanders Equals Hillary Clinton's Campaign Fundraising," CNN, April 21, 2016, https://www.cnn.com/2016/04/21/politics/2016-bernie-sanders-fundraising-hillary-clinton/index.html.
58. Tessa Berenson, "Bernie Sanders Breaks Fundraising Record," *Time,* December 21, 2015, https://time.com/4157904/bernie-sanders-fundraising-donations-record/; Yoon, "$182 Million."
59. Cappella and Jamieson, *Spiral of Cynicism.*
60. Emily Atkin, "Bernie Sanders is Using His Coveted Donor List to Fundraise for Senate Democrats," *Circa,* August 30, 2016, https://www.circa.com/story/2016/08/30/politics/bernie-sanders-is-using-his-coveted-donor-list-to-fundraise-for-senate-democrats; Gabriel Debenedetti and Darren Samuelsohn, "The Desperate Scramble for Bernie's Secret Weapon," *Politico,* April 23, 2016, https://www.politico.com/story/2016/04/bernie-sanders-fundraising-list-222342; Julia Glum, "Bernie Sanders To Keep Email List of Donors, Use It To Raise Money for Senate Candidates: Report," *International Business Times,* August 29, 2016, https://www.ibtimes.com/bernie-sanders-keep-email-list-donors-use-it-raise

-money-senate-candidates-report-2408518; Sam Stein and Jason Cherkis, "Bernie Sanders' Team Explains Why He Won't Hand Over His Donor List," *Huffington Post,* June 29, 2017, https://www.huffingtonpost.com/entry/bernie-sanders-donor-list_us_5952776fe4b05c37bb799b97.

61. Cassidy, "What Bernie Sanders Has Achieved."
62. Corasaniti, "Viral Moments."
63. Budowsky, "Sanders' Small Donors."
64. Bouie, "Bernie's Change."
65. Corasaniti, "Viral Moments"; Ivan Levingston, "As Sanders Campaign Wraps Up, Down-Ballot Candidates Reap Big Bern Rewards," CNBC, June 15, 2016, https://www.cnbc.com/2016/06/15/as-sanders-campaign-wraps-up-down-ballot-candidates-reap-big-bern-rewards.html.
66. Fred Wertheimer, "U.S. Politics Are Rigged. It's Time for a Small-Donor Revolution," NBC, October 29, 2017, https://www.nbcnews.com/think/opinion/u-s-politics-are-rigged-it-s-time-small-donor-ncna815181.
67. Debenedetti and Samuelsohn, "Scramble."
68. Ibid.
69. Ibid.
70. Christine Mai-Duc, "Fighting for the Progressive Cause Got a Little Easier Thanks to This Bernie Sanders-Affiliated Group," *Los Angeles Times,* December 9, 2016, http://www.latimes.com/politics/la-pol-ca-our-revolution-bernie-sanders-california-20161209-story.html?outputType=amp; Andrew McGill, "Will Bernie Sanders Give Away His Supporters' Data?" *Atlantic,* June 10, 2016, https://www.theatlantic.com/politics/archive/2016/06/bernie-sanders-email-list-clinton/486284/.
71. Ben Geier, "Clinton Doesn't Yet Have Sanders' Most Valuable Chip," *Fortune,* July 13, 2016, http://fortune.com/2016/07/13/sanders-email-list/.
72. Daniel Marans, "Bernie Sanders Has a Massive Email List. But He Has Good Reason to Think Twice about Sharing It," *Huffington Post,* February 9, 2017, https://www.huffingtonpost.com/entry/bernie-sanders-email-list_us_589c9862e4b0c1284f2b0285.
73. Debenedetti and Samuelsohn, "Scramble."
74. Edward-Isaac Dovere, "DNC Overhaul Struggles as Sanders-Clinton Rivalries Persist," *Politico,* January 16, 2018, https://www.politico.com/story/2018/01/16/democrats-clinton-sanders-reforms-340616; Mai-Duc, "Fighting"; Mark Sullivan, "Even More Valuable That His Endorsement, Bernie May Have Started Sharing Data," *Fast Company,* July 14, 2016, https://amp.fastcompany.com/3061788/even-more-valuable-than-his-endorsement-bernie-may-have-started-sharing-data.
75. Al Urbanski, "How Digital Marketing Will Decide the Next President," DMNEWs, February 16, 2016, https://www.dmnews.com/channel-marketing/news/13055395/how-digital-marketing-will-decide-the-next-president.
76. Levingston, "Rewards."
77. Michael Fraase, "Whither Bernie's Database?" Arts & Farces LLC, December 18, 2016, https://www.farces.com/whither-bernies-database/ (author has since deleted content); Kyle Griffin (@kylegriffin1), "Sanders campaign confirms to NBC they have not handed over their valuable email list to Team Clinton. No word on if/when that will change," Twitter, July 13, 2016, https://twitter.com/kylegriffin1/status/753283747429093376?ref_src=twsrc%5Etfw; McGill, "Supporters' Data."
78. Atkin, "Coveted"; Dave Maass, "Voter Privacy: What You Need to Know About Your Digital Trail During the 2016 Election," Electronic Frontier Foundation,

February 29, 2016, https://www.eff.org/deeplinks/2016/02/voter-privacy-what-you-need-know-about-your-digital-trail-during-2016-election.

79. Griffin, "Confirms."
80. Maass, "Voter Privacy."
81. Ibid.
82. Tim Murphy, "Democrats Are Desperate for Bernie Sanders' Email List," *Mother Jones,* February 6, 2017, https://www.motherjones.com/politics/2017/02/democrats-desperate-bernie-sanders-email-list/.
83. Dovere, "DNC Overhaul"; Murphy, "Desperate."
84. McGill, "Supporters' Data."
85. Robin Curran et al., "The Incredible Inside Story of How Bernie Sanders Raised $218 Million Online," audio interview by Jason Cherkis and Sam Stein, Candidate Confessional (podcast), *Huffington Post,* June 28, 2017, https://www.acast.com/candidateconfessional/theinsidestoryhowberniesandersraised-218milliononline.
86. Nicole Gaudiano, "Bernie Sanders Will Launch Organizations to Spread Progressive Message," *USA Today,* July 15, 2016, https://www.usatoday.com/story/news/politics/elections/2016/07/15/bernie-sanders-progressive-message/87073052/; Griffin, "Confirms."
87. Sasha Issenberg, "The Meticulously Engineered Grassroots Network Behind the Bernie Sanders Revolution," *Bloomberg,* February 24, 2016, https://www.bloomberg.com/news/features/2016-02-24/behind-bernie-sanders-revolution-lies-a-meticulously-engineered-grassroots-network; Sarah Jaffe, "Enough with Big Data: Knock on Doors and Talk to Voters," BillMoyers.com, June 8, 2017, https://billmoyers.com/story/enough-big-data-knock-doors-talk-voters/; Micah Sifry, "How the Sanders Campaign Is Reinventing the Use of Tech in Politics," *Nation,* March 14, 2016, https://www.thenation.com/article/how-the-sanders-campaign-is-reinventing-the-use-of-tech-in-politics/.
88. Matthew Artz, "Can Sanders Keep His Political Revolution Alive?" *Santa Cruz Sentinel,* June 18, 2016, http://www.santacruzsentinel.com/article/NE/20160618/NEWS/160619728.
89. Mehta et al., "Who Gives Money to Bernie Sanders?"

CHAPTER FOUR

Amending the US Constitution with Transparent Deliberation

1. "Writing the 28th Amendment—Boston, MA," filmed on March 27, 2018, at Suffolk University Law School in Boston, Massachusetts, streamed by Move to Amend on Facebook Live, https://www.facebook.com/watch/live/?v=1988368064714282&ref=watch_permalink; "Writing the 28th Amendment," featuring H.R. Res. 2, 116th Congress (2019), American Promise, accessed April 27, 2021, https://americanpromise.net/take-action/join-a-program/writing-the-28th-amendment/?fbclid=IwAR3csoqOHj3C4YfX1UyaIacMai15jiacOT2nIJBI9vxwQo68liNbbU_gKjA.
2. "Writing the 28th Amendment," American Promise.
3. Clements, *Corporations Are Not People.*
4. "Constitutional Amendments," United for the People, accessed May 18, 2021, http://united4thepeople.org/amendments/.
5. "Move to Amend's Proposed 28th Amendment to the Constitution," Move to Amend, accessed May 19, 2021, https://www.movetoamend.org/amendment.
6. "Constitutional Amendments."

7. "Move to Amend's Proposed 28th Amendment to the Constitution."
8. "What is the 28th Amendment?" American Promise, accessed May 18, 2021, https://www.americanpromise.net/who-we-are/the-28th-amendment/.
9. Sara Swann, "Amendment to Nullify Citizens United Finally Gets Air Time in the House," The Fulcrum, February 6, 2020, https://thefulcrum.us/campaign-finance/citizens-united-28th-amendment; Nicole Zerillo, "Nonprofit Advocates Ramp Up Efforts to Reverse Citizens United," *Nonprofit Quarterly*, January 25, 2021, https://nonprofitquarterly.org/nonprofit-advocates-ramp-up-efforts-to-reverse-citizens-united/.
10. "Other Amendments," Move to Amend, accessed May 19, 2021, https://www.movetoamend.org/other-amendments.
11. Proposing an Amendment to the Constitution of the United States Providing that the Rights Extended by the Constitution are the Rights of Natural Persons Only, H.R. Res. 48, 116th Congress (2019), Congress.gov, https://www.congress.gov/bill/116th-congress/house-joint-resolution/48/=.
12. Hartmann, *Unequal Protection.*
13. Ritz, ed., *Defying Corporations, Defining Democracy.*
14. Grossman, "Corporations Must Not Supplant 'We the People.'"
15. "Why Abolish All Corporate Constitutional Rights," Move to Amend, accessed November 19, 2020, https://movetoamend.org/why-abolish-all-corporate-constitutional-rights, page appears to have been removed since access date.
16. Ibid.
17. Ibid.
18. Ibid.
19. "Welcome Address from National Director Kaitlin Sopoci-Belknap & Representative Rick Nolan," filmed on June 8, 2018, at the National Leadership Summit in Washington, DC, streamed by Move to Amend on Facebook Live, accessed April 27, 2021, https://www.facebook.com/watch/live/?v=1988368064714282&ref=watch_permalink.
20. "The Peoples Movement Assemblies Offer Spaces for Us to Practice Community Governance and to Coordinate Together across Multiple Strategies and Multiple Geographies," Project South, accessed April 27, 2021, https://projectsouth.org/global-movement-building/peoples-movement-assemblies/.
21. "Movement Education Program," Move to Amend, accessed April 27, 2021, https://www.movetoamend.org/education3.
22. Clements, *Corporations Are Not People.*
23. Winkler, *We the Corporations.*
24. Winkler, *We the Corporations,* 387.
25. As noted above, American Promise hosted a series of mass conference calls in 2017 that included various leaders and supporters of different constitutional amendments. Recordings of the mass conference calls were initially made publicly available through the organization's website. After a year or so, however, the recordings were inexplicably taken offline, contradicting the organization's initial commitment to transparency and open, "informational" deliberation. The retraction of the recordings seems to have been the result of concerns about how conflicts between participants stymied the deliberations and undercut the ethos of American Promise. The calls were downloaded by the author on September 20, 2018. To cite these calls, we include the name of speaker(s) (when relevant), name of the organization, number of the call, date of the call, and date of download. Adam Winkler

speaking during American Promise conference call, October 31, 2017, downloaded September 20, 2018.

26. Leo E. Strine Jr. speaking during American Promise conference call 5a, October 31, 2017, downloaded September 20, 2018; Winkler, *We the Corporations.*
27. Strine and Winkler, call 5a.
28. American Promise conference call 1, May 30, 2017, downloaded September 20, 2018.
29. "Summary for Working Group—Writing the 28th Amendment," American Promise, accessed September 24, 2018, http://www.americanpromise.net/writing_the_28th_amendment, page appears to have been removed since access date.
30. Lessig, *Republic, Lost;* Teachout, "The Anti-corruption Principle."
31. Lawrence Lessig, "What It REALLY Means to Call for an Article V Convention. Prof. Larry Lessig," filmed at Wolf PAC Warrior Workshop 2018, posted August 24, 2018, by The Young Turks, YouTube video, 36:24, https://www.youtube.com/watch?v=arwhpwRNekE.
32. Ibid.
33. "Summary for Working Group—Writing the 28th Amendment."
34. "Summary for Working Group—Writing the 28th Amendment."
35. "National Business Network," American Promise, accessed November 28, 2020, https://americanpromise.net/take-action/join-a-program/national-business-network/.
36. Hartelius, *The Rhetoric of Expertise.*
37. "Writing the 28th Amendment," American Promise.
38. Gutmann and Thompson, *Democracy and Disagreement;* Gutmann and Thompson, *Why Deliberative Democracy?*
39. Curato et al., "Twelve Key Findings in Deliberative Democracy Research."
40. Andrejevic, *Infoglut.*
41. Young, "Activist Challenges to Deliberative Democracy."
42. Chambers, "Rhetoric and the Public Sphere," 331; Young, "Activist Challenges to Deliberative Democracy."
43. Mouffe, "Deliberative Democracy or Agonistic Pluralism?"
44. Chambers, "Rhetoric and the Public Sphere."
45. See, for example, Fishkin, *Democracy When the People Are Thinking.*
46. Hauser, *Vernacular Voices,* 27.
47. Chambers, "Rhetoric and the Public Sphere."
48. Young, *Inclusion and Democracy.*
49. Asen, *Democracy, Deliberation, and Education.*
50. Mouffe, *The Democratic Paradox.*
51. Fishkin, *Democracy When the People Are Thinking,* 18.
52. Fraser, "Rethinking the Public Sphere"; Sanders, "Against Deliberation"; Young, "Activist Challenges to Deliberative Democracy."
53. Brown, *Undoing the Demos*; Foucault, *The Birth of Biopolitics.*
54. Young, "Activist Challenges to Deliberative Democracy."
55. Deliberative democratic theorists, including James Fishkin, embrace the ideal of the people ruling itself through thoughtful deliberation about issues of consequence. Such theorists have been far slower, however, to cede democratic control over the ideals and goals guiding the *design* of deliberative bodies. Robert Dahl, a founding thinker of deliberative democratic theory, argues that the people should have control over "how matters are to be placed on the agenda of matters that

are to be decided by the means of the democratic process"; see Dahl, *Democracy and Its Critics,* 113. Deliberative mini-publics such as those advocated by Fishkin, however, are still designed and tightly controlled by experts who often determine the questions, agenda, standards of decorum, possible outcomes, and sources of information and evidence available to participants. This means that, in effect, most deliberative democracy fails to meet the criterion laid out by Dahl that a rigorously democratic process must allow the people to set its own agenda and determine the rules of the democratic process itself.

56. Bray, *Translating Anarchy;* Gitlin, *Occupy Nation.*
57. Young, "Activist Challenges to Deliberative Democracy."
58. "Movement Education Program," Move to Amend.
59. Ibid.
60. The conference calls happened monthly during late 2017 and early 2018. American Promise, "Summary for Working Group—Writing the 28th Amendment."
61. American Promise, call 1.
62. "Summary for Working Group—Writing the 28th Amendment," 3.
63. Ibid, 4.
64. Ibid, 1.
65. Ibid, 1.
66. Ibid.
67. Ibid.
68. Clements, *Corporations Are Not People.*
69. American Promise, call 1.
70. American Promise, call 1.
71. Ben Manski, speaking during call 1.
72. Jeffrey Clements speaking during American Promise conference call 1.
73. David Cobb speaking during American Promise conference call 1.
74. Jeffrey Clements, speaking during American Promise conference call 2, June 27, 2017, downloaded September 20, 2018.
75. Habermas, *The Structural Transformation of the Public Sphere.*
76. American Promise conference call 3, August 29, 2017, downloaded September 20, 2018.
77. Clements, speaking during conference call 1.
78. American Promise conference call 6, November 28, 2017, downloaded September 20, 2018.
79. Ibid.
80. Ibid.
81. Ibid.
82. Kaitlin Sopoci-Belknap speaking during American Promise conference call 7, January 30, 2018, downloaded September 20, 2018.
83. Lee Ketelson, speaking during American Promise conference call 7, January 30, 2018, downloaded September 20, 2018.
84. Sopoci-Belknap, speaking during call 7.
85. Ibid.
86. Keyan Bliss, speaking during call 6.
87. Keyan Bliss, speaking during call 7.
88. Robert Kerr and Craig Klevidence, speaking during call 7.
89. American Promise, "Our Organizations/Board Members," accessed September 12, 2021, https://americanpromise.net/who-we-are/about-us/staff/; American Promise,

"Why We Fight Against Money in Politics" (video), published May 5, 2021, https://youtu.be/BDjqPkZU2DE.

90. American Promise, "Build Support in Your State," accessed September 12, 2021, https://americanpromise.net/take-action/see-whats-happening/.
91. American Promise, "Events," accessed September 12, 2021, https://americanpromise.net/events/.

CHAPTER FIVE

Rural Community Democracy and the Radicalism of Instrumental Reason

1. Thimsen, "The Lessons of Community Rights Ordinances for Democratic Philosophizing."
2. Thomas Linzey, "Hey Liberal, You're Late, but Welcome to the Local-Control Party," *In These Times*, March 1, 2018, http://inthesetimes.com/rural-america/entry/20950/community-rights-thomas-linzey-celdf-think-globally-enact-locally.
3. Linzey, "Hey Liberal."
4. "Rights of Nature Symposium – Panel 2, Part 2: U.S. Perspective," recorded on October 27, 2017, at Tulane Law School in New Orleans, Louisiana by the Community Environmental Legal Defense Fund (CELDF), YouTube video, 45:20, https://www.youtube.com/watch?v=clcUYSqzGzE.
5. Jacob Baynham, "The Mother of All Anti-Fracking Tools," *Outside*, May 26, 2017, https://www.outsideonline.com/outdoor-adventure/environment/mother-all-anti-fracking-tools/; Laura Legere, "'No Is No Is No': A Tiny Township's Fight Against Oil and Gas Waste Disposal," *Pittsburgh Post-Gazette*, November 13, 2017, https://www.post-gazette.com/business/powersource/2017/11/13/Grant-Township-Indiana-County-Pennsylvania-fight-oil-gas-waste-disposal-underground-shale-fracking/stories/201711120039; Justin Nobel, "How a Small Town Is Standing Up to Fracking," *Rolling Stone*, May 22, 2017, https://www.rollingstone.com/politics/politics-news/how-a-small-town-is-standing-up-to-fracking-117307/.
6. Peters, *Speaking into the Air.*
7. Barron, "Reclaiming Home Rule."
8. Luke Mogelson, "The Militias against Masks," *New Yorker*, August 17, 2020, https://www.newyorker.com/magazine/2020/08/24/the-militias-against-masks.
9. Dustin Hornbeck, "State Efforts to Ban Mask Mandates in Schools Mirror Resistance to Integration," The Conversation, https://theconversation.com/state-efforts-to-ban-mask-mandates-in-schools-mirror-resistance-to-integration-167026.
10. Article about how CELDF tries to maintain human rights protections while critiquing Dillon's rule: Simon Davis-Cohen, "Progressive Wins in Virginia Are Limited as Long as 'Dillon's Rule' Is on the Books," *Scalawag*, November 13, 2019, https://scalawagmagazine.org/2019/11/virginia-property-discrimination/.
11. *Constitution of the Republic of Ecuador*, published by the Official Ecuadorian Register on October 20, 2008, last updated on January 31, 2011, accessed on the Georgetown University Political Database of the Americas, http://pdba.georgetown.edu/Constitutions/Ecuador/english08.html.
12. Thomas Linzey, "Thomas Linzey—Challenging Corporations," filmed February 10, 2005, in Seattle, WA, YouTube video, 45:37, https://www.youtube.com/watch?v=HowKoNmODNY.
13. Linzey with Campbell, *Be the Change.*

14. Dewey, *The Public and Its Problems.*
15. Ben Price, "Press Release, Pittsburg Bans Natural Gas Drilling," Community Environmental Legal Defense Fund (website), November 16, 2010, https://celdf.org/2010/11/press-release-pittsburgh-bans-natural-gas-drilling/.
16. Tom Shepstone, "Pool Hall Hustlers and Influence Peddlers," Energy in Depth, September 2, 2011, https://www.energyindepth.org/pool-hall-hustlers-and-influence-peddlers/.
17. "Citizens United," Community Environmental Legal Defense Fund (website), accessed January 8, 2013, http://www.celdf.org/citizens-united.
18. Community Environmental Defense Fund, "Statement on Efforts to Amend the U.S. Constitution following Citizens United," CELDF (website), January 1, 2012, accessed December 17, 2012, https://celdf.org/2012/01/statement-on-efforts-to-amend-the-u-s-constitution-following-citizens-united/.
19. Community Environmental Legal Defense Fund, "Statement on Efforts to Amend."
20. Ibid.
21. Ibid.
22. Community Environmental Legal Defense Fund, "Democracy School Curriculum," CELDF (website), accessed February 5, 2020, https://celdf.org/how-we-work/education/democracy-school/democracy-school-curriculum/.
23. Community Environmental Legal Defense Fund, "Democracy School Curriculum."
24. Ibid.
25. Thimsen, "Lessons of Community Rights Ordinances."
26. Tamaqua Borough, "Sewage Sludge Ordinance," Community Environmental Legal Defense Fund (website), accessed 2006, http://www.celdf. org/downloads/Ordinance-Mt_1.pdf. The community rights ordinances referenced throughout this chapter were formerly publicly available in an archive on the website of the Community Environmental Legal Defense Fund. After a complete overhaul of this organization's web presence in 2015, the ordinances are no longer available to the public. All ordinances cited in this article were archived by the author prior to 2015.
27. Borough, "Sewage."
28. "Rights of Nature Symposium."
29. Linzey and Campbell, *Be the Change.*
30. Thomas Linzey, "Legal Defense Fund Turns Fifteen in 2010," article in *Susquehanna: A Publication of the Community Environmental Defense Fund* 11, no. 4 (December 2012): 7, https://celdf.org/wp-content/uploads/2015/08/December-2009-Susquehanna.pdf.
31. Gail Darrell, "Live Free or What?" article in *Susquehanna: A Publication of the Community Environmental Defense Fund* 12, no. 1 (March 2010): 4, http://celdf.org/wp-content/uploads/2015/08/March-2010-Susquehanna.pdf.
32. Hauser, *Vernacular Voices: The Rhetoric of Publics and Public Spheres*; Tracy, *Everyday Talk: Building and Reflecting Identities.*
33. Thimsen, "Lessons of Community Rights Ordinances."
34. Linzey and Campbell, *Be the Change.*
35. Ibid.
36. Ibid, 80.
37. Ibid, 37.

38. Ibid, 46.
39. Lee, "Electoral Politics and Visions of Community: Jimmy Carter, Virtue, and the Small Town Myth."
40. Gail Darrell, "Overcoming the Obstacles to Community Organizing," article in *Susquehanna: A Publication of the Community Environmental Defense Fund* 14, no. 2 (Summer 2012): 2–3, http://celdf.org/wp-content/uploads/2015/08/Susquehanna_Summer_2012.pdf.
41. Ibid, 8.
42. Daniel E. Brannan Jr., "Wagon Mound Self-Government Movement Falters," article in *Susquehanna: A Publication of the Community Environmental Defense Fund* 13, no. 2 (Summer 2011): 4, http://celdf.org/wp-content/uploads/2015/08/Susquehanna-Newsletter-Summer-2011.pdf.
43. Linzey and Campbell, *Be the Change*, 53.
44. Ibid.
45. Ibid, 33.
46. Ibid, 86.
47. Linzey, "Challenging Corporations."
48. In 2020, the cofounders of CELDF left the organization to start a new nonprofit organization focused more on the rights of nature. See Community Environmental Legal Defense Fund, "A New Phase," article *in Moments of Transition: a special edition of the Susquehanna Newsletter* 23, no. 3 (Winter 2015): 1–2, accessed January 4, 2021, https://celdf.org/2021/01/newsletter-moments-of-transition/; "Our Team," Center for Democratic and Environmental Rights, accessed January 4, 2021, https://www.centerforenvironmentalrights.org/team.
49. Thomas Linzey and Mari Margil, "Thomas Linzey & Mari Margil: Occupy the Law | Bioneers 2016," address given October 21, 2016, at 2016 National Bioneers Conference, https://www.youtube.com/watch?v=QiXjzgRiAEw.
50. Peterson and Schmid, *We the People 2.0*.
51. Jackson Barnett, "What is Denver Initiative 300: Right to Survive," *Denver Post*, April 12, 2019, https://www.denverpost.com/2019/04/12/denver-initiative-300-camping-ban-homeless/.
52. "Group Organization," Denver Homeless Out Loud, website, accessed February 6, 2020, https://denverhomelessoutloud.org/group-orginization/; Chris Walker, "Confusion Over Right to Survive Initiative Isn't Easy to Put to Rest," *Westword*, April 2, 2019, https://www.westword.com/content/printView/11292222.
53. Walker, "Confusion Over Right to Survive Initiative."
54. Chris Walker, "Right to Survive Opposition Includes Some of the Biggest Names in Development," *Westword*, February 18, 2019, https://www.westword.com/news/together-denver-campaign-fighting-denvers-right-to-survive-ballot-initiative-11235097.
55. Terese Howard and Ben Price, "Media Statement: A Human Right to Survive is Born in Denver," Community Environmental Legal Defense Fund (website), May 8, 2019, https://celdf.org/2019/05/media-statement-a-human-right-to-survive-is-born-in-denver/.
56. Community Environmental Legal Defense Fund, *On Community Civil Disobedience in the Name of Sustainability: The Community Rights Movement in the United States* (Oakland, CA: PM Press, 2015), a pamphlet published by the CELDF.
57. Peters, *Speaking into the Air*, 33.
58. Peterson and Schmid, *We the People 2.0*.

59. Ibid.
60. Linzey and Campbell, *Be the Change;* Linzey and Campbell, *We the People.*
61. Linzey and Campbell, *We the People,* 79.
62. Ibid, *We the People,* 22.
63. Community Environmental Legal Defense Fund, *On Community Civil Disobedience,* 24.
64. Ibid, 27.
65. Ibid, 21–22.
66. Ibid, 23.
67. Thomas Linzey, "Can the Community Rights Movement Fix Capitalism?" *In These Times,* December 29, 2017, https://inthesetimes.com/rural-america/entry/20795/capitalism-community-rights-corporate-power-democracy-rights-of-nature.
68. Community Environmental Legal Defense Fund, *On Community Civil Disobedience,* 22.

Conclusion

1. Brown, "Resisting Left Melancholy"; Mudge, *Leftism Reinvented.*
2. Hall, *Road to Renewal.*
3. Laclau, *On Populist Reason;* Mouffe, *Democratic Paradox;* Mouffe, *Left Populism;* Mouffe, *Return of the Political.*
4. Brown, *Ruins of Neoliberalism;* Brown, "Interview with Wendy Brown," interview by Burgum, Raza, and Vasquez.
5. Grossberg, *We All Want to Change the World.*
6. Zemlicka and Hazeltine, "The Reality of Contingency."
7. Michael Levitin, "The Triumph of Occupy Wall Street," *Atlantic,* June 10, 2015, accessed June 23, 2017, https://www.theatlantic.com/politics/archive/2015/06/the-triumph-of-occupy-wall-street/395408/; Emily Stewart, "We Are (Still) the 99 Percent," *Vox,* April 30, 2019, https://www.vox.com/the-highlight/2019/4/23/18284303/occupy-wall-street-bernie-sanders-dsa-socialism; Tribune News Services, "Measuring Occupy Wall Street's Impact, 5 Years Later," *Chicago Tribune,* September 17, 2016, https://www.chicagotribune.com/nation-world/ct-occupy-wall-street-s-impact-20160917-story.html.
8. Sitrin, *Everyday Revolutions.*
9. Banet-Weiser, "Convergence on the Street"; Hallsby, "Psychoanalysis Against WikiLeaks"; Shumway, "Authenticity."
10. Taylor, *The Ethics of Authenticity.*
11. Banet-Weiser, "Convergence on the Street"; Shumway, "Authenticity."
12. White, *Tropics of Discourse.*
13. White, *Tropics of Discourse.*
14. Burke, "Four Master Tropes," 435.
15. McCarthy, "Private Irony and Public Decency"; Rorty, "Contingency, Irony, and Solidarity."
16. Mercieca, "The Irony of Democratic Style."
17. Gitlin, *Occupy Nation;* Polletta, *Freedom is an Endless Meeting.*
18. Emahunn Raheem Ali Campbell, "A Critique of the Occupy Movement from a Black Occupier."
19. John Metta, "The Problem of Performative Activism," *Al Jazeera,* July 20, 2020, https://www.aljazeera.com/opinions/2020/7/20/the-problem-of-performative-activism.

WORKS CITED

Alinsky, Saul D. *Rules for Radicals: A Practical Primer for Realistic Radicals.* New York: Vintage Books, 1972.

Amossy, Ruth. "Ethics at the Crossroads of Disciplines: Rhetoric, Pragmatics, and Sociology." *Poetics Today* 22, no. 1 (Spring 2001): 1–23.

Andrejevic, Mark. *Infoglut: How Too Much Information Is Changing the Way We Think and Know.* Abingdon, UK: Routledge, 2013.

———. *iSpy: Surveillance and Power in the Interactive Era.* Lawrence: University Press of Kansas, 2007.

Asen, Robert. *Democracy, Deliberation, and Education.* University Park: Pennsylvania State University Press, 2015.

Asen, Robert, and Daniel C. Brouwer. "Introduction: John Dewey and the Public Sphere." *Argumentation and Advocacy* 39, no. 3 (2003): 157–60.

Austin, J. L. *How to Do Things with Words.* Cambridge, MA: Harvard University Press, 1962.

Azzellini, Dario, and Marina Sitrin. *They Can't Represent Us! Reinventing Democracy from Greece to Occupy.* London: Verso, 2014.

Bakunin, Mikhail Aleksandrovich. *Bakunin on Anarchism.* Edited, translated, and with an introduction by Sam Dolgoff. Montreal: Black Rose Books, 1980.

Baldwin, James. "A Report from Occupied Territory." *Nation,* July 11, 1966. https://www.thenation.com/article/archive/report-occupied-territory/.

Baldwin-Philippi, Jessica. *Using Technology, Building Democracy: Digital Campaigning and the Construction of Citizenship.* New York: Oxford University Press, 2015.

Banet-Weiser, Sarah. "Convergence on the Street." *Cultural Studies* 25, no. 4–5 (2011): 641–58.

Barron, David J. "Reclaiming Home Rule." *Harvard Law Review* 116, no. 8 (June 2003): 2255–386.

Barthes, Roland. *Mythologies.* 2nd ed. CITY: Hill & Wang, 2013.

Baudrillard, Jean. *Simulacra and Simulation.* Translated by Sheila Faria Glaser. Ann Arbor: University of Michigan Press, 2006.

Biesecker, Barbara A. "Guest Editor's Introduction: Toward an Archaeogenealogy of Post-truth." *Philosophy & Rhetoric* 51, no. 4 (2018): 329–41.

Biesecker, Barbara A., and William Trapani. "Escaping the Voice of the Mass/ter: Late Neoliberalism, Object-Voice, and the Prospects for a Radical Democratic Future." *Advances in the History of Rhetoric* 17, no. 1 (2014): 25–33.

Boggs, Carl. "Marxism, Prefigurative Communism, and the Problem of Workers' Control." *Radical America* 11, no. 6 (Winter 1977–78): 99–121.

Bond, Becky, and Zack Exley. *Rules for Revolutionaries: How Organizing Can Change Everything.* White River Junction, VT: Chelsea Green, 2016.

Bowers, Christopher J., and Matthew Robert Kerbel. *Next Generation Netroots: Realignment and the Rise of the Internet Left.* New York: Routledge, 2016.

Bray, Mark. *Translating Anarchy.* Winchester, UK: Zero Books, 2013.

Brennan Center for Justice. "Policy Solutions: The Case for Small Donor Financing in New York." New York University School of Law. February 26, 2019. http://www.brennancenter.org/publication/small-donor-public-financing-ny.

Brown, Wendy. "American Nightmare: Neoliberalism, Neoconservatism, and De-democratization." *Political Theory* 34, no. 6 (2006): 690–714.

———. "Interview with Wendy Brown." Interview by Samuel Burgum, Sebastian Raza, and Jorge Vasquez. *Theory, Culture & Society.* Published on June 8, 2017. https://www.theoryculturesociety.org/interview-wendy-brown/.

———. "Neo-liberalism and the End of Liberal Democracy." *Theory & Event* 7, no. 1 (2003). https://doi.org/10.1353/tae.2003.0020.

———. "Resisting Left Melancholy." *boundary 2* 26, no. 3 (1999): 19–27.

———. *In the Ruins of Neoliberalism: The Rise of Antidemocratic Politics in the West.* New York: Columbia University Press: 2019.

———. *Undoing the Demos: Neoliberalism's Stealth Revolution.* New York: Zone Books, 2015.

Buckley, Robert M. "The Arc of Communism: Lessons for Occupy Wall Street?" In *The Occupy Handbook,* edited by Janet Byrne, 184–95. New York: Little, Brown, 2012.

Burke, Kenneth. "Four Master Tropes." *Kenyon Review* 3, no. 4 (1941): 421–38.

———. *A Grammar of Motives.* New York: Prentice Hall, 1952.

Butler, Judith. *Notes toward a Performative Theory of Assembly.* Cambridge, MA: Harvard University Press, 2015.

Butler, Judith, and Gayatri Chakravorty Spivak. *Who Sings the Nation-State? Language, Politics, Belonging.* London: Seagull Books, 2007.

Campbell, Emahunn Raheem Ali. "A Critique of the Occupy Movement from a Black Occupier." *The Black Scholar* 41, no. 4 (2011): 42–51.

Capella, Joseph N., and Kathleen Hall Jamieson. "News Frames, Political Cynicism, and Media Cynicism." *Annals of the American Academy of Political and Social Science* 546, no. 1 (Summer 1996): 71–84.

———. *Spiral of Cynicism: The Press and the Public Good.* New York: Oxford University Press, 1997.

Carey, James W. "Commentary: Communication and the Progressives." *Critical Studies in Mass Communications* 6, no. 3 (1989): 264–82.

———. "The Mass Media and Democracy: Between the Modern and the Postmodern." *Journal of International Affairs* 41, no. 1 (Summer 1993): 1–21.

Castañeda, Ernesto. "The Indignados of Spain: A Precedent to Occupy Wall Street." *Social Movement Studies* 11, no. 3–4 (2012): 309–19.

Castells, Manuel. *Networks of Outrage and Hope: Social Movements in the Internet Age.* Cambridge, UK: Polity, 2012.

Chambers, Simone. "Rhetoric and the Public Sphere: Has Deliberative Democracy Abandoned Mass Democracy?" *Political Theory* 37, no. 3 (2009): 323–50.

Chaput, Catherine. "Rhetorical Circulation in Late Capitalism: Neoliberalism and the Overdetermination of Affective Energy." *Philosophy & Rhetoric* 43, no. 1 (2010): 1–25.

Chávez, Karma R. "Counter-Public Enclaves and Understanding the Function of Rhetoric in Social Movement Coalition-Building." *Communication Quarterly* 59, no. 1 (2011): 1–18.

Cherniavsky, Eva. *Neocitizenship: Political Culture after Democracy.* New York: New York University Press, 2017.

Cintron, Ralph. *Democracy as Fetish.* University Park: Pennsylvania State University Press, 2020.

Clements, Jeffrey D. *Corporations Are Not People: Reclaiming Democracy from Big Money and Global Corporations.* 2nd ed. San Francisco: Berrett-Koehler, 2014.

Clough, Nathan, and Renata Blumberg. "Toward Anarchist and Autonomist Marxist Geographies." *ACME: An International Journal for Critical Geographies* 11, no. 3 (2012): 335–51.

Connolly, William. *The Ethos of Pluralization.* Minneapolis: University of Minnesota Press, 1995.

Cram, E., Melanie Loehwing, and John Lucaites. "Civic Sights: Theorizing Deliberative and Photographic Publicity in the Visual Public Sphere." *Philosophy & Rhetoric* 49, no. 3 (2016): 227–53.

Curato, Nicole, John S. Dryzek, Selen A. Ercan, Carolyn M. Hendriks, and Simon Niemeyer. "Twelve Key Findings in Deliberative Democracy Research." *Daedalus* 146, no. 3 (2017): 28–38.

Dahl, Robert A. *Democracy .and Its Critics.* New Haven, CT: Yale University Press, 1989.

Danisch, Robert. *Building a Social Democracy: The Promise of Rhetorical Pragmatism.* Lanham, MD: Lexington Books, 2015.

Dean, Jodi. *Democracy and Other Neoliberal Fantasies: Communicative Capitalism and Left Politics.* Durham, NC: Duke University Press, 2009.

Debord, Guy. *Society of the Spectacle.* Translated Donald Nicholson-Smith. New York: Zone Books, 1995.

della Porta, Donatella. *Social Movements in Times of Austerity: Bringing Capitalism Back into Protest Analysis.* Cambridge, UK: Polity, 2015.

DeLuca, Kevin. *Image Politics: The New Rhetoric of Environmental Activism.* New York: Routledge, 1999.

DeLuca, Kevin, Sean Lawson, and Ye Sun. "Occupy Wall Street on the Public Screens of Social Media: The Many Framings of the Birth of a Protest Movement." *Communication, Culture & Critique* 4, no. 4 (November 2012): 483–509.

Derrida, Jacques. *Dissemination.* Translated Barbara Johnson. Chicago: University of Chicago Press, 1983.

Deseriis, Marco. "The People's Mic as a Medium in Its Own Right: A Pharmacological Reading." *Communication and Critical/Cultural Studies* 11, no. 1 (2014): 42–51.

Dewey, John. *The Public and Its Problems: An Essay in Political Inquiry.* Edited by Melvin L. Rogers. University Park: Pennsylvania State University Press, 2012.

Dixon, Chris. *Another Politics Is Possible: Talking Across Today's Transformative Movements.* Oakland: University of California Press, 2014.

Doxtader, Erik W. "Characters in the Middle of Public Life: Consensus, Dissent, and Ethos." *Philosophy & Rhetoric* 33, no. 4 (2000): 336–69.

Ewalt, Joshua P., Jessy J. Ohl, and Damien Smith Pfister. "Activism, Deliberation, and Networked Public Screens: Rhetoric Scenes from the Occupy Moment in Lincoln, Nebraska." *Cultural Studies, Critical Methodologies* 13, no. 3 (2013): 173–90.

Ewell, Audrey, Aaron Aites, Lucian Read, and Nina Krstic, dir. *99%: The Occupy Wall Street Collaborative Film.* Beverly Hills, CA: Participant Media, 2013.

Fishkin, James S. *Democracy When the People Are Thinking: Revitalizing Our Politics through Public Deliberation.* Oxford: Oxford University Press, 2018.

Foss, Sonja K., and Cindy L. Griffin. "Beyond Persuasion: A Proposal for an Invitational Rhetoric." *Communication Monographs* 62 no. 1 (1995): 2–18.

Foucault, Michel. *The Birth of Biopolitics: Lectures at the Collège de France, 1978–1979.* Translated by Graham Burchell. Edited by Michel Senellart. New York: Picador, 2010.

Frank, Thomas. "To the Precinct Station." *Baffler*, November 2012. https://thebaffler.com/salvos/to-the-precinct-station.

Fraser, Nancy. "The End of Progressive Neoliberalism." *Dissent*, January 2, 2017. https://www.dissentmagazine.org/online_articles/progressive-neoliberalism-reactionary-populism-nancy-fraser.

———. "Rethinking the Public Sphere: A Contribution to the Critique of Actually Existing Democracy." *Social Text* 25/26 (1990): 56–58.

Freeman, Jo. "The Tyranny of Structurelessness." *Berkeley Journal of Sociology* 17 (1972–73): 151–64.

Gaonkar, Dilip Parameshwar. "The Idea of Rhetoric in the Rhetoric of Science." *Southern Communication Journal* 58, no. 4 (1993): 258–95.

Garsten, Bryan. *Saving Persuasion: A Defense of Rhetoric and Judgment.* Cambridge, MA: Harvard University Press, 2006.

Gitlin, Todd. *Occupy Nation: The Roots, The Spirit, and The Promise of Occupy Wall Street.* It Books, 2012.

Graeber, David. *The Democracy Project: A History, a Crisis, a Movement.* New York: Spiegel & Grau, 2013.

Greene, Ronald Walter. "Rhetorical Capital: Communicative Labor, Money/Speech, and Neo-liberal Governance." *Communication and Critical/Cultural Studies* 4, no. 3 (2007): 327–31.

Greene, Ronald Walter, and Kevin Douglas Kuswa. "'From the Arab Spring to Athens, from Occupy Wall Street to Moscow': Regional Accents and the Rhetorical Cartography of Power." *Rhetoric Society Quarterly* 42, no. 3 (2012): 271–88.

Gross, Alan G., and William M. Keith, eds. *Rhetorical Hermeneutics: Invention and Interpretation in the Age of Science.* Albany: State University of New York Press, 1997.

Grossberg, Lawrence. *Under the Cover of Chaos: Trump and the Battle for the American Right.* London: Pluto Press, 2018.

———. *We All Want to Change the World: The Paradox of the U.S. Left.* Self-published, Creative Commons, 2015. https://www.academia.edu/13048909.

Grossman, Richard L. "Corporations Must Not Supplant 'We the People.'" In *Defying Corporations, Defining Democracy: A Book of History and Strategy,* edited by Dean Ritz. New York: Apex Press, 2001.

Gutmann, Amy, and Dennis F. Thompson. *Democracy and Disagreement.* Cambridge, MA: Belknap Press, 1996.

———. *Why Deliberative Democracy?* Princeton, NJ: Princeton University Press, 2004.

Habermas, Jürgen. *The Structural Transformation of the Public Sphere: An Inquiry into a Category of Bourgeois Society.* Translated by Thomas Burger with the assistance of Frederick Lawrence. Cambridge, MA: MIT Press, 1991.

Halkin, Alexandra. "Outside the Indigenous Lens: Zapatistas and Autonomous Videomaking." In *Global Indigenous Media: Cultures, Poetics, and Politics,* edited by Pamela Wilson and Michelle Stewart, 160-82. Durham, NC: Duke University Press, 2008.

Hall, Stuart. *The Hard Road to Renewal: Thatcherism and the Crisis of the Left.* London: Verso, 1988.

Halloran, S. Michael. "Aristotle's Concept of Ethos, or If Not His Somebody Else's." *Rhetoric Review* 1, no. 1 (1982): 58–63.

Hallsby, Atilla. "Psychoanalysis against WikiLeaks: Resisting the Demand for Transparency." *Review of Communication* 20, no. 1 (2020): 69–86.

Hammond, John L. "The Anarchism of Occupy Wall Street." *Science & Society* 79, no. 2 (Spring 2015): 288–313.

Happe, Kelly E. "Parrhesia, Biopolitics, and Occupy." *Philosophy & Rhetoric* 48, no. 2 (2015): 211–23.

Hardt, Michael, and Antonio Negri. *Multitude: War and Democracy in the Age of Empire.* New York: Penguin, 2005.

Hariman, Robert. "Allegory and Democratic Public Culture in the Postmodern Era." *Philosophy & Rhetoric* 35, no. 4 (2002): 267–96.

Hartelius, Johanna E. *The Rhetoric of Expertise.* Lanham, MD: Lexington Books, 2011.

Hartmann, Thom. *Unequal Protection: How Corporations Became "People"—And You Can Fight Back.* 2nd ed. San Francisco: Berrett-Koehler, 2010.

Hauser, Gerard A. *Vernacular Voices: The Rhetoric of Publics and Public Spheres.* Columbia: University of South Carolina Press, 1999.

Herman, Edward S., and Noam Chomsky. *Manufacturing Consent: The Political Economy of the Mass Media.* New York: Pantheon Books, 2011.

———. *Change the Word without Taking Power.* London: Pluto Press, 2010.

Hyde, Michael J. "Introduction." In *The Ethos of Rhetoric,* edited by Michael J. Hyde, 1–34. Columbia: University of South Carolina Press, 2004.

Jackson, Brian, and Gregory Clark. *Trained Capacities: John Dewey, Rhetoric, and Democratic Practice.* Columbia: University of South Carolina Press, 2014.

Jasanoff, Sheila. "Future Imperfect: Science, Technology, and the Imaginations of Modernity." In *Dreamscapes of Modernity: Sociotechnical Imaginaries and the Fabrication of Power,* edited by Sheila Jasanoff and Sang-Hyun Kim. Chicago: University of Chicago Press, 2015.

Jones, John. "Compensatory Division in the Occupy Movement." *Rhetoric Review* 33, no. 2 (2014): 148–64.

Joosse, Paul. "Elves, Environmentalism, and 'Eco-Terror': Leaderless Resistance and Media Coverage of the Earth Liberation Front." *Crime, Media, Culture* 8, no. 1 (2012): 75–93.

Judis, John B. *The Populist Explosion: How the Great Recession Transformed American and European Politics.* New York: Columbia Global Reports, 2016.

Juris, Jeffrey S., Michelle Ronayne, Firuzeh Shokooh-Valle, and Robert Wengronowitz. "Negotiating Power and Difference within the 99%." *Social Movement Studies* 11, no. 3–4 (2012): 434–40.

Karpf, David. "Digital Politics after Trump." *Annals of the International Communication Association* 41, no. 2 (2017): 198–207.

Kavada, Anastasia. "Creating the Collective: Social Media, the Occupy Movement and Its Constitution as a Collective Actor." *Information, Communication & Society* 18, no. 8 (2015): 872–86.

Kelp-Stebbins, Katherine, and Allison M. Schifani. "The Medium Is the Masses: Embodied Amplification, Urban Occupation." *Media Fields Journal,* no. 9 (2015). http://mediafieldsjournal.org/the-medium-is-the-masses/2015/8/21/the-medium-is-the-masses-embodied-amplification-urban-occupa.html.

Kerbel, Matthew Robert, and Christopher J. Bowers. *Next Generation Netroots: Realignment and the Rise of the Internet Left.* New York: Routledge, 2016.

Laclau, Ernesto. *On Populist Reason.* London: Verso, 2005.

Lee, Ronald. "Electoral Politics and Visions of Community: Jimmy Carter, Virtue, and the Small Town Myth." *Western Journal of Communication* 59, no. 1 (1995): 39–60.

Leonard, Thomas C. *Illiberal Reformers: Race, Eugenics, and American Economics in the Progressive Era.* Princeton, NJ: Princeton University Press, 2016.

Lessig, Lawrence. *America, Compromised.* Chicago: University of Chicago Press, 2018.

———. *Republic, Lost: How Money Corrupts Congress—And a Plan to Stop It.* New York: Twelve, 2011.

———. *The USA Is Lesterland: The Nature of Congressional Corruption.* Seattle: Create Space, 2014.

Linzey, Thomas, with Anneke Campbell. *Be the Change: How to Get What You Want in Your Community.* Layton, UT: Gibbs-Smith, 2009.

———. *We the People: Stories from the Community Rights Movement in the United States.* Oakland, CA: PM Press, 2016.

Lundberg, Christian, and Loshua Gunn. "'Ouija Board, Are There Any Communications?' Agency, Ontotheology, and the Death of the Humanist Subject, or, Continuing the ARS Conversation." *Rhetoric Society Quarterly* 35, no. 4 (2005): 83–105.

Maharajah, Manissa. "Standing Up." In *Occupy! Scenes From Occupied America*, edited by Astra Taylor, Keith Gessen, and the Editors from *n+1, Dissent, Triple Canopy,* and *The New Inquiry,* 34–40. New York: Verso, 2011.

Maharawal, Manissa McCleave. "Occupy Wall Street and a Radical Politics of Inclusion." *Sociological Quarterly* 54, no. 2 (2013): 159–228.

Marcuse, Herbert. "Some Social Implications of Modern Technology." In *The Essential Frankfurt School Reader,* edited by Andrew Arato and Eike Gebhardt, 138–62. New York: Continuum, 1982.

Markovits, Elizabeth. *The Politics of Sincerity: Plato, Frank Speech, and Democratic Judgment.* University Park: Pennsylvania State University Press, 2008.

Martinez-Torres, Maria Elena. "Civil Society, the Internet, and the Zapatistas." *Peace Review* 13, no. 3 (2001): 347–55.

May, Matthew S., and Daniel Synk. "Contradiction and Overdetermination in Occupy Wall Street." *Communication and Critical/Cultural Studies* 11, no. 1 (2014): 74–84.

McCarthy, Thomas. "Private Irony and Public Decency: Richard Rorty's New Pragmatism." *Critical Inquiry* 16, no. 2 (Winter 1990): 355–70.

Mercieca, Jennifer R. "The Irony of Democratic Style." *Rhetoric and Public Affairs* 11, no. 3 (2008): 441–49.

Miller, Carolyn R. "Technology as a Form of Consciousness: A Study of Contemporary Ethos." *Central States Speech Journal* 29, no. 4 (1978): 228–36.

Min, Seong-Jae. "Occupy Wall Street and Deliberative Decision-Making: Translating Theory to Practice." *Communication, Culture & Critique* 8, no. 1 (2015): 73–89.

Mouffe, Chantal. "Deliberative Democracy or Agonistic Pluralism?" *Social Research* 66, no. 3 (1999): 745–58.

———. *For a Left Populism.* London: Verso, 2019.

———. *The Democratic Paradox.* London: Verso, 2009.

———. *The Return of the Political.* London: Verso, 1993.

Mudge, Stephanie L. *Leftism Reinvented: Western Parties from Socialism to Neoliberalism.* Cambridge, MA: Harvard University Press, 2018.

Mumford, Lewis. "Authoritarian and Democratic Technics." *Technology and Culture* 5, no. 1 (Winter 1964): 1–8.

Murray, Billie. "The Sphere, the Screen, and the Square: 'Locating' Occupy in the Public Sphere." *Communication Theory* 26, no. 4 (July 2016): 450–68.

Nail, Thomas. "Zapatismo and the Global Origins of Occupy." *Journal for Cultural and Religious Theory* 12, no. 3 (Spring 2013): 20–38.

Ober, Josiah. *Demopolis: Democracy before Liberalism in Theory and Practice.* Cambridge, UK: Cambridge University Press, 2017.

Osborne, Robin. *Athens and Athenian Democracy.* New York: Cambridge University Press, 2010.

Parson, Sean. "Breaking Bread, Sharing Soup, and Smashing the State: Food Not Bombs and Anarchist Critiques of the Neoliberal Charity State." *Theory in Action* 7, no. 4 (2014): 33–51.

Pason, Amy. "Phenomenon or Meaning? A Tale of Two Occupies." In *What Democracy Looks Like: The Rhetoric of Social Movements and Counterpublics,* edited by Christina Foust, Amy Pason, and Kate Zittlow Rogness, 107–28. Tuscaloosa: University of Alabama Press, 2017.

———. "The Revolution Will Not Be (Food) Reviewed: Politics of Agitation and Control of Occupy Kitchen." In *The Political Language of Food,* edited by Samuel Boerboom, 45–70. Lanham, MD: Lexington Books, 2015.

Perlman, Michael, dir. *The 99%: Occupy Everywhere.* Los Angeles: FilmBuff, 2013.

Peters, John Durham. "Satan and Savior: Mass Communication in Progressive Thought." *Critical Studies in Mass Communication* 6, no. 3 (1989): 247–63.

———. *Speaking into the Air: A History of the Idea of Communication.* Chicago: University of Chicago Press, 2001.

Peterson, Leila Conners, and Mathew Schmid, dir. *We the People 2.0.* Portland, OR: Santa Monica: Tree Media, 2017. https://www.treemedia.com/we-the-people-2-0.

Pezzullo, Phaedra. *Toxic Tourism: Rhetorics of Pollution, Travel, and Environmental Justice.* Tuscaloosa: University of Alabama Press, 2009.

Pietrucci, Pamela. "YES WE CAMP! Protest Rhetoric in Times of Disaster: Citizens' Activism in Post-earthquake L'Aquila." *Comunicazione Politica* 1 (April 2015): 43–65.

Pleyers, Geoffrey, and Alain Touraine. *Alter-globalization: Becoming Actors in a Global Age.* Cambridge, UK: Polity, 2010.

Polletta, Francesca. *Freedom Is an Endless Meeting.* Chicago: University of Chicago Press, 2002.

Polletta, Francesca, and Katt Hoban. "Why Consensus?" *Journal of Social and Political Psychology* 4, no. 1 (2016): 286–301.

Protevi, John. "Semantic, Pragmatic, and Affective Enactment at OWS." *Theory & Event* 14, no. 4 (2011 Supplement). 10.1353/tae.2011.0061.

Radovac, Lillian. "Mic Check: Occupy Wall Street and the Space of Audition." *Communication and Critical/Cultural Studies* 11, no. 1 (March 2014): 34–41.

Rancière, Jacques. *Disagreement: Politics and Philosophy.* Translated by Julie Rose. Minneapolis: University of Minnesota Press, 1999.

Rancière, Jaques, Davide Panagia, and Rachel Bowlby. "Ten Theses on Politics." *Theory & Event* 5, no. 3 (2001). doi:10.1353/tae.2001.0028.

Rasza, Maple John. "Beyond 'Riot Porn': Protest Video and the Production of Unruly Subjects." *Ethnos* 79, no. 4 (2014): 496–524.

Rehmann, Jan. "Occupy Wall Street and the Question of Hegemony: A Gramscian Analysis." *Socialism and Democracy* 21, no. 1 (2013): 1–18.

Reich, Adam D. "The Organizational Trace of an Insurgent Moment: Occupy Wall Street and New York City's Social Movement Field, 2004 to 2015." *Socius* 3 (2017): 1–21.

Reich, Robert B. "Occupy Democracy." In *The Occupy Handbook,* edited by Janet Byrne, 362–369. Boston: Back Bay Books, 2012.

———. *Saving Capitalism: For the Many, Not the Few.* New York: Knopf, 2015.

Ritz, Dean, ed. *Defying Corporations, Defining Democracy: A Book of History and Strategy.* New York: Apex Press, 2001.

Rorty, Richard. *Contingency, Irony, and Solidarity.* Cambridge, UK: Cambridge University Press, 1989.

Rose, Nikolas. *Inventing Ourselves: Psychology, Power, and Personhood.* Cambridge, UK: Cambridge University Press, 1996.

Rowe, James K., and Myles Carroll. "Reform or Radicalism: Left Social Movements from the Battle of Seattle to Occupy Wall Street." *New Political Science* 36, no. 2 (2014): 149–71.

Ryan, Kathleen J., Nancy Myers, and Rebecca Jones, eds. *Rethinking Ethos: A Feminist Ecological Approach to Rhetoric.* Carbondale: Southern Illinois University Press, 2016.

Sanders, Bernie. *Our Revolution: A Future to Believe In.* New York: Thomas Dunne Books, 2017.

Sanders, Lynn M. "Against Deliberation." *Political Theory* 25, no. 3 (1997): 347–76.

Sattler, William. "Conceptions of *Ethos* in Ancient Rhetoric." *Speech Monographs* 14, no. 1–2 (1947): 55–65.

Schmitt, Mark. "Philanthropy, Politics, and Democracy." *Society* 52, no. 6 (December 2015): 549–51.

Schneider, Nathan. *Thank You, Anarchy: Notes from the Occupy Apocalypse.* Berkeley: University of California Press, 2013.

Selfa, Lance, and Ashley Smith. "The Sanders Campaign and the Left." *New Politics* 15, no. 4 (Winter 2016): 13–20.

Shein, Rebecca. "Whose Occupation? Homelessness and the Politics of Park Encampments." *Social Movement Studies* 11, no. 3–4 (Summer 2012): 335–41.

Shumway, David R. "Authenticity: Modernity, Stardom, and Rock & Roll." *Modernism/Modernity* 14, no. 3 (2007): 527–33.

Sitrin, Marina. *Everyday Revolutions: Horizontalism and Autonomy in Argentina.* London: Zed Books, 2012.

Smith, Jackie, and Bob Glidden. "Occupy Pittsburgh and the Challenges of Participatory Democracy." *Social Movement Studies* 11, no. 3–4 (Summer 2012): 288–94.

Stiegler, Bernard. *Technics and Time.* Stanford, CA: Stanford University Press, 1998.

Stuckey, Mary E. "Rethinking the Rhetorical Presidency and Presidential Rhetoric." *Review of Communication* 10, no. 1 (2010): 38–52.

Taussig, Michael. "I'm So Angry I Made a Sign." *Critical Inquiry* 39, no. 1 (Fall 2012): 56–88.

Taylor, Astra, Keith Gessen, and the Editors from n+1, eds. *Occupy!: Scenes From Occupied America.* New York: Verso, 2011.

Taylor, Charles. *The Ethics of Authenticity.* Cambridge, MA: Harvard University Press, 1992.

Taylor, Diana. *The Archive and the Repertoire: Performing Cultural Memory in the Americas.* Durham, NC: Duke University Press, 2003.

Teachout, Zephyr. "The Anti-corruption Principle." *Cornell Law Review* 94, no. 2 (January 2009): 342–408.

———. *Corruption in America: From Benjamin Franklin's Snuff Box to Citizen's United.* Cambridge, MA: Harvard University Press, 2014.

Thimsen, A. Freya. "The Lessons of Community Rights Ordinances for Democratic Philosophizing." *Philosophy & Rhetoric* 51, no. 3 (2018): 245–68.

Tracy, Karen. *Everyday Talk: Building and Reflecting Identities.* New York: Guilford Press, 2002.

Trilling, Lionel. *Sincerity and Authenticity.* Cambridge, MA: Harvard University Press, 1972.

van de Sande, Mathijs. "Fight with Tools: Prefiguration and Radical Politics in the Twenty-First Century." *Rethinking Marxism* 27, no. 2 (2015): 177–94.

Varga, Joseph. "Occupying the Picket Line: Labor and Occupy in South Central Indiana." *Journal of Working-Class Studies* 3, no. 1 (2018): 81–103.

Vivian, Bradford. "Neoliberal Epideictic: Rhetorical Form and Commemorative Politics on September 11, 2002." *Quarterly Journal of Speech* 92, no. 1 (2006): 1–26.

Vlastos, Gregory. "Socratic Irony." *Classical Quarterly* 37, no. 1 (1987): 79–96.

Vogel, Shane. *Stolen Time: Black Fad Performance and the Calypso Craze.* Chicago: University of Chicago Press, 2018.

Vogelaar, Alison. "Staging Revolution: The OWS Encampment at Zuccotti Park." *Media Fields Journal,* no. 9 (2015). http://mediafieldsjournal.org/staging-revolution.

Wanzer-Serrano, Darrel. *The New York Young Lords and the Struggle for Liberation.* Philadelphia: Temple University Press, 2015.

Weaver, Jeff. *How Bernie Won: Inside the Revolution That's Taking Back Our Country and Where We Go from Here.* New York: St. Martin's Press, 2018.

West, Isaac. *Transforming Citizenships: Transgender Articulations of the Law.* New York: New York University Press, 2014.

White, Hayden V. *Tropics of Discourse: Essays in Cultural Criticism.* Baltimore: Johns Hopkins University Press, 1985.

White, Micah. *The End of Protest: A New Playbook for Revolution.* Toronto: Knopf Canada, 2016.

Winkler, Adam. *We the Corporations: How American Businesses Won Their Civil Rights.* New York: Liveright, 2018.

Winslow, Luke. "'Not Exactly a Model of Good Hygiene': Theorizing an Aesthetic of Disgust in the Occupy Wall Street Movement." *Critical Studies in Media Communication* 34, no. 3 (February 2017): 278–92.

Wolfson, Todd. "From the Zapatistas to Indymedia: Dialectics and Orthodoxy in Contemporary Social Movements." *Communication, Culture and Critique* 5, no. 2 (June 2012): 149–70.

Young, Iris Marion. "Activist Challenges to Deliberative Democracy." *Political Theory* 29, no. 5 (2001): 670–90.

———. *Inclusion and Democracy.* Oxford: Oxford University Press, 2000.

Zemlicka, Kurt, and Marjorie Hazeltine. "The Reality of Contingency: Performance as Materialized Trope and the Theorization of Rupture." *Liminalities: A Journal of Performance Studies* 10, no. 3/4 (2014): 1–22.

Zivi, Karen. "Rights and the Politics of Performativity." In *Judith Butler's Precarious Politics: Critical Encounters,* edited by Terrell Carver and Samuel Allen Chambers, 157–70. Abingdon, UK: Routledge, 2008.

INDEX